Critical Criminological Perspectives

Series Editors
Reece Walters, Faculty of Law, Deakin University,
Burwood, VIC, Australia
Deborah H. Drake, Department of Social Policy &
Criminology, The Open University, Milton Keynes, UK

The Palgrave Critical Criminological Perspectives book series aims to showcase the importance of critical criminological thinking when examining problems of crime, social harm and criminal and social justice. Critical perspectives have been instrumental in creating new research agendas and areas of criminological interest. By challenging state defined concepts of crime and rejecting positive analyses of criminality, critical criminological approaches continually push the boundaries and scope of criminology, creating new areas of focus and developing new ways of thinking about, and responding to, issues of social concern at local, national and global levels. Recent years have witnessed a flourishing of critical criminological narratives and this series seeks to capture the original and innovative ways that these discourses are engaging with contemporary issues of crime and justice. For further information on the series and to submit a proposal for consideration, please get in touch with the Editor: Josephine Taylor, Josephine.Taylor@palgrave.com.

Aleš Završnik · Katja Simončič
Editors

Artificial Intelligence, Social Harms and Human Rights

Editors
Aleš Završnik
Institute of Criminology at the Faculty
of Law
Ljubljana, Slovenia

Katja Simončič
Ministry of Labour, Social Affairs
and Equal Opportunities of the Republic
of Slovenia
Ljubljana, Slovenia

ISSN 2731-0604 ISSN 2731-0612 (electronic)
Critical Criminological Perspectives
ISBN 978-3-031-19151-0 ISBN 978-3-031-19149-7 (eBook)
https://doi.org/10.1007/978-3-031-19149-7

© The Editor(s) (if applicable) and The Author(s), under exclusive license to Springer Nature
Switzerland AG 2023
This work is subject to copyright. All rights are solely and exclusively licensed by the Publisher,
whether the whole or part of the material is concerned, specifically the rights of reprinting, reuse
of illustrations, recitation, broadcasting, reproduction on microfilms or in any other physical way,
and transmission or information storage and retrieval, electronic adaptation, computer software, or
by similar or dissimilar methodology now known or hereafter developed.
The use of general descriptive names, registered names, trademarks, service marks, etc. in this
publication does not imply, even in the absence of a specific statement, that such names are exempt
from the relevant protective laws and regulations and therefore free for general use.
The publisher, the authors, and the editors are safe to assume that the advice and information in
this book are believed to be true and accurate at the date of publication. Neither the publisher
nor the authors or the editors give a warranty, expressed or implied, with respect to the material
contained herein or for any errors or omissions that may have been made. The publisher remains
neutral with regard to jurisdictional claims in published maps and institutional affiliations.

This Palgrave Macmillan imprint is published by the registered company Springer Nature Switzerland
AG
The registered company address is: Gewerbestrasse 11, 6330 Cham, Switzerland

Preface

Artificial Intelligence (AI) brings numerous benefits to individuals, businesses, and countries, for example, when social networks recommend friends, when algorithms perform transactions on stock exchanges, when AI helps law enforcement agencies predict crime or the military search for potential terrorists. However, all these examples demonstrate how these AI systems may violate fundamental human rights codified in constitutions and binding international rules. This is in addition to the violation of ethical commitments, for example when algorithms cause "flash crashes" as a result of non-transparent "black-boxed" high-frequency trading; or when minority communities are disproportionally more policed than others due to the "vicious circle" effects of predictive police software, or a false target recognition of military targets in the so-called "signature strikes" based on the presumed resemblances of mobile phone movement records of targets to the records of known terrorists. The threats may be specific to a single domain of use of AI, such as in insurance, banking, the judiciary, or law enforcement, but several common threats exist in all domains. Examples of AI usage suggest that the new presumably objective tools, often presented as "pure" math,

Preface

raise many legal and ethical challenges: at the micro level, AI used in decision-making systems regarding individuals' rights and obligations may interfere with individual human rights, such as privacy and personal data protection, the principle of equality and social justice, and the individual's autonomy and dignity. On the meso and macro levels, AI influences the functioning of democracy, exacerbates global social and economic inequalities, and increases the social sorting of the population.

The book's initial premise is that AI inevitably enters a specific social, cultural, and political space. It is the product of a particular socioeconomic and cultural milieu that the tools in turn help reshape. Therefore, AI can be used to enhance "negative" social changes, for example, by increasing economic inequality at a global level, expanding socially disruptive and hostile policies, or as a means to prevent such social changes. This book's overall objective is to critically explore to what extent and how AI can infringe on human rights in various domains and may lead to individual, social, and ecological harmful consequences. Seeing that the European Union has outlined its efforts to use big data, machine learning, and AI to tackle several inherently social problems, such as poverty, climate change, social inequality, and criminality, this book advocates that the developments in AI must take place in an appropriate ethical and legal framework. It also offers recommendations in various fields of law, especially international human rights law, personal data protection law, anti-discrimination law and even space law, and indicates the direction for such a framework should take in order to increase the existing levels of respect for human rights and fundamental freedoms of individuals, consolidate legitimate democratic processes and ensure economic and political stability.

The first part of the book addresses human rights violations and harms that may occur in relation to AI tools in the criminal justice and law enforcement domain, modern warfare, and horizontal private law relationships, such as in employment. It analyses the impacts AI has in these selected domains on specific human rights. The book offers insights into the effects on legal rights and also goes beyond legally defined rights to support positive values such as increasing well-being and the socially beneficial development and use of AI.

The second part of the book offers insights into the governance of AI, spanning from ethics to international human rights law, together with an analysis of the private business responsibilities *de lege lata* and critical reflections on the collision of politics, academia, and the AI industry in "surveillance capitalism". Here, the contributions propose ways in which AI development, implementation, and use can be governed by various types and strands of ethics and law. One aspect of the ethical implications of AI is also technological, which refers to an analysis of the "computability" of different ethical frameworks, a commonly used analytical tool in computer analysis. The book finally situates the development of AI in a specific capitalist constellation of power that generates social harm and offers a reflection of the embeddedness of AI in the social-economic constellations of power.

The aspects of this book that make it distinctive are, firstly, the fact that it covers a broad range of subjects related to AI and human rights and ethics on one hand, and secondly, its solution-oriented contributions to the discussion of the governance of AI, on the other. It does so by diving into existing legal rules, such as regarding businesses' responsibilities under international human rights law; the existing general guidelines and space law provisions governing the prevention of harm that can serve as an example for governing the use of AI also on Earth, and the rules on the processing of personal data in the computer vision domain.

The book outlines the direction of the development and use of AI tools to avoid harm and human rights violations, which is particularly important for raising awareness about the issue and educating future generations, as well as for researchers and practitioners, such as computer science engineers, who play a role in policy making and in developing AI tools.

The book is of interest to academics, students, and practitioners in law, criminology, sociology, anthropology, political science, computer science, and emerging AI studies. It appeals to researchers and practitioners analysing technology and its societal and legal ramifications and the implications of AI for society, law, and ethics. These can be sociologists, scholars in STS studies, security studies scholars, criminologists, and legal scholars. The book is also of interest to the general public

viii **Preface**

because it provides an easy-to-read analysis of the risks AI poses for individuals and their rights and points to measures necessary to prevent or remedy harm that already exists in law, such as antidiscrimination law, international human rights law, and personal data protection law. The book aims at counter-balancing AI scholarly articles and books permeated with techno-enthusiastic sentiments and adding to the more critical voices about AI's consequences for society, individuals, and the environment. The advantage of the book is that it offers new insights into how to avoid potential human rights violations and social harm by using existing laws and human rights regimes and not only resorting to self-regulatory regimes which are difficult to enforce.[1]

Ljubljana, Slovenia   Aleš Završnik

---

[1] Part of the research leading to this book was funded by the Slovenian Research Agency, research project "Human Rights and Regulation of Trustworthy Artificial Intelligence" (no. V5-1930, 2019–2021), led by Professor Aleš Završnik. In case contributors of individual chapters conducted their research in the context of other research projects, this fact is indicated in their respective chapters or the acknowledgment to the Agency left out.

Acknowledgements

We would like to express our gratitude to all the authors who supported the initial idea for the book. They were ready to write their chapters, format and revise them after the reviews, and engage in the peer-reviewing process for the other chapters. The writing of their chapters and their reviews are most appreciated!

We are extremely grateful to the book reviewers, who made helpful comments and encouraged our discussion on how to focus our book more precisely. Much appreciation goes to editor Ms Josie Taylor and Ms Abarna Antonyraj and their team at Palgrave Macmillan, Springer Nature, for their patience and big support in the process.

We would like to express our gratitude to all attendees of the conference "Artificial Intelligence, Human Rights and Social Harm" held in Ljubljana on 15 June 2021 and attendees of the Autumn School "Law and Challenges of Digital (R)evolution" in October 2020 and 2021 for their stimulating talks and discussions that impacted our line of thought and development of arguments for our book. We would also like to express our gratitude to our colleagues at the Institute of Criminology at the Faculty of Law, University of Ljubljana, for insightful and vivid discussions.

Finally, great gratitude goes to our loved ones who supported us throughout the process of stumbling and sometimes struggling while completing our work. This book would not have been possible without them.

Ljubljana, Slovenia
August 2022

Aleš Završnik
Katja Simončič

Contents

Part I AI in Different Domains: AI, Repression and Crime

1 Artificial Intelligence and Sentencing from a Human Rights Perspective   3
*Johannes Kaspar, Stefan Harrendorf, Felix Butz,
Katrin Höffler, Lucia Sommerer, and Stephan Christoph*

2 Technical and Legal Challenges of the Use of Automated Facial Recognition Technologies for Law Enforcement and Forensic Purposes   35
Patricia Faraldo Cabana

Part II AI in Different Domains: Impacts of AI on Specific Rights

3 Artificial Intelligence, International Law and the Race for Killer Robots in Modern Warfare   57
Kristian Humble

xi

xii   Contents

4   Artificial Intelligence and the Prohibition
      of Discrimination in the EU: A Private Law
      Perspective   77
      Karmen Lutman

Part III   Policy, Regulation, Governance: AI and Ethics

5   In Defence of Ethics *and* the Law in AI Governance:
      The Case of Computer Vision   101
      Aleš Završnik

6   What Role for Ethics in the Law of AI?   141
      Mariavittoria Catanzariti

7   Introduction to Computational Ethics   161
      Ljupčo Todorovski

**Part IV   Policy, Regulation, Governance: AI and Harm
            Prevention**

8   Artificial Intelligence and Human Rights: Corporate
      Responsibility Under International Human Rights
      Law   183
      Lottie Lane

9   As Above so Below: The Use of International Space
      Law as an Inspiration for Terrestrial AI Regulation
      to Maximize Harm Prevention   207
      Iva Ramuš Cvetkovič and Marko Drobnjak

10   Democratizing the Governance of AI: From Big Tech
      Monopolies to Cooperatives   239
      Katja Simončič and Tonja Jerele

Index   269

Contributors

Felix Butz Department of Criminal Law, Criminal Procedure and Criminology, University Leipzig, Leipzig, Germany

Mariavittoria Catanzariti Robert Schuman Centre for Advanced Studies, European University Institute, Fiesole, Italy

Stephan Christoph Department of Criminal Law, Criminal Procedure, Criminology and Penology, University of Augsburg, Augsburg, Germany

Marko Drobnjak Institute of Criminology at the Faculty of Law, Ljubljana, Slovenia

Patricia Faraldo Cabana Facultad de Derecho, Campus de Elviña, A Coruña, Spain

Stefan Harrendorf Department of Criminology, Criminal Law, Criminal Procedure and Comparative Criminal Law and Justice, University of Greifswald, Greifswald, Germany

Kristian Humble School of Law and Criminology, Faculty of Liberal Arts and Sciences, University of Greenwich, London, UK

Katrin Höffler Department of Criminal Law, Criminal Procedure and Criminology, University Leipzig, Leipzig, Germany

Tonja Jerele Faculty of Social Sciences, University of Ljubljana, Ljubljana, Slovenia

Johannes Kaspar Department of Criminal Law, Criminal Procedure, Criminology and Penology, University of Augsburg, Augsburg, Germany

Lottie Lane Department of Transboundary Legal Studies, Faculty of Law, University of Groningen, Groningen, The Netherlands

Karmen Lutman Faculty of Law, University of Ljubljana, Ljubljana, Slovenia

Iva Ramuš Cvetkovič Institute of Criminology at the Faculty of Law, Ljubljana, Slovenia

Katja Simončič Ministry of Labour, Social Affairs and Equal Opportunities of the Republic of Slovenia, Ljubljana, Slovenia

Lucia Sommerer Criminology, Criminal Compliance, Risk Management and Penal Law, Martin Luther University Halle-Wittenberg, Halle, Germany

Ljupčo Todorovski Faculty of Mathematics and Physics, University of Ljubljana, Ljubljana, Slovenia;
Department of Knowledge Technologies, Jožef Stefan Institute, Ljubljana, Slovenia

Aleš Završnik Institute of Criminology at the Faculty of Law, Ljubljana, Slovenia

Part I

AI in Different Domains: AI, Repression and Crime

1

Artificial Intelligence and Sentencing from a Human Rights Perspective

Johannes Kaspar, Stefan Harrendorf, Felix Butz, Katrin Höffler, Lucia Sommerer, and Stephan Christoph

1 Introduction: "The Advent of AI Sentencing"

The progressing technological development of legal tech including different forms of "artificial intelligence" (AI) has also reached (criminal) justice systems. AI in this context means "weak" AI, i.e. sectoral systems solving specific problems based on algorithms that can recognize patterns in data and use them to optimize decisions and outcomes, for

J. Kaspar · S. Christoph
Department of Criminal Law, Criminal Procedure, Criminology and Penology, University of Augsburg, Augsburg, Germany

S. Harrendorf (✉)
Department of Criminology, Criminal Law, Criminal Procedure and Comparative Criminal Law and Justice, University of Greifswald, Greifswald, Germany
e-mail: stefan.harrendorf@uni-greifswald.de

© The Author(s), under exclusive license to Springer Nature Switzerland AG 2023
A. Završnik and K. Simončič (eds.), *Artificial Intelligence, Social Harms and Human Rights*, Critical Criminological Perspectives,
https://doi.org/10.1007/978-3-031-19149-7_1

example based on self-learning mechanisms. Russell and Norvig (2021: vii) in this context refer to "intelligent [...] agents that receive percepts from the environment and perform actions".

The potential use of AI within criminal sentencing is increasingly discussed, not only in the US, where especially automated risk assessment tools are already used (see Cyphert 2020; Rudin et al. 2020), but also in European countries like Germany (see e.g. Kaspar et al. 2020; Rostalski & Völkening 2019; Ruppert 2021; Kohn 2021; for the European context generally see Quattrocolo 2019). The question arises if the area of sentencing is apt for the use of this technology. As Quattrocolo has rightly pointed out, with potentially disruptive technologies like AI, we as scholars have to pose the right questions from the beginning, such as: "Why do we need (...) AI in our court rooms? Can [it] improve the quality of criminal justice? Is this compliant with fundamental rights?" (Quattrocolo 2019: 1548).

To answer these questions, we have to keep in mind that the process of sentencing is pivotal for the future of the offender. Once a criminal is found guilty and the punishment has to be decided upon, this decision (obviously) embodies a direct interference with fundamental rights. In a constitutional state governed by the rule of law, there is a need for certainty, equality, and proportionality in sentencing. The rules of sentencing must be clearly defined by law and applied equally by judges when determining sentencing decisions. However, this is not always guaranteed. Take the example of Germany, where many of the legal provisions relating to sentencing provide for a large margin of discretion and considerable regional differences in the sentencing of comparable cases have been found (Grundies 2016, 2018; Herz 2020). Against this backdrop, it might seem like a good idea to promote the use of AI to

---

F. Butz · K. Höffler
Department of Criminal Law, Criminal Procedure and Criminology, University Leipzig, Leipzig, Germany

L. Sommerer
Criminology, Criminal Compliance, Risk Management and Penal Law, Martin Luther University Halle-Wittenberg, Halle, Germany

support or maybe even replace the humans in charge of sentencing to promote efficiency and transparency, provide more consistent control over sentencing decisions, and—above all—prevent sentencing disparities, thus contributing to equal and fair decisions. On the other hand, depending of course on the concrete shape of the system and the way the interaction of humans and AI is construed, AI-supported sentencing may as well threaten fundamental rights. In this article, we will discuss these issues especially with regard to the European Convention on Human Rights (ECHR).

2 Sentencing in Europe: Structural Features and Possibilities for AI Use

First, it is necessary to take a look at sentencing in European countries in general, in order to find out how AI-supported sentencing decisions could be implemented in different legal systems and to assess the different forms AI support of sentencing might take in Europe. Therefore, we will briefly outline the sentencing law of several European countries (1.). Then we will explore the potential added value and possibilities of AI use in criminal sentencing in Europe; this will also include a comparison with the US criminal justice system where (sometimes AI-supported) algorithmic decision-support systems are increasingly used to prepare judicial decisions (2.).

2.1 Sentencing in Europe

Sentencing systems in Europe differ with regard to their structures, e.g. regarding the borderline drawn between criminal and administrative sanctions or the use of preventive measures in addition to guilt-based punishment, and theoretical background (Satzger et al. 2020), e.g. concerning the legal sources of sentencing or the question of criminal liability of legal persons (Lindner et al. 2020). Such "macro-structural" differences between EU member states, however, are contrasted by common foundations; the countries "even show some remarkable similarities in detail" (Lindner et al. 2020: 518). These range from the definition of a criminal sanction as culpable behavior, which is punished to communicate society's disapproval after criminal proceedings, to the fact that legal systems in Europe grade their sentences according to the severity of the offense; the sentencing decision itself is usually governed by at least some statutory stipulations (Lindner et al. 2020). In many states the sentencing practices of the courts, especially higher courts, also play an important role (see for example Hinkkanen & Lappi-Seppälä, 2011; Steinborn 2020; Bogdan 2020).

The methods by which judges apply the different frameworks to cases and reach a sentencing decision are, however, again rather specific to the respective legal systems. In France judges have a very large margin of discretion to decide on punishment (Lindner et al. 2020), while Spanish judges use a rather strict mathematical calculation model (Nieto-Martín et al. 2020). In most legal systems sentencing decisions are structured around offense-related or offender-related factors that are to be considered when determining the sentence; a further distinction is then made between aggravating and mitigating circumstances (Lindner et al. 2020).

From an empirical perspective, the available and predominant sanction types as well as the severity of sentences are differing strongly across Europe (just see Aebi et al. 2021: 217–271). Sentencing studies using case vignettes have also shown large discrepancies in the types of formal and informal sanctions and the sentence severity typically used in different scenarios (Elsner et al. 2008; Jehle et al. 2021).

The existing disparities have invoked international efforts to harmonize sentencing in Europe or, respectively, the European Union (EU) member states—like the category model described in European Criminal Policy Institute 2020.

2.2 Scenarios of AI-Based Decision-Support Systems for Sentencing in Europe

Could the described sentence disparities within and across countries be reduced by the use of AI? Could therefore AI truly contribute to equal and fair sentencing decisions in Europe? Before exploring the legal boundaries and also the legally relevant technical restrictions of AI use in sentencing, it is first necessary to cast a brief glance on the general potential of AI to harmonize sentencing.

First of all, we will take a look at regional sentencing disparities within a country. Typically, these are not intended and can easily be identified as endangering the fairness and equality of sentencing decisions (just see Herz 2020). To reduce such disparities, AI solutions are by far not the only option. Instead, there are also other legal, judicial or technical possibilities. From a legal perspective, sentencing guidelines might be such an option. Technical solutions to harmonize sentencing also do not necessarily have to rely on AI. These could also be simple sentencing databases, as in the case of the Japanese Saiban'in system, or algorithms that are not AI-based, but rely on "normal" mathematical models (cf. Kaspar et al. 2020).

The added value of an AI-based system to assist sentencing will therefore also depend on the extent to which other approaches to harmonize sentencing are already in use. In the US, for example, a quite formalized approach toward sentencing is applied—regardless of the vast differences between the criminal law systems of the different states and on the federal level (Satzger 2020). Widespread reliance on sentencing guidelines reduces the utility of an AI-based assistance to sentencing. Therefore, judicial decision-support systems in the US typically focus on a single aspect of the sentencing decision: recidivism risk assessment (see Butz et al. 2021). This risk-based approach has a long-standing tradition within the US (Završnik 2018) and complements the formalized sentencing guidelines (Christin 2019). Yet even these systems do not necessarily rely on AI. The best-known automated risk assessment system, COMPAS,[1] is simply a statistical actuarial tool utilizing mathematical formulas which are theory-based (Rudin et al. 2020). Research shows, however, that AI-based risk assessment tools are feasible—the predictive power of them is already better than classical approaches to the prediction of recidivism (Duwe & Kim 2017; Ghasemi et al. 2021).

---

[1] The acronym stands for "Correctional Offender Management Profiling for Alternative Sanctions.".

However, in a full-fledged sentencing support system, recidivism risk would only be one factor among many others that might help judges better classify the case at hand. Such an automated system has, according to media reports, recently been developed and tested in Shanghai, China, although not for sentencing, but for indictments, thus able to replace the prosecutor for several typical offenses (Chen 2021). The human rights issues raised by such full-fledged AI-based systems might even be more pronounced than for mere risk assessment tools. For the latter, there is already an intense ongoing discussion, focusing mainly on bias and lack of transparency (just see Angwin et al. 2016; Rudin et al. 2020), two problems that will also be associated with systems that assist or even take over the whole sentencing decision (see discussion below).

While the applicable sentencing laws vary significantly across Europe, there is a general tendency toward categorization, following a similar logic of a penalty range for a certain offense or group of offenses. Not only margins of discretion, but also more generally any decisions relying on a categorization of output variables based on the values of several input variables can be analyzed and supported by AI. Therefore, it can be assumed that European systems, as far as they are not already completely dominated by sentencing guidelines (like the US system), could harmonize their sentencing practices further, based on AI-based decision-support systems.

Finally, when it comes to sentencing disparities in Europe, AI sentencing might at least be of relevance for such offenses that have already been subject to EU-wide harmonization and standardization.

3 A European Human Rights Perspective on AI-Supported Sentencing

Which problems does AI-supported sentencing pose with a view to European human rights? Under which circumstances, if at all, might AI-based decision-support systems be admissible in sentencing? And might—provided technology development allows for this in the future—human judges eventually be replaced by AI-guided computers? We will discuss these questions regarding the European Convention of Human Rights (ECHR).

The ECHR is applicable within the jurisdictions of all 47 Council of Europe (CoE) member states (Art. 1 ECHR). The EU as such is not yet a signatory of the ECHR. Protocol No. 14 of the ECHR, however, expressly permits its accession and negotiations between EU and CoE are currently taking place (see overview at CoE 2021).

Since the EU Charter of Fundamental Rights is, due to its Article 51, still of limited importance in criminal law, we solely focus on the ECHR.

3.1 Art. 3 ECHR: Inhuman and Degrading Treatment

Opacity and the lack of a sufficient "human element" in the sentencing decision lead to the question if criminal sanctions based on AI support constitute an "inhuman or degrading treatment or punishment" (Art. 3 ECHR). Algorithms can be considered opaque if their inherent logic and decision mechanism are no longer comprehensible to humans (including experts). AI-based decision (support) systems, but also other automated assessment tools predominating decisions in an area sensitive to human rights have often been criticized for their lack of transparency (see, for example, Rudin et al. 2020 on the COMPAS risk assessment algorithm). For AI-based applications, this is, first of all, due to the fact that these are often based on machine learning and the automated identification of patterns by big data analytics. This often leads to a "black box" type construction of AI algorithms. Opacity can even be increased by secrecy interests of private companies and public administrations (Burrell 2016; Kehl et al. 2017).

Art. 3 ECHR prohibits inhuman or degrading punishment (i.e. measures of a sanctioning nature) or treatment (i.e. all other forms of state action). According to Art. 15 (2) ECHR, Art. 3 is (together with Art. 4 (1) and Art. 7) one of only three provisions that even in times of emergency are not subject to derogation. Adding to the "absolute nature" of Art. 3 is the impossibility of lawful exceptions from it (Mavronicola 2015: 723), forbidding inhuman and degrading treatment even in the criminal justice systems' arguably most challenging areas (like terrorism or organized crime; Grabenwarter & Pabel 2021, § 20 mn. 41).

A treatment is inhuman if it intentionally inflicts severe mental or physical suffering, thus causing feelings of fear and humiliation (Grabenwarter & Pabel 2021, § 20 mn. 44). Degrading treatment, on the other hand, captures subjection under state measures that are severe due to inherent elements of humiliation and debasement (Vorhaus 2002). Treatment is considered degrading when it "humiliates or debases an individual showing a lack of respect for, or diminishing, his or her human dignity or arouses feelings of fear, anguish or inferiority capable of breaking an individual's moral and physical resistance" (ECtHR, 29.04.2002, *Pretty v United Kingdom*, No 2346/02, § 52). This includes situations that cause a feeling of vulnerability, powerlessness and insult for the individual (ECtHR, 28.07.2009, *Rachwalski and Ferenc v Poland*, No 47709/99, § 61). It is important to note that when deciding cases based upon Art. 3, the ECtHR regularly refers to the principle of human dignity even though it is not explicitly mentioned in Art. 3 (see, for example, ECtHR, 04.03.2001, *Keenan v United Kingdom*, No. 27229/95, § 112).

According to the Court, the assessment of the threshold of Art. 3 "is, in the nature of things, relative; it depends on all the circumstances of the case, such as the duration of the treatment, its physical or mental effects and, in some cases, the sex, age and state of health of the victim" (ECtHR, 18.01.1978, *Ireland v United Kingdom*, No 5310/71, § 162). Additionally, this can include the type of treatment or punishment or the context in which it takes place (ECtHR, 23.09.1998, *A v United Kingdom*, No 25599/94, § 20).

Degrading treatment involves a certain level of objectification of another human being by state actors, either in the form of instrumentalizing a person for an objective or in the form of disregard for a person's subjective wishes and needs. Cases involving AI use or big data analysis in connection with a possible objectification have not reached the ECtHR so far.

How the Court would decide an issue of AI-supported sentencing brought before it in the context of Art. 3 ECHR cannot be predicted with certainty. Yet, the issue is to be taken seriously. A study by Lee on the use of algorithms in the selection of applicants for a job showed that participants described the evaluation of humans merely by algorithms to be "humiliating" and "dehumanizing" (Lee 2018: 12). A 2017 survey of more than 1000 technology experts, scientists, practitioners and government officials also found that the dehumanizing character of algorithmic decision-making is a major concern (Rainie & Anderson 2017: 42–43; Simmons 2018: 1094). Indeed, human dignity demands that people are not made a mere object of machines when processing information (Botha 2009; Duwell 2014). According to Sommerer (2020), the threshold for objectification is crossed in the context of government-led data processing when opaque algorithms are used to produce forecasts in an area sensitive to other fundamental rights, such as the area of crime control (also see Butz et al. 2021). This also applies to sentencing decisions, which have at least similarly grave impact on individuals as police decisions in crime control. It can be assumed that the issue of degrading objectification by opaque data AI-based assessment methods will be an issue of concern for the ECtHR judges in the future.

AI does, however, not necessarily have to be opaque. Researchers are working on "explainable AI" solutions, in which the output of the system can be traced back by human users to certain factors and thus be explained (Deeks 2019). Such programs have even already been tested for the assessment of recidivism risks and deliver promising results (just see Wang et al. 2020; critical towards the positive impact of explainable AI on the quality of human decision-making Poursabzi-Sangdeh et al. 2018; Alufaisan et al. 2021). As long as the explanation of the suggestions and decisions of such algorithms is not only available to the owners of the technology, but also accessible for those who have been sentenced based on the use of such an algorithm, explainable AI tools might help to reduce the problems with regard to Art. 3 ECHR (also see the discussion below, re Art. 6, 8). But even if you know the reason why a machine decides your case in a certain way, it is still a machine which does so.

3.2 Art. 6 ECHR: Fair Trial

Art. 6 ECHR is the provision of the Convention with the highest relevance in decisions of the ECtHR by far (see ECtHR 2021: 37.7% of all violation judgements between 1959 and 2020). The different procedural safeguards it provides are also of key importance for the admissibility of AI-based tools in civil or criminal proceedings in any European country (just see Alfaia Sampaio et al. 2019; CEPEJ 2018; Dymitruk 2019; Fair Trials 2020; Reiling 2020; Ulenaers 2020; Završnik 2020). The fair trial principle actually comprises several separate procedural rights of persons in judicial proceedings and, specifically, criminal proceedings (Dymitruk 2019).

Of these different procedural rights, quite a few might also be infringed by AI-supported sentencing. Let us begin with the most general one: Would an automated, completely AI-based sentencing decision still be one made by a tribunal? The ECtHR so far never had a chance to decide whether replacing a human judge with an automated AI-based judgment system would violate the guarantee of a "tribunal" in the meaning of Art. 6 (1) ECHR. The in-depth study found in annex I of the European Ethical Charter on the use of Artificial Intelligence in judicial systems and their environment (CEPEJ 2018) simply states sub paragraph 8 that there is a "right to a natural judge established by law", but does not discuss this at all. Sourdin (2018), Nink (2021) and Ulenaers (2020) doubt that an electronic system can be able to take over the work and functions of a judge, as this would be too complex for a machine. A machine would also be incapable of exercising discretion, according to the authors. Both is surely true for the time being, but it might change in some later future (also see Sourdin 2018). Anyway, such objections against a "robot judge" refer to feasibility, not to legitimacy.

Hence, the question is still open: technical feasibility presumed, could a "robot judge" be a legitimate "tribunal" in line with Art. 6 (1) ECHR? The ECtHR holds that a tribunal "is characterised [...] by its judicial function, [...] determining matters within its competence on the basis of rules of law and after proceedings conducted in a prescribed manner" (ECtHR, 29.04.1988, *Belilos v Switzerland*, No 10328/83, § 64). In a more recent decision, the ECtHR emphasized that the members of a court also need to be selected on basis of merit. Technical competence and moral integrity are seen to be of paramount importance here (ECtHR, 01.12.2020, *Guðmundur Andri Ástráðsson v Iceland*, No 26374/18, § 220).

Selection on basis of merit can be adapted to the situation of automated judgments by AI. *Technical competence* would require here that the AI solution has to be chosen based on its ability to solve cases, in principle, flawlessly, i.e. it would have to show very low rates of wrong decisions. The error rate needs to be similarly low than for a typical, qualified human judge, the quality of legal reasoning should be similarly high (also see Nink 2021). It is also not per se excluded that an AI may act on grounds of morality or that morality might be attributed to AI (just see Danaher 2020; Lara & Deckers 2020; Shank et al. 2019; Tigard 2021), but still the term *moral integrity* needs to be somehow "translated" into the AI context. For example, currently it is hard to imagine that an AI could be bribed or act selfish in other ways. But moral integrity can refer to the AI code and algorithm, which should—in addition to being non-discriminating, a requirement addressed in more detail below—not consider irrelevant factors for its decision or have any hidden functions that allow to override the regular way a decision is reached according to law. A robot judge therefore only fulfills the "tribunal" requirement of Art. 6 (1) if it reaches a level of technical competence and moral integrity similar to human judges. This merit threshold has not yet been reached, but it cannot be ruled out for the future that it will be. Such a highly competent AI judge would, according to Nink (2021), still be illegitimate, since as a result the process of judgment would be dehumanized, lack social competence and empathy. He, however, implicitly assumes that future AI judges would not be able to act ethically and understand social rules and/or that robots should not be afforded significant moral status by humans, which in itself requires discussion (see Danaher 2020; Tigard 2021).

If a "robot judge" is ever implemented, it will, of course, have to be "established by law", as foreseen in Art. 6 (1) ECHR. But could a robot judge also act independently and impartially? And how about dangers for the independence and impartiality of human judges in the case of AI-supported decisions? Independence of a court especially requires "safeguards against outside pressures" and an "appearance of indepence" (ECtHR, 22.06.2000, *Coëme and others v Belgium*, No 32492/96 and others, § 120). Independence of the court from the executive, the parliament and the parties involved in a case (ECtHR, 28.06.1984, *Campbell and Fell v United Kingdom*, No 7819/77 and 7878/77, § 78; ECtHR, 18.04.1999, *Ninn-Hansen v Denmark*, No 28972/95) is also a necessary requirement for sentencing (ECtHR, 16.12.1999, *T. v United Kingdom*, No 24724/94, § 108).

In case of a "robot judge", the requirement of independence would refer to the AI itself. This would not hinder the financing of such a program by a Ministry of Justice (MoJ) or the passing of a law that introduces such a system, same as it does not hinder per se that judges are appointed by the executive (ECtHR, 28.06.1984, *Campbell and Fell v United Kingdom*, No 7819/77 and 7878/77, § 79) or the parliament (ECtHR, 18.04.1999, *Ninn-Hansen v Denmark*, No 28972/95), but it hinders direct influence on the development of the algorithm by the other powers, as it would lead to an appearance of dependence. Safeguards against outside pressures would, in addition, require that neither the other powers nor the parties can alter the AI algorithm or change any outcome of an AI-based procedure in an irregular way, i.e. by backdoor or override functions included in the system. In order to also secure the appearance of independence, a certification procedure, concluded by some kind of technical sealing of the robot against irregular influences seems to be appropriate.

In cases in which an AI system is not meant to replace a human judge, but shall merely assist her or him, independence is not provided in cases in which the executive (e.g. the MoJ) or parliament orders to blindly follow any AI sentencing suggestions (see Kohn 2021), since this would amount to outside pressure. It must be up to the individual judge or court chamber to decide if the AI-based sentencing support system is used and if the suggestion provided by the system is followed (Nink 2021). Judges shall not be pressured to do so (Ulenaers 2020) and shall not face disciplinary or other negative consequences for failure to use such an algorithm or follow its suggestions (CEPEJ 2018).

To secure the appearance of independence, it would also be necessary that neither the other powers nor any of the parties, namely the public prosecutor, are involved in the concrete development of the algorithm (similar to the situation of an AI judge, see above; also see Kohn 2021). This also applies to the parliament (contrary to Kohn 2021), although it has the power to alter sentencing laws and also to introduce an AI-based sentencing support tool. Ideally, the actual "fieldwork" needs to be done under the auspices of a commission of the judiciary (also see Kohn 2021).

As regards, finally, impartiality, i.e. "the absence of prejudice or bias" (ECtHR, 10.08.2006, *Schwarzenberger v Germany*, No 75737/01, § 38), the Court applies two different tests, a subjective and an objective one. The subjective test refers to "the personal conviction and behaviour of a particular judge in a given case" (ibid.), while the objective one consists of "ascertaining whether he or she offered sufficient guarantees to exclude any legitimate doubt in this respect" (ibid.). With regard to the subjective test, personal impartiality is assumed if there is no proof of the contrary, e.g. by showing hostility or ill will, leading to a rather minor relevance of this test compared to the objective one (ECtHR 15.12.2005, *Kyprianou v Cyprus*, No 73797/01, § 119).

In the case of a "robot judge" having full command over the sentencing decision, impartiality is lacking if it can be proved that the algorithm is biased (subjective test), but also if there is serious evidence pointing to such bias, because then legitimate doubts regarding impartiality are in place (objective test). AI systems are prone to learn prejudice and bias from prejudiced or biased training data. In the same line of argument, judges using AI-based sentencing support tools will fail the objective test of impartiality if the system used is biased. This bias issue also affects Art. 14 ECHR and will therefore be discussed in detail below.

While AI systems might alleviate certain human biases (Sourdin 2018; Ulenaers 2020), the use of AI-based sentencing support tools (as opposed to a fully automated sentencing decision by a "robot judge") may also lead to another form of bias: automation bias. Several studies show that humans tend to trust systems that were designed to support their decisions so much that they often simply take over an AI suggestion as if it would be binding for them (Butz et al. 2021; Nink 2021). Automation bias does not occur in all constellations and further research is still necessary, but meta-analysis has shown that this type of bias increases with task verification complexity (Lyell & Coiera 2017). Therefore, although automation bias shown by a judge would raise serious issues with regard to his or her impartiality, it is more than plausible that it may occur in a complex field like sentencing, especially when decisions have to be made quickly due to time constraints. Unfortunately, it is not so easy to reduce automation bias—raising awareness is not sufficient; instead it seems to be necessary to design decision environments in order to "free up additional cognitive resources" (Lyell & Coiera 2017: 430), e.g. by reducing time constraints or the amount of parallel tasks to be carried out.

Further problems and possible violations of Art. 6 ECHR by AI-based sentencing, be it by a "robot judge" or by computer-assisted humans, refer to the black box problem addressed above: opacity of AI-based or AI-supported decisions may infringe the right of confrontation (Art. 6 (3) lit. d ECHR; Završnik 2020), the rights to a public hearing (Ulenaers 2020) and to a reasoned judgment (Dymitruk 2019; Ulenaers 2020) and endanger the overall equality of arms between defense and prosecution (Fair Trials 2020).

The ECtHR interprets the procedural guarantee laid down in Art. 6 (3) lit. d ECHR extensively and does not only apply it to witnesses, but to all persons testifying before a court, e.g. expert witnesses (ECtHR, 26.03.1996, *Doorson v The Netherlands*, No 20524/92, § 81–82), and also to evidence laid down in documents or computer files (ECtHR, 11.12.2008, *Mirilashvili v Russia*, No 6293/04, § 158–159). Therefore, the provision could also be applied to AI systems used by judges at the sentencing stage, as long as they are involved in the assessment of evidence in any way. This would at least be the case for systems which also include elements of recidivism risk assessment, since insofar such systems not only assist judges, but also replace expert witnesses. This justifies that their assessments can be contested in the same way as any other evidence presented before the courts, which would also include contesting the correct functioning of the algorithm, etc. Završnik (2020) has compared the situation with the admission of anonymous or absent witnesses or undisclosed documentary evidence and has rightly pointed to the fact that such evidence is not excluded per se, as long as sufficient counterbalancing measures were taken.

1 Artificial Intelligence and Sentencing from a Human ... 17

To include such evidence, a three-pronged test (known as the "Al-Khawaja test") is required to check whether a) there was "a good reason for the non-attendance of a witness" (ECtHR, 15.12.2011, *Al-Khawaja and Tahery v United Kingdom*, No 26766/05 and 22228/06, § 119), b) if the "conviction is based solely or decisively on the evidence of absent witnesses" (ibid., § 147) and c) "whether there are sufficient counterbalancing factors in place, including measures that permit a fair and proper assessment of the reliability of that evidence to take place" (ibid.). Obviously, this test would not directly apply to the situation of AI-based sentencing, but it might give hints to solve the problem at hand. The use of an opaque algorithm for risk assessment at the sentencing stage would need a good reason and the algorithmic risk assessment should not be the decisive evidence on which to base the conviction of a defendant, if not sufficient counterbalancing measures were taken. In principle, it will be necessary to provide the defendant with insights on the way the algorithm works, which variables it assesses and how risk scores are computed (Završnik 2020).

AI-based sentencing support systems, however, do not only act as a new form of evidence during criminal proceedings, but might also provide assessments based on former judgments of other courts to assist judges in the finding of a fair and adequate punishment. Yet, a court might not be able to give reasons for its sentencing decision, if it is mainly based on the suggestion of an opaque AI-based algorithm (Dymitruk 2019; Ulenaers 2020). The same could happen in case of a "robot judge" taking over the whole sentencing decision. The ECtHR, however, requires courts to "adequately state the reasons on which they are based" (ECtHR 27.09.2001, *Hirvisaari v Finland*, No 49684/99, § 30)—another argument against the use of opaque algorithms and in favor of "explainable AI" (see already above).

Further support for the need of explainable AI in sentencing can be found in the requirement of a public hearing. A sentencing decision mainly or solely based on an opaque algorithm cannot be discussed in a public hearing, but will always have an air of secrecy (Ulenaers 2020). Finally, it has also been brought up whether the use of an opaque algorithm might endanger the equality of arms between defense and prosecution (Fair Trials 2020), which is an important factor in criminal proceedings (just see ECtHR, 28.08.1991, *Brandstetter v Austria*, No 11170/84 and others, § 66–67). This would especially be the case if opacity is not due to inherent qualities of the algorithm, but is based on governmental secrecy. In such a situation, the prosecutor might have more detailed insights in the functioning of the algorithm than the defense, which would be problematic vis-à-vis the equality of arms, if the prosecution therefore would be able to prepare and tailor the presentation of evidence in a way which suits the algorithm best, while the defense cannot do the same.

On a more general level, the overall equality of arms between defense and prosecution might also be endangered if the defense does not have access to equivalent means or opportunities to analyze an AI-based sentencing system as the prosecution (see Alfaia Sampaio et al. 2019; CEPEJ 2018; Staffler & Jany 2020; Ulenaers 2020). The ECtHR has already acknowledged such a right in a comparable case: for keyword search in computer data that could be used as potential evidence and had been pre-selected and scanned for relevance only by the prosecution (ECtHR, 04.06.2019, *Sigurður Einarsson and others v Iceland*, No 39757/15, § 87–91). It also needs to be taken into account that the ability to substantially question the functioning of an AI-based support system will depend on the financial means of defendants, since those who are wealthy or are supported by a company could afford to pay the necessary computer experts, while a "normal" defendant (and in many cases also the prosecution service) could not (see CEPEJ 2018; Staffler & Jany 2020; Ulenaers 2020).

All in all, Art. 6 ECHR does not completely rule out the use of opaque algorithms in sentencing, but restricts their use very strongly. Transparent, explainable AI systems, on the other hand, theoretically pose less problems regarding the overall fairness of proceedings, but perhaps one has to keep in mind whether the accused can really understand *in practice* how the AI calculates, explainable or not, so that the problem of equality of arms will still remain to be solved.

3.3 Art. 7 ECHR: "Nullum Crimen, Nulla Poena Sine Lege"

Art. 7 ECHR regulates the principle "nullum crimen, nulla poena sine lege". Therefore, this guarantee not only applies to crimes, but also to punishments (ECtHR, 29.10.2013, *Varvara v Italy*, No 17475, § 54), which also need to be fixed by law before the criminal act in question. The provision explicitly also forbids retroactive aggravation of punishment (Art. 7 (1), second sentence).

The implementation of a robot judge in sentencing or of an AI-based sentencing support system will, as mentioned above, remove (in the first case) or reduce (in the second case) human discretion in sentencing. As a side effect, an AI-based sentencing system will inevitably change the concrete sentencing patterns that are in use across a given country or region so far. Some offenders will receive a more lenient punishment, but others will be punished more severely than before. This aggravation of punishment requires a (material) legal basis. Hence, the implementation of an AI-based sentencing system needs to be established by law also with a view to Art. 7 and for both variants—as a robot judge and as sentencing support. This requires that the use or option to use such a system is regulated in criminal law, alongside the key factors that shall be considered by it. Such a regulation needs to be clear enough to be legally certain, without going too much into the details, since this might endanger judicial independence (see above). Art. 7 does not necessarily require rigid provisions, regulations may also be vague and gradually clarified by the courts (ibid., § 141). A certain punishment is, however, not foreseeable anymore, if a law "was not formulated with sufficient precision as to enable the applicant to discern, even with appropriate advice, to a degree that was reasonable in the circumstances, the scope of the penalty [...] and the manner of its execution" (ibid., § 150). Any future regulation of AI sentencing would have to meet these standards.

3.4 Art. 8 ECHR: Privacy and Data Protection

The use of AI within sentencing might also interfere with the right to privacy guaranteed in Art. 8 ECHR, which also comprises the right to data protection (Meyer-Ladewig & Nettesheim 2017, Art. 8 mn. 32). According to the ECtHR, the protection of personal data is of fundamental importance to a person's enjoyment of his or her right to respect for private and family life (ECtHR, 27.06.2017, *Satakunnan Markkinapörssi Oy and Satamedia Oy v Finland*, No 931/13, § 133). Data protection and privacy are also highly important for an individual's right to self-determination and his or her free development of personality. This refers not only to a systematic collection and storage of personal data, even if these data are publicly available (ECtHR, 04.05.2000, *Rotaru v. Romania*, No 28341/95), but also to the possible inferences drawn from the collected raw data by an intelligent system (see Wachter and Mittelstadt 2019). Especially if the processes behind the automatic decision-making of an AI and the probable outcome remain opaque for the individual, possible chilling effects of the unpredictable consequences of data processing may (on multiple levels) affect that person's way of life negatively (Wachter and Mittelstadt 2019). Any AI system used by state agencies which analyzes personal data to come to certain results interferes with Art. 8 ECHR. A violation of this right, however, depends on the concrete shape of the AI system that is installed and the way data are collected, stored and processed.

An interference can be justified under the circumstances listed in Art. 8 (2) ECHR. The measure in question has to be regulated by national law, has to serve one of the legitimate purposes (including the"prevention of disorder or crime") and has to be necessary (Meyer-Ladewig & Nettesheim 2017, Art. 8 mn. 101), i.e. correspond to a pressing social need and be proportionate to a legitimate aim pursued (ECtHR, 04.06.2013, *Peruzzo and Martens v Germany*, No 7841/08 and 57900/12).

The legal foundation must be accessible, foreseeable and compatible with the rule of law. For the latter, the legal basis needs to sufficiently protect against arbitrary infringements and to contain safeguards against misuse (ECtHR, 02.09.2010, *Uzun v Germany*, No 35623/05), a need which is increased in cases of automatic processing of data, not least when such data are used for police purposes (ECtHR, 04.12.2008, *S. and Marper v the United Kingdom*, No 30562/04 and 30566/04, § 103).

For data protection, the right guaranteed in Art. 8 ECHR must be balanced with the public interest in the collection and use of the respective data. Concerning criminal law enforcement, public interest increases with the gravity of the offense at stake (ECtHR, 02.09.2010, *Uzun v Germany*, No 35623/05); in cases involving suspected terrorists, the ECtHR has found that states enjoy a wider margin of appreciation, especially with regard to the retention of information on individuals previously involved in terrorist activities (ECtHR, 06.09.2006, *Segerstedt-Wiberg and Others v Sweden*, No 62332/00, § 88; also see ECtHR, 17.03.2010, *Gardel v France*, No 16428/05, § 58 for an entry in a national sex-offenders database). These decisions are, however, related to the prediction and prevention of future crimes, so it is doubtful if they can also be applied to sentencing in general. In favor of such a view it could be argued that AI-supported sentencing, if able to overcome sentencing disparities, also furthers fair and equal sentencing decisions, thus improving the realization of the fair trial principle (Art. 6 ECHR) and reducing discrimination (Art. 14 ECHR; but also see the discussion on the possible infringements of these guarantees in this text). In addition, the general preventive functions of punishment (deterrence and reassurance of norm validity) might be impaired if sentencing disparities become too pronounced, thus calling the whole penal system into question. Although "courts dealing with criminal matters are particularly likely to process sensitive data" (CEPEJ 2018: 26), it is another dimension of collecting and combing data. Therefore, individual interests at stake here will regularly be substantial and call for a strict assessment of proportionality.

When it comes to the use of modern scientific techniques in the criminal justice system (which would also include the use of AI), the Court has stressed that the protection provided by Art. 8 ECHR "would be unacceptably weakened if such techniques were allowed at any cost and without carefully balancing the potential benefits of the extensive use of such techniques against important private-life interests". Any state claiming a pioneering role in the development of new technologies bears a "special responsibility" for striking the right balance in this regard (ECtHR, 04.12.2008, *S. and Marper v the United Kingdom*, No 30562/04 and 30566/04, § 112).

This became also relevant in a recent decision of the District Court of The Hague in the so-called "SyRI"-Case (Rechtbank Den Haag, 5 February 2020, ECLI:NL:RBDHA:2020:1878; see Bygrave 2020; Gipson Rankin 2021). "SyRI" (i.e. "Systeem Risico Indicatie") was an automated risk indication system used by the Dutch government to detect tax and social security fraud cases, which used structured data sets collected and kept by government agencies to produce a risk report concerning the person in question. In the Dutch case, the balancing demanded by the ECtHR was rejected due to a lack of sufficient publicly available information about the inner logic of the system, the amount of personal data processed by it, and a deficient review mechanism. Therefore, the system was seen to violate Art. 8 (2) ECHR.

Art. 8 ECHR also provides for the right to a kind of "informational self-determination". It comprises the right of each person to know how and to what purpose his or her data are stored and used by the state. It resembles the concept of "cognitive sovereignty" described by Bygrave as "a human being's ability and entitlement to comprehend with a reasonable degree of accuracy their environs and their place therein, particularly the implications these hold for their exercise of choice" (Bygrave 2020, 9). The European Ethical Charter on the use of Artificial Intelligence in judicial systems and their environment argues similarly: "The party concerned should have access to and be able to challenge the scientific validity of an algorithm, the weighting given to its various elements and any erroneous conclusions it comes to whenever a judge suggests that he/she might use it before making his/her decision. Moreover, this right of access is also covered by the fundamental principle of personal data protection" (CEPEJ 2018, 55). This legal position is endangered if an AI system uses personal data to produce a certain result (e.g. the prediction of recidivism as part of a sentencing decision), while at the same time the affected person cannot understand how the system works and makes use of his or her data.

The need for transparency (see e.g. Carlson 2017; CEPEJ 2018; Commissioner for Human Rights 2019; Ünver 2018; Reiling 2020) is not only part of the discussion of Art. 3 and Art. 6 ECHR (see supra), but also relates strongly to the question of a violation of Art. 8 ECHR.

3.5 Art. 14 ECHR: Discrimination

Another fundamental aspect that has to be considered when using intelligent algorithms in the field of criminal sentencing is the possibility of evident or hidden forms of discrimination that may violate Art. 14 ECHR. According to this provision, the enjoyment of rights and freedoms set forth in the ECHR shall be secured without discrimination on any grounds such as sex, race, color, language, religion, political or other opinions, national or social origin, association with a national minority, property, birth or other status.

Art. 14 ECHR does not contain a general principle prohibiting unequal treatment, but has to be understood as an accessory rule and amendment of other rights and freedoms of the Convention (ECtHR, 27.10.1975, *National Union of Belgian Police v Belgium*, No 4464/70, § 44).[2] Thus, it is only applicable if the facts at issue fall within the ambit of at least one of the substantive provisions of the Convention (ECtHR, 25.10.2005, *Okpisz v Germany*, No 59140/00, § 30; ECtHR, 21.02.1997, *Van Raalte v the Netherlands*, No 20060/92, § 33). As the ECtHR frequently states, Art. 14 applies whenever "the subject-matter of the disadvantage [...] constitutes one of the modalities of the exercise of a right guaranteed" or if a contested measure is "linked to the exercise of a right guaranteed" (ECtHR, 27.10.1975, *National Union of Belgian Police v Belgium*, No 4464/70, § 45).

Using AI based or other automated algorithms in criminal sentencing that "treat" people differently due to one or more characteristics mentioned above without any plausible justification may constitute a violation of the prohibition of discrimination in Art. 14 ECHR, as

---

[2] Art. 1 of the Protocol No. 12 to the ECHR contains a general prohibition of discrimination that encompassed the equal enjoyment of every right set forth by law. However, the Protocol has only been ratified by 20 member states so far (inter alia not by France, Germany, the UK).

the persons discriminated against do not enjoy the right to a fair trial (Art. 6 ECHR) to the same degree as other individuals. The danger of disparate punishment or unjustified differences in probation decisions is real and has to be taken seriously. A quite famous example, where potential racial discriminations by an automated risk assessment program are claimed, concerns COMPAS, a tool used in some states of the US for the prediction of recidivism of criminal offenders (already seen above). Here, external analysis led some authors to the conclusion that the software systematically rates the risk of recidivism higher, when offenders of African American descent are involved (Angwin et al. 2016). Whether those allegations are justified has remained controversial (Dressel & Farid 2018; Rudin et al. 2020), but the discussion has for sure raised the awareness for racial or other discrimination issues that might occur in connection with the usage of AI in the legal system. This problem is also strongly linked to system opacity, since it is difficult to assess if, whom and to what extent a "black box AI" system or similarly opaque algorithm does indeed discriminate (see Rudin et al. 2020).

If we assume that there is indeed some danger that algorithms (AI-based or not) can show signs of racial, gender or other biases, it has to be clear though, that it is not the software as such which is racist, xenophobic, misogynistic or homophobic (cf. Bagaric et al. 2020; Chander 2017). Discriminatory tendencies mainly occur if the input data by itself, which is or has been used during the training phase of the AI, contained (evidently or subliminally) certain forms of bias (Carlson 2017; MSI-NET 2018; Ünver 2018).

The algorithmic programming can also be deficient if the defaults of the software focus too much on factors that are strongly linked to special characteristics of minorities or particular groups of people in a population (Fair Trials 2020; Zuiderveen Borgesius 2018). In other words, it is not the mere usage of an AI-based tool that leads to a possible violation of Art. 14 ECHR, it is rather the wrong conceptual design and selection of input data that can bring forth undesirable results. As Brayne and Christin (2021) point out, predictive technologies might not only reflect existing biases, but also produce new discrimination by "creating" the predicted event in some kind of a "feedback loop": if a person is considered to be a high-risk offender, an increased surveillance will follow with an increased likelihood of detecting criminal behavior (also see Završnik 2020).

Disparities in criminal sentencing already exist in our current legal systems and thus can be directly or indirectly transported into and perpetuated in algorithms based on machine learning or other forms of big data analysis. Several empirical studies already examined effects of extralegal circumstances like gender (Bontrager et al. 2013), race and ethnicity (Mitchell 2005; Wooldredge et al. 2015) or an interaction of several factors (Steffensmeier et al. 2017) influencing the treatment of defendants. Despite the vast number of studies conducted in this field, it is still quite unknown in which stadium of the legal process such factors come into play and how they exactly influence the outcome of criminal proceedings (Spohn 2015).

In order to avoid any form of discrimination violating Art. 14 ECHR, the data selection for the learning phase of the algorithm as well as the design of the program itself has to be thoroughly adjusted (also see Commissioner for Human Rights 2019). Contents and parameters that may lead to biased results need to be identified and excluded or de-biased by weighing procedures or other measures in the first place. Yet, it is difficult to clearly identify such factors and circumstances that may provoke disparate treatment and unjustified differences in criminal sentencing. Further empirical research is necessary. We may even be able to use AI systems to identify patterns of discrimination in our legal systems that have not been revealed so far and thus make the legal process even more transparent, equal and fair.

4 Discussion and Conclusion

As the paper has demonstrated, the introduction of AI applications into the criminal justice process in general and sentencing in particular raises a multitude of complex legal questions that are either a continuation of known problems or completely novel issues, like the question of whether the use of an algorithm in a sentencing decision might constitute degrading treatment. However, the ECHR does, in our opinion, not form an insurmountable barrier against using algorithmic systems within sentencing. What it does, however, is narrow the path of possible technological designs for said instruments. Any sentencing algorithm will have to meet high standards of transparency and fairness and needs to be based in material law. Autonomous AI-based sentencing systems ("robot judges") require further scrutiny with regard to the guarantee of an independent and impartial tribunal in Art. 6 (1) ECHR. Their admission requires a degree of merit equal to that of human judges regarding both technical competence and moral integrity. And even if an autonomous system reaches this threshold (fundamentally doubting this Greco 2020), the fact remains that human beings would then be judged by computers. This might lead to feelings of dehumanization, even if explainable AI is used, and human communication, that is otherwise inherent in the verdict and that may be of importance for the rehabilitation of the offender, is missing.

The use of AI-based sentencing support systems or an adherence to their suggestions, on the other hand, cannot be made a binding requirement for human judges—this has to be a voluntary decision. As soon as AI-based sentencing (support) systems are emerging, they will be subject to further examination by the ECtHR as well as other courts and judicial entities tasked with establishing and safeguarding the normative framework for the deployment of AI in the societies of Europe.

But before laws allowing for AI sentencing are created, democratic process could, and in our view should, take one step further back and deliberate thoroughly whether there is, in fact, a need for the use of AI applications in sentencing decisions. Even though technological advancements, especially as seemingly groundbreaking as AI, often appear to be pre-determined in their path, it is always worth pondering alternatives, as "there is absolutely no inevitability, so long as there is a willingness to contemplate what is happening" (McLuhan & Fiore 2001: 25). And while there might be a need for technological tools to help judges make sense of the sheer quantities of information theoretically at their disposal, there is more to sentencing. As, for example, the Finnish case illustrates (Lappi-Seppälä 2007), sentencing issues can also be addressed without the newest technological fixes. A robust legal culture that is focused on improving sentencing practice through processes of deliberation and experimentation—which at times also might include technological experiments—might be something legal systems should try to foster rather than replace it with technology solutions that put humans increasingly out of the loop.

References

Aebi, M.F., Caneppele, S., Harrendorf, S., Hashimoto, Y.Z., Jehle, J.-M., Khan, T.S., Kühn, O., Lewis, C., Molnar, L., Smit, P., Þórisdóttir, R. and the ESB Network of National Correspondents (2021). *European sourcebook of crime and criminal justice statistics—2021* (6 ed.). Göttingen University Press: Göttingen.

Alfaia Sampaio, E., Seixas, J.J. & Gomes, P.J. (2019). Artificial Intelligence and the judicial ruling. Themis Competition 2019, Semi-Final D, Team Portugal I. https://www.ejtn.eu/PageFiles/17916/TEAM%20PORTUGAL%20I%20TH%202019%20D.pdf. Accessed 3 February 2022.

Alufaisan, Y., Marusich, L. R., Bakdash, J. Z., Zhou, Y. & Kantarcioglu, M. (2021). Does explainable artificial intelligence improve human decision-making? In: *Proceedings of the AAAI Conference on Artificial Intelligence*, 35(8), 6618–6626. https://www.ojs.aaai.org/index.php/AAAI/article/view/16819. Accessed 20 April 2022.

Angwin, J., Larson, J., Mattu, S. & Kirchner, L. (2016). Machine bias. There's software used across the country to predict future criminals. And it's biased against blacks. https://www.propublica.org/article/machine-bias-risk-assessments-in-criminal-sentencing. Accessed 22 November 2021.

Bagaric, M., Hunter, D. & Stobbs, N. (2020). Erasing the bias against using artificial intelligence to predict future criminality. Algorithms are color blind and never tire. *University of Cincinnati Law Review*, 88, 1037–1082.

Bagaric, M., Svilar, J., Bull, M., Hunter, D. and Stobbs, N. (2021). The solution to the pervasive bias and discrimination in the criminal justice. Transparent artificial intelligence. https://ssrn.com/abstract=3795911. Accessed 22 November 2021.

Bogdan, S. (2020). Country Report Romania. In: Satzger, H. (ed.) *Harmonisierung strafrechtlicher Sanktionen in der Europäischen Union (Harmonisation of Criminal Sanctions in the European Union*. Nomos: Baden-Baden, 427–453.

Bontrager, S., Barrick, K., & Stupi, E. (2013). Gender and sentencing. Meta-analysis of contemporary research. *Journal of Gender, Race and Justice*, 16, 349–372.

Botha, H. (2009). Human dignity in comparative perspective. *Stellenbosch Law Review*, 20, 171–220.

Brayne, S. & Christin, A. (2021). Technologies of crime prediction. Reception of algorithms in policing and criminal courts. *Social Problems*, 68, 608–624

Burrell, J. (2016). How the Machine 'Thinks'. Understanding Opacity in Machine Learning Algorithms. *Big Data & Society*, 3, 1–12.

Butz, F., Christoph, S., Sommerer, L., Harrendorf, S., Kaspar, J. & Höffler, K. (2021). Automatisierte Risikoprognosen im Kontext von Bewährungsentscheidungen. *Bewährungshilfe*, 68, 241–259.

Bygrave, L.A. (2020). Machine learning, cognitive sovereignty and data protection rights with respect to automated decisions. https://papers.ssrn.com/sol3/papers.cfm?abstract_id=3721118. Accessed 22 November 2020.

Carlson, A.M. (2017). The need for transparency in the age of predictive sentencing algorithms. *Iowa Law Review*, 103, 303-329.

Chander, A. (2017). The racist algorithm? *Michigan Law Review*, 115, 1023–1045.

Chen, S. (2021). Chinese scientists develop AI 'prosecutor' that can press its own charges. South China Morning Post, 26 December 2021. https://www.scmp.com/news/china/science/article/3160997/chinese-scientists-develop-ai-prosecutor-can-press-its-own. Accessed 24 January 2022.

Christin, A. (2019). Predictive algorithms and criminal sentencing. In: Bessner D and Guilhot N (eds.) *The Decisionist Imagination. Sovereignty, Social Science, and Democracy in the 20th Century*, Berghahn Books: New York, 272–294.

Commissioner for Human Rights. (2019). Unboxing artificial intelligence. 10 steps to protect Human Rights. Council of Europe. https://rm.coe.int/unboxing-artificial-intelligence-10-steps-to-protect-human-rights-reco/1680946e64. Accessed 22 November 2021.

Committee of Experts on Internet Intermediaries (MSI-NET). (2018). Algorithms and human rights. Study on the human rights dimensions of automated data processing techniques and possible regulatory implications. Council of Europe study, DGI(2017)12. https://rm.coe.int/algorithms-and-human-rights-study-on-the-human-rights-dimension-of-aut/1680796d10. Accessed 3 February 2022.

Council of Europe. (2021). EU accession to the ECHR. https://www.coe.int/en/web/human-rights-intergovernmental-cooperation/accession-of-the-european-union-to-the-european-convention-on-human-rights. Accessed 24 January 2022.

Cyphert, A.B. (2020). Reprogramming recidivism. The First Step Act and algorithmic prediction of risk. *Seton Hall Law Review*, 51, 331–381.

Danaher, J. (2020). Welcoming robots into the moral circle: A defence of ethical behaviourism. *Science and Engineering Ethics,* 26, 2023–2049.

Deeks, A. (2019). The judicial demand for explainable artificial intelligence. *Columbia Law Review*, 119, 1829–1850.

Dressel, J. & Farid, H. (2018). The accuracy, fairness, and limits of predicting recidivism. *Science Advances*, 4.

Duwe, G. & Kim, K. (2017). Out with the old and in with the new? An empirical comparison of supervised learning algorithms to predict recidivism. *Criminal Justice Policy Review*, 28, 570–600.

Duwell, M. (2014). Human Dignity: Concept, Discussions, Philosophical Perspectives: Interdisciplinary Perspectives. In: Duwell, M., Braarvig, J., Brownsword, R. & Mieth, D. (eds.) *Cambridge Handbook on Human Dignity.* Cambridge: Cambridge University Press, 23–50.

Dymitruk, M. (2019). The right to a fair trial in automated civil proceedings. *Masaryk University Journal of Law and Technology*, 13, 27-44.

Elsner, B., Aebi, M.F., Aubusson de Cavarlay, B., Gillieron, G., Hakeri, H., Jehle, J.-M., Killias, M., Lewis, C., Peters, J., Roth, E., Smit, P., Sobota, P., Turkovic, K., Wade, M. & Zila, J. (2008). The Criminal Justice Approach: Case Examples. *European Journal on Criminal Policy and Research*, 14, 123-132.

European Commission for the Efficiency of Justice (CEPEJ). (2018). European Ethical Charter on the use of artificial intelligence (AI) in judicial systems and their environment. https://rm.coe.int/ethical-charter-en-for-publication-4-december-2018/16808f699c. Accessed 22 November 2021.

European Court of Human Rights (ECtHR) (2021). Overview 1959–2020 ECHR. https://www.echr.coe.int/Documents/Overview_19592020_ENG.pdf. Accessed 1 February 2022.

European Criminal Policy Institute (2020). Category model for the harmonisation of criminal sanctions in Europe. In Satzger, H. (ed.) *Harmonisierung strafrechtlicher Sanktionen in der Europäischen Union – Harmonisation of Criminal Sanctions in the European Union.* Nomos: Baden-Baden, 707–742.

Fair Trials (2020). Regulating artificial intelligence for use in criminal justice systems in the EU. Policy paper. https://www.fairtrials.org/sites/default/files/RegulatingArtificialIntelligenceforUseinCriminalJusticeSystems-FairTrials.pdf. Accessed 3 February 2022.

Ghasemi, M., Anvari, D., Atapour, M., Wormith, J.S., Stockdale, K.C. & Spiteri, R.J. (2021). The application of machine learning to a general risk-need assessment instrument in the prediction of criminal recidivism. *Criminal Justice and Behavior*, 48, 518–538.

Gipson Rankin, S.M. (2021). Technological tethered. Potential impact of untrustworthy artificial intelligence in criminal justice risk assessment instruments. *Washington and Lee Law Review*, 78, 647–724.

Grabenwarter, C. & Pabel, K. (2021). *Europäische Menschenrechtskonvention* (7th ed.). München: C.H. Beck.

Greco, L. (2020). Richterliche Macht ohne richterliche Verantwortung. Warum es den Roboter-Richter nicht geben darf. *Rechtswissenschaft*, 11, 29–62.

Grundies, V. (2016). Gleiches Recht für alle? – Eine empirische Analyse lokaler Unterschiede in der Sanktionspraxis in der Bundesrepublik Deutschland. In Neubacher, F. & Bögelein, N. (eds.) *Krise – Kriminalität – Kriminologie*, Mönchengladbach: Forum Verlag Godesberg, 511–525.

Grundies, V. (2018). Regionale Unterschiede in der gerichtlichen Sanktionspraxis in der Bundesrepublik Deutschland. Eine empirische Analyse. In Hermann, D. & Pöge, A. (eds.) Kriminalsoziologie. Nomos: Baden-Baden, 295–316.

Herz, C. (2020). Striving for consistency: Why German sentencing needs reform. German Law Journal, 21, 1625–1648.

Hinkkanen, V. & Lappi-Seppälä, T. (2011). Sentencing theory, policy, and research in the nordic countries. *Crime and Justice*, 40, 349–404.

Jehle, J.-M., Lewis, C., Nagtegaal, M., Palmowski, N., Pyrcak-Górowska, M., van der Wolf M. & Zila, J. (2021). Dealing with dangerous offenders in Europe. A comparative study of provisions in England and Wales, Germany, the Netherlands, Poland and Sweden. *Criminal Law Forum*, 32, 181–245.

Kaspar, J., Höffler, K. & Harrendorf, S. (2020). Datenbanken, Online-Votings und künstliche Intelligenz—Perspektiven evidenzbasierter Strafzumessung im Zeitalter von "Legal Tech". *Neue Kriminalpolitik*, 32, 35–56.

Kehl, D., Guo, P. & Kessler, S. (2017). Algorithms in the criminal justice system. Assessing the use of risk assessments in sentencing. http://nrs.harvard.edu/urn-3:HUL.InstRepos:33746041. Accessed 22 November 2021.

Kohn, B. (2021). Künstliche Intelligenz und Strafzumessung, Baden-Baden: Nomos.

Länderarbeitsgruppe. (2019). Legal Tech: Herausforderungen für die Justiz. Abschlussbericht. https://www.schleswig-holstein.de/DE/Landesregier ung/II/Minister/Justizministerkonferenz/Downloads/190605_beschluesse/ TOPI_11_Abschlussbericht.pdf?__blob=publicationFile&v=1. Accessed 8 February 2022.

Langford, M. (2020). Taming the digital leviathan: Automated decision-making and international human rights. *American Journal of International Law Unbound*, 114, 141–146.

Lappi-Seppälä, T. (2007). Penal policy in Scandinavia. *Crime and Justice*, 36, 217–295.

Lara, F. & Deckers, J. (2020). Artificial intelligence as a Socratic assistant for moral enhancement. *Neuroethics*, 13, 275–287.

Lee, M. K. (2018). Understanding perception of algorithmic decisions: Fairness, trust, and emotion in response to algorithmic management. *Big Data & Society*, 5, 1–16.

Lindner, B., Neumann, L. & Pohlmann, S. (2020). Comparative Conclusion. In Satzger, H. (ed.) *Harmonisierung strafrechtlicher Sanktionen in der Europäischen Union—Harmonisation of Criminal Sanctions in the European Union*. Nomos: Baden-Baden, pp. 517–540.

Lyell, D. & Coiera, E. (2017). Automation bias and verification complexity. A systematic review. *Journal of the American Medical Informatics Association*, 24, 423–431.

Mavronicola, N. (2015). Crime, Punishment and Article 3 ECHR: Puzzles and Prospects of Applying an Absolute Right in a Penal Context. *Human Rights Law Review*, 15, 721–743.

Meyer-Ladewig, J. & Nettesheim, M. (2017). Artikel 8 EMRK. Recht auf Achtung des Privat—und Familienlebens. In: Meyer-Ladewig, J., Nettesheim, M. & v. Raumer, S. (eds.) *EMRK: Europäische Menschenrechtskonvention—Handkommentar* (4 ed.) Nomos: Baden-Baden.

McLuhan, M. & Fiore, Q. (2001). The Medium is the Message. An Inventory of Effects, Corte Madera: Gingki Press Inc.

Mitchell, O. (2005). A meta-analysis of race and sentencing research. Explaining the inconsistencies. *Journal of Quantitative Criminology*, 21(4), 439–466.

Nieto-Martín, A., Muñoz de Morales Romero, M. & Rodríguez Yagüe, C. (2020). Country Report Spain. In: Satzger, H. (ed.) *Harmonisierung strafrechtlicher Sanktionen in der Europäischen Union—Harmonisation of Criminal Sanctions in the European Union*. Nomos: Baden-Baden, 149–183.

Nink, D. (2021). *Justiz und Algorithmen. Über die Schwächen menschlicher Entscheidungsfindung und die Möglichkeiten neuer Technologien in der Rechtsprechung.* Nomos: Baden-Baden.

Poursabzi-Sangdeh, F., Goldstein, D. G., Hofman, J. M., Vaughan, J. W. & Wallach, H. (2018). Manipulating and measuring model interpretability. In: *Proceedings of the 2021 CHI Conference on Human Factors in Computing Systems (CHI '21). Association for Computing Machinery*, New York, NY, USA, 237, 1–52.

Quattrocolo, S. (2019). An introduction to AI and criminal justice in Europe. *Revista Brasileira de Direito Processual Penal,* 5, 1519–1554.

Rainie, L. & Anderson, J. (2017). Code-dependent: Pros and cons of the algorithm age. https://apo.org.au/node/74277. Accessed 7 November 2022.

Reiling, A.D. (2020). Courts and artificial intelligence. *International Journal for Court Administration,* 11, Art. 8.

Rostalski, F. & Völkening, M. (2019). Smart Sentencing. Ein neuer Ansatz für Transparenz richterlicher Strafzumessungsentscheidungen. *Kriminalpolitische Zeitschrift,* 265–273.

Ruppert, F. (2021). Strafzumessung am Scheideweg? Legal Tech und Strafzumessung, *Kriminalpolitische Zeitschrift,* 90–98.

Rudin, C., Wang, C. & Coker, B. (2020). The age of secrecy and unfairness in recidivism prediction. Harvard Data Science Review 2.1. https://hdsr.mit press.mit.edu/pub/7z10o269/release/4. Accessed 22 November 2021.

Russell, S.J. & Norvig, P. (2021). *Artificial Intelligence. A Modern Approach* (4 ed.). Pearson: Hoboken.

Satzger, H. (2020). Strafzumessung in den USA. In: Satzger, H. (ed.) *Harmonisierung strafrechtlicher Sanktionen in der Europäischen Union—Harmonisation of Criminal Sanctions in the European Union.* Nomos: Baden-Baden, 541–563.

Satzger, H., Lindner, B. & Pohlmann, S. (2020). Research Report. In: Satzger, H. (ed.) *Harmonisierung strafrechtlicher Sanktionen in der Europäischen Union—Harmonisation of Criminal Sanctions in the European Union.* Nomos: Baden-Baden, 35–45.

Shank, D.B., DeSanti, A. & Maninger, T. (2019). When are artificial intelligence versus human agents faulted for wrongdoing? Moral attributions after individual and joint decisions. *Information, Communication & Society,* 22, 648–663.

Simmons, R. (2018). Big Data, Machine Judges, and the Legitimacy of the Criminal Justice System. *UC Davis Law Review,* 1067–1118.

Sommerer, L. (2020). *Personenbezogenes Predictive Policing. Kriminalwissenschaftliche Untersuchung über die Automatisierung der Kriminalprognose.* Baden-Baden: Nomos.

Sourdin, T. (2018). Judge v robot? Artificial intelligence and judicial decision-making. *UNSW Law Journal*, 41, 1114–1133.

Spohn, C. (2015). Evolution of sentencing research. *Criminology and Public Policy*, 14, 225–232.

Staffler, L. & Jany, O. (2020). Künstliche Intelligenz und Strafrechtspflege—eine Orientierung, Zeitschrift für Internationale Strafrechtsdogmatik, 15, 164–177.

Steffensmeier, D., Painter-Davis, N. & Ulmer, J. (2017). Intersectionality of race, ethnicity, gender, and age on criminal punishment. *Sociological Perspectives*, 60, 810–833.

Steinborn, S. (2020). Länderbericht Polen. In: Satzger, H. (ed.) *Harmonisierung strafrechtlicher Sanktionen in der Europäischen Union—Harmonisation of Criminal Sanctions in the European Union.* Nomos: Baden-Baden, 333–377.

Tigard, D.W. (2021). Artificial moral responsibility: How we can and cannot hold machines responsible. *Cambridge Quarterly of Healthcare Ethics*, 30, 435–447.

Ulenaers, J. (2020). The impact of artificial intelligence on the right to a fair trial. Towards a robot judge? *Asian Journal of Law and Economics*, 11, article number: 20200008.

Ünver, H.A. (2018). Artificial Intelligence, Authoritarianism and the Future of Political Systems, Centre for Economics and Foreign Policy Studies. https://www.jstor.org/stable/resrep26084. Accessed 22 November 2021.

Vorhaus (2002). Part One: Article 3 of the European Convention on Human Rights. *Common Law World Review*, 31, 374–399.

Wachter, S. & Mittelstadt, B. (2019). A right to reasonable inferences: re-thinking data protection law in the age of big data and AI. *Columbia Business Law Review*, 494–620.

Wang, C., Han, B., Patel, B., Mohideen, F. & Rudin, C. (2020). In pursuit of interpretable, fair and accurate machine learning for criminal recidivism prediction. https://arxiv.org/abs/2005.04176. Accessed 24 January 2022.

Wooldredge, J., Frank, J., Goulette, N. & Travis, L. (2015). Is the impact of cumulative disadvantage on sentencing greater for black defendants? *Criminology and Public Policy*, 14, 187–223.

Završnik, A. (2018). Algorithmic crime control. In: Završnik A (ed.) *Big Data, Crime and Social Control*, Routledge: New York, 131–153.

Završnik, A. (2020). Criminal justice, artificial intelligence systems and human rights, *ERA Forum,* 20, 567–583.

Zuiderveen Borgesius, F. (2018). Discrimination, artificial intelligence and algorithmic decision-making. https://rm.coe.int/discrimination-art ificial-intelligence-and-algorithmic-decision-making/1680925d73. Accessed 22 November 2021.

2

Technical and Legal Challenges of the Use of Automated Facial Recognition Technologies for Law Enforcement and Forensic Purposes

Patricia Faraldo Cabana🆔

1 Introduction

Biometrics covers a variety of automated technologies used for the identification and authentication of individuals based on their behavioral, physical and biological characteristics. The main biometric methods that are in use today are still fingerprint and DNA technologies. As computational power and techniques improve and the resolution of sensor modules increases, it seems clear that many benefits could be derived through the application of a wider range of biometric techniques for law enforcement and forensic purposes. Facial recognition technology (FRT), taking advantage of our improved understanding of the human body and advanced sensing techniques, makes it possible to uniquely identify individuals. It provides advantages over traditional identification methods,

---

P. Faraldo Cabana (✉)
Facultad de Derecho, Campus de Elviña, A Coruña, Spain
e-mail: patricia.faraldo@udc.es

© The Author(s), under exclusive license to Springer Nature
Switzerland AG 2023
A. Završnik and K. Simončič (eds.), *Artificial Intelligence, Social Harms
and Human Rights*, Critical Criminological Perspectives,
https://doi.org/10.1007/978-3-031-19149-7_2

35

since (1) it is based upon who the person is and inherent characteristics that exist within the human body, which are much harder to replicate than a passport or a social security card, allowing to avoid circumvention, that is, copy or imitation by using artefacts; and (2) it is possible to capture facial images in unconstrained environments, using, for instance, video surveillance cameras or multimedia content available on social networking sites, such as photos or video recordings. Facial biometric systems are increasingly used as security and surveillance mechanisms in Europe, but there are many difficulties in using such evidence to secure convictions in criminal cases. Some are related to their technical shortcomings, which impact their utility as evidence, while others to the need to provide safeguards and protection to human rights, which has led to the EU and national legislatures putting restrictions upon the storage, processing and usage of facial biometric data, since people's facial images are recognized as sensitive data. Moreover, the use of automatic systems, which compare images and generate a matching score, with no human intervention, adds its own challenges. As a result, examples of national law enforcement authorities in the EU using such systems are still quite sparse,[1] even though several are testing their potential.

This paper looks at the technical (Sect. 2) and legal challenges of FRT (Sect. 3), focusing on its use for law enforcement and forensic purposes in criminal matters. Recognizing that automated facial recognition has the potential to revolutionize the identification process, facilitate crime detection and reduce misidentification of suspects, the aim of this paper is to improve its usefulness as intelligence data in police investigations and as forensic evidence in the criminal justice system by highlighting the critical issues that hinder a wider use. This fills an important gap in literature. Certainly, there is a vast amount of research into the area

---

[1] FRT in relation to criminal investigations has been implemented in 11 EU member states and in two international police cooperation organizations, Europol and Interpol. Currently, 7 member states expect to implement it until 2022 (TELEFI, 2021, p. 22). FRT is much more frequent in the USA. Already in 2012 the FBI launched the Interstate Photo System Facial Recognition Pilot project in three states, a system fully deployed as of June 2014, now integrated in the Next Generation Identification System, which provides the US criminal justice community with the world's largest electronic repository of biometric and criminal history information. For other applications at state and local level, see New York City Bar Association (2020).

of application of biometric techniques in forensic investigations. It has been boosted in the last two decades by computational intelligence techniques replacing manual identification approaches in forensic sciences (Saini & Kapoor, 2016) and the wide range of applications for traditional and cybercrime detection (Dilek et al., 2015). Much has been said about how automated biometric technologies in general, and FRT in particular, provide advantages over traditional identification methods. A combined analysis of technical shortcomings and legal limits of the identification of facial images for their use for investigative purposes, however, have largely escaped scientific scrutiny. The combination of both technical and legal approaches is necessary to recognize and identify the main potential risks arising from the use of FRT, in order to prevent both possible errors due to technological misassumptions and threats to fundamental rights, including, among others, human dignity, the right to respect for private life, the protection of personal data, non-discrimination, the rights of the child and the elderly, the rights of people with disabilities, and the right to an effective remedy and to a fair trial (FRA 2019). On the one hand, a good part of the controversies and contingencies surrounding the credibility and reliability of facial biometrics for law enforcement and forensic purposes is intimately related to its technical shortcomings. On the other hand, data acquisition and protection, database custody, transparency, fairness, accountability and trust are relevant legal issues that might raise problems when using FRT results as traces that target individuals and trigger police action which may have a very significant impact on their lives and freedoms.

The topic is definitely a timely one. The EU General Data Protection Regulation 2016/679[2] (henceforth GDPR), which came into force in 2018, created a complex set of new rules for the collection, storage and retention of personal data. It introduces several categories of personal data to which different regimes apply. The GDPR prohibits the processing of biometric data for the purpose of uniquely identifying natural persons—interestingly, verification, one-to-one comparison, is

---

[2] Regulation (EU) 2016/679 of the European Parliament and of the Council of 27 April 2016 on the protection of natural persons with regard to the processing of personal data and on the free movement of such data, and repealing Directive 95/46/EC (General Data Protection Regulation) [2016] OJ L119/89.

another kind of use and purpose than identification, or one-to-many comparison (Kindt, 2018, pp. 526–527). Such a processing is considered very privacy intrusive and likely to result in a high risk to the rights and freedoms of natural persons. Therefore, only if the processing operation falls within one of the exemptions under article 9(2) GDPR or the relevant national legislation—the GDPR grants EU member states some discretion to adopt or modify existing legal rules—it is possible to process biometric data for the purpose of uniquely identifying individuals. There is a new obligation for the controllers to assess the impact and risks of such operations in a data protection impact assessment and to take safeguards, and if needed, to consult with the supervisory authority and obtain authorization. In the same line, Directive 2016/680[3] (henceforth LED, Law Enforcement Directive) prohibits automated decisions that produce adverse legal effects concerning the data subject or significantly affect him or her, unless such decisions are authorized by EU or member state law and include appropriate safeguards for the rights and freedoms of the data subject. Therefore, it is not sufficient to circumscribe the pertinent assessment to a reading of the GDPR. It is necessary to move toward an assessment of national legislation that either specifies the GDPR requirements or implements the LED, as member states might adopt exemptions or derogations that modulate the safeguards eventually available to individuals when their data are processed for law enforcement and forensic purposes. Therefore, the current legal landscape is fragmented. These contingencies have led to a lack of clarity on the legal requirements surrounding the automated processing of personal biometric data (Kindt, 2018).

---

[3] Directive (EU) 2016/680 of the European Parliament and of the Council of 27 April 2016 on the protection of natural persons with regard to the processing of personal data by competent authorities for the purposes of the prevention, investigation, detection or prosecution of criminal offences or the execution of criminal penalties, and on the free movement of such data, and repealing Council Framework Decision 2008/977/JHA [2016] OJ L119/89.

2 Technical Shortcomings of FRT

Although facial biometrics have achieved satisfactory results in controlled environments, various factors such as expression, pose and occlusion, as well as sensor quality and calibration limit the practical application of this technology. Due to different positioning on the acquiring sensor, imperfect imaging conditions, environmental changes, bad user interaction with the sensor, etc., it is impossible that two samples of the same face, acquired in different sessions, exactly coincide, even if they are photographs of a suspect taken under controlled conditions (Tistarelli et al., 2014; Zeinstra et al., 2018, p. 24). There are also variations due to aging or physical changes like beard, glasses, change in hairstyle, etc. For this reason, a facial biometric matching systems' response is also typically a matching score that quantifies the similarity between the input and the database template representations. Therefore, the automated recognition of individuals offered by facial biometric systems must be tempered by an awareness of the uncertainty associated with that recognition.

In fact, in the capture or acquisition stage, due to the natural changes in the face and expression over time as well as other challenges such as varying illuminations, poor contrast and non-cooperative approach by subjects, FRT may lead to limited recognition performances (Sarangi et al., 2018; Zeinstra et al., 2018). Facial recognition in many instances has proved unreliable for visual surveillance and identification systems. Certainly, facial biometrics are related to physical features, but there are cases in which facial features are not available, for example, for religious or sanitary reasons—e.g., Islamic veil, face mask or surgical mask—or because those who are planning to commit crimes are aware of the fact that visual surveillance mechanisms are in operation in the area and therefore they take steps to avoid detection from the cameras by hiding their faces or disguising their physical appearance through 3D masks, make-up, facial hair, glasses or surgical operations. On the other hand, reliable acquisition of the input signal is another challenge. Changes in scale, location and in-plane rotation of the face, as well as rotation in depth—facing the camera obliquely—may seriously affect performance. Sensor quality and calibration also play an important role.

Captured video image data of facial figures may have many shortcomings. For example, a too low resolution in order to reliably identify the subject from his or her facial characteristics (Bouchrika, 2016; Singh & Prasad, 2018, p. 537), or a too far distance to the subject, since facial features may not be recovered from a given distance. There are, though, some promising approaches using 3D face recognition systems (Zhou & Xiao, 2018) and night vision capacities based on thermal facial imagery (Riggan et al., 2018).

Once acquired, the raw biometric data of an individual is first assessed and, when needed, subjected to signal enhancement algorithms to improve its quality. In this phase, algorithms can be manipulated, either to escape detection or to create impostors. For example, knowledge of the feature extraction algorithms can be used to design special features in presented biometric samples to cause incorrect features to be calculated.[4] Subsequently, the initial biometric sample is transformed into a digital template that contains only the information needed to run the pattern recognition algorithm. In the comparison stage, the template is compared with another registered template in the system to produce a score-based likelihood ratio or matching ratio, according to which the identification of a person or the verification of her or his identity is validated or rejected. At this stage, the false non-match rate (FNMR) and the false match rate (FMR) are functions of the system threshold: If the designer decreases the acceptance threshold to make the system more tolerant to input variations, FMR increases, while if the acceptance threshold is raised to make the system more secure, FNMR increases accordingly (Fish et al., 2013). In short, designers can set the acceptance threshold value at will (Kotsoglou & Oswald, 2020, p. 88). In

---

[4] This section concentrates on system vulnerabilities which are part of the biometric processing itself. Since biometric systems are implemented on server computers, they are vulnerable to all cryptographic, virus and other attacks which plague any computer system. For example, biometric data may be stored locally on hardware within the organization, or externally at an unknown location within the cloud (Tomova, 2009), both vulnerable to hacking. The training dataset may be subject to intentional manipulations, such as data poisoning attacks (Papernot et al., 2018) and backdoor injections (Chen et al., 2017). Vulnerabilities of data storage concern modifying the storage (adding, modifying or removing templates or raw data), copying data for secondary uses (identity theft or directly inputting the information at another stage of the system to achieve authentication) and modifying the identity to which the biometric is assigned. We are aware of these issues, but do not intend to cover them in this paper.

order to do it, however, the task, purpose and context of the FRT use is important: When applying the technology in places visited by millions of people—such as airports or train stations—a relatively small proportion of errors still means that hundreds of individuals are wrongly flagged, that is, either they are incorrectly identified or incorrectly rejected as a match. The consequences of these two errors are different depending on the situation. For example, if the police use a facial recognition algorithm in their efforts to locate a fugitive, a false positive can lead to the wrongful arrest of an innocent person, while a false negative may help the suspect to slip through. Each case requires a determination of the cost of different kinds of errors, and a decision on which kind of errors to prioritize. Accordingly, industrial settings such as the mentioned acceptance threshold should reflect the institutional architecture of the criminal process including its overriding objectives, i.e. acquitting the innocent, convicting the guilty and the acceptable rate of errors/trade-off between these objectives. The renowned Blackstone-ratio, stressing the 'fundamental value [...] of our society that it is far worse to convict an innocent man than to let a guilty man go free' (Blackstone, 1769 [1893], p. 358), illustrates this point.

The probabilistic nature of facial biometric systems also means that the measured characteristics of the population of those subjects in the system are designed to recognize matter and affect design and implementation. A large amount of training data is required to obtain good accuracy. Because of the biased composition of police datasets, mostly white, male-dominated, but with an overrepresentation of ethnic and racial minorities, algorithms trained with these data increase the risk of false identification of women and minorities. Unequal error rates are not always indicative of bias, but they may reflect a pre-existing societal bias and can lead to inaccurate outcomes that infringe on people's fundamental rights, including equality and non-discrimination (Eubanks, 2018).

Furthermore, the utility of facial recognition software is dependent on practitioners' understanding of how to use it. The algorithmic process renders a match between a face captured on video and an image on the database, but then there are two possibilities. In the first one, the system operator, i.e. a human being (police officer, forensic expert), has to intervene and make his or her assessment by reviewing the 'match'. Without specialized training, personnel reviewing matches may achieve false results. This training is not regulated. In the second one, whenever a human is not reviewing the match a confidence threshold should be introduced to prevent adverse effects on those being misidentified, requiring the algorithm to only return a result if it is x% certain of its findings. However, there are no existing standards for police, the courts and the public to assess the accuracy of facial biometric systems. There is a lack of methodological standardization and empirical validation, notably when using automatic systems (Jacquet & Champod, 2020). Despite extensive research in the area, automated FRT is still struggling to achieve sufficient reliability and repeatability for its use in forensic identifications. Moreover, regarding criminal databases, the requirements for facial images and the practices used for quality assurance show significant variations between EU member states, most of which do not apply quality standards for image capture or database entry, performed neither by human intervention nor automatically by the software (TELEFI, 2021, pp. 29–30).

Even though in the last years there have been massive steps forward in the technology's performance (Galbally et al., 2019), no current system can claim to handle all of these problems well. Moreover, only limited studies have been done on accuracy and reproducibility. To overcome reliability issues of FRT and increase the possibility of recognition and verification, a multimodal fusion of a selection of biometric modalities or multiple aspects of the same feature has been proposed (Ross et al., 2006; Saini & Kapoor, 2016; Tistarelli et al., 2014). Recent advances in facial biometric technologies suggest complementing facial recognition systems with facial soft biometric traits (Arigbabu et al., 2015; Dantcheva et al., 2011). These traits can be typically described using human understandable labels and measurements, allowing for retrieval and recognition solely based on verbal descriptions. They can be physical—such as eye and hair color, skin, presence of facial hair (beard, moustache), scars, marks and tattoos, sex, body geometry, height and weight—or behavioral—like gait or keystroke. Soft biometrics are only relatively useful to identify individuals—they lack of sufficient permanence and distinctiveness (Tome et al., 2015)—but they can complement the performance of facial recognition systems. For example, these additional techniques remove the difficulties inherent to facial biometric techniques due to expression, occlusion and pose. They take advantages of high resolution images and rely upon micro-features in the face to increase reliability. These techniques, however, still fail to overcome the difficulties that arise when the face is obscured by the suspect. Moreover, although data fusion may involve the same biometric trait—face—acquired from different devices, little effort has been devoted to the multimodal integration and fusion of data from multiple sensor modules (Tistarelli et al., 2014).

3 Legal Challenges of FRT

FRT is coveted as a mechanism to address the perceived need for increased security, but there are many aspects of these technologies that give rise to legal concerns regarding their use for law enforcement and forensic purposes. The first problem is related to the taking of the biometric sample from the individual through image capture (Benzaoui et al., 2017). Fingerprint and DNA methods, while being long-standing methods of being used as proof of crimes, require invasive methods for their collection. Hence, only those who have already been suspected or convicted of crimes have their information stored in a database, which limits the detection of crime to existing offenders. By contrast, facial recognition is unique from other forms of biometric surveillance in that it tracks one's face, that is, something that is difficult to hide and easy to observe in the open, without the consent of the observed person. Researches in the field of FRT appear to regard the ability to obtain biometric data by non-invasive means and without the requirement to obtain consent from the data subject as a benefit (see, for instance, Singh & Prasad, 2018, p. 537). Certainly, depending on the perspective, the reduced requirement for human subject compliance may be an advantage of this method (New York City Bar Association, 2020, p. 2; Arigbabu et al., 2015). Capture without constraint is a prerequisite in surveillance environments and lightens the workload of criminal investigations. It allows authorities to circumvent the legal limitations inherent within the collection of DNA and fingerprint evidence. At the same time, it subjects these techniques to significant privacy concerns about the collection of such data (Kindt, 2013, 2018, pp. 297–306), which in turn leads to significant civil and political resistance against such a collection due to its high potential for misuse.

The second concern regards the processing of the acquired image, including, whether or not by automated means, collecting, recording and storing (Article 4.2 GDPR). In respect of data protection, the processing of a subject's image with FRT individualizes him or her from others. Since this act constitutes the processing of sensitive personal data, data protection principles apply. As a general principle, the processing of biometric data for the purpose of uniquely identifying a natural person, as the processing of all other special categories of personal data, is forbidden for all entities falling under the material scope of the GDPR, including public authorities, governments and private organizations (Article 9.1 GDPR). However, several exemptions from the prohibition exist (Article 9.2 GDPR). Moreover, for law enforcement agencies (LEAs) a separate regime applies. They are allowed to process biometric data for unique identification under three cumulative conditions: (i) if 'strictly necessary', (ii) if subject to appropriate safeguards for the rights and freedoms of the data subject and only (iii) (a) where authorized by Union or member state law; (b) to protect the vital interests of the data subject or of another natural person; or (c) where such processing relates to data which are manifestly made public by the data subject (Article 10 LED). Therefore, for LEAs, further national law is awaited implementing Directive 2016/680, which does not prohibit per se the use of biometric data for identification purposes. Such national law is still not enacted in many countries or does not offer clear guidance on police collection and use of biometric data.

The third problem is related to the storage of the image or template in a database. Challenges are similar to those posed by human genetics databases (Sutrop, 2010). Retention of all available data on those who have committed serious crimes seems to be unproblematic (Bichard, 2004). It leads to the improved detection of crime and act as a deterrent. Conversely, retention of biometric data of individuals who have not been convicted of a criminal offence, even if deemed dangerous, has been subjected to successful legal challenge in some jurisdictions, such as the United Kingdom[5] or France.[6] Furthermore, the European Court of Human Rights clearly stated in S. and Marper[7] that already the mere retention of fingerprints—because objectively containing unique information about the individual concerned allowing his or her identification with precision in a wide range of circumstances—by LEAs amounts to an interference with the right to respect for private life. This applies even more when such data undergo automatic processing and are retained and used for police purposes for an indeterminate period without appropriate guarantees, such as the prospect of a successful request to be removed.[8] Since European and national case law tends to favor a strict interpretation of the necessity and proportionality tests as they apply to law enforcement use, the critical issue therefore is how to achieve the correct balance between the needs of LEAs to detect those responsible for serious crimes and the needs of the public to keep their own personal data private and protected from misuse.

The fourth concern regards the use of facial biometric data for purposes other than the one for which they were originally captured and stored. The gradual widening of the use of a technology or system beyond the purpose for which it was originally intended is known as

---

[5] For example, in S & Marper v United Kingdom [2008] ECHR 1581, the European Court on Human Rights found the retention by the British police of DNA samples of individuals who had been arrested but had later been acquitted, or who had had the charges against them dropped, to be a violation of their right to privacy under Article 8 ECHR (Sampson 2018). Furthermore, in some EU member states the indefinite retention of biometric samples, including DNA evidence and fingerprints of data subjects, has been successfully challenged, except for in exceptional circumstances. See, for the (pre-Brexit) UK, R (on the application of GC & C) v The Commissioner of Police of the Metropolis [2011] UKSC 21. Also in the UK the High Court of Justice (England and Wales) was called upon to determine whether the current legal regime in that country was 'adequate to ensure the appropriate and non-arbitrary use of automated facial recognition in a free and civilized society'. In R (Bridges) v Chief Constable of the South Wales Police [2019] EWHC 2341 (Admin), the judgment was that the use of FRT was not 'in accordance with law' and implied a breach of Article 8 (1) and (2) ECHR and of data protection law, and it failed to comply with the public sector equality duty.

[6] The Constitutional Court in France stated that the keeping of a database with biometric identity information allowing identification interferes with the fundamental right to respect of privacy. Cons. const. (France) no. 2012–652, 22 March 2012 (Loi protection de l'identité), Article 6.

[7] ECtHR, S. and Marper v. United Kingdom, nos. 30562/04 and 30566/04, 4 December 2008, Articles 84 and 86.

[8] ECtHR, M.K. v. France, no.19522/09, 18 April 2013, Articles 44–46 ('ECtHR, M.K. 2013').

'function creep'. It occurs whenever the original purpose for which the data collection is justified is overreached and the biometric data is used for other purposes (Mordini & Massari, 2008, p. 490). Such an expansion to other domains entails both technical and legal risks. One example of the former is using the data collected in a domain purely for the sake of convenience in a domain that demands high data integrity, assuming incorrectly that collected data are of greater fidelity than they really are (National Research Council, 2010, p. 4). For the latter, vast name and face databases of law-abiding citizens already in existence (i.e. driver's license records, ID photos, databases relating to aliens, asylum seekers or missing persons), which were created for purposes other than investigative ones, may be used to access facial images that allow the identification of persons not in custody for which reasonable suspicion of criminal involvement may not be present. Currently, the police of some EU member states has legal access to non-criminal databases containing facial images that can be used for facial recognition in criminal investigations (TELEFI, 2021, p. 31). Such a police seizure of a person registered in these civil databases for the purpose of subjecting that person to an identification procedure does implicate the right to privacy.

The fifth concern is related to the impact of these technologies on racial and ethnic minorities and other vulnerable and disadvantaged groups. On a general level, facial recognition software trained with police databases has a higher chance of disproportionately affecting racial and ethnic minorities when used for law enforcement purposes. Members of these minorities are more likely to be enrolled in these database systems as they are arrested and subject to criminal law proceedings at a higher rate than their population share. This disproportion leads to a vicious circle in which more members of minorities are detected, which in turn amplifies the need to police minority groups already heavily over-policed. In turn, if trained with other biometric data sets, facial recognition software is usually built around whiteness, maleness and ability as default categories (Browne, 2015, p. 113), showing disproportionate failure at 'the intersection of racialized, queered, gendered, classed, and disabled bodies' (Magnet, 2011, p. 50), where the characteristic uncertainty of facial biometrics is greater (Abdurrahim et al., 2018; Beveridge et al.,

2009; Howard & Etter, 2013). Moreover, the attempt to reduce identity to a bodily characteristic is especially problematic for subjects who are already in a marginalized position (Wevers, 2018). In fact, biometric technologies do not recognize that identities and faces have social and cultural dimensions (Sharp, 2000), and that identity is much more than a face or a bodily appearance.

Last but not least, scores generated by AI-based software have proved to be highly influential on human decision-makers, who may find it difficult to bypass the system output (Cooke & Michie, 2013). In general, many studies have shown that police officers, courts and jurors have difficulties in discerning reliable biometric evidence from unreliable evidence, and as a consequence they place too high a probative value on such evidence (Cummings, 2014; Freeman, 2016; Garrett & Mitchell, 2013; Maeder et al., 2017; Završnik, 2020). The reliability problem is not unique to these so-called second generation forensic techniques (Murphy, 2007), such as facial and iris-based biometric systems (Keenan, 2015; Thompson, 2018), automated speaker recognition (Bonastre et al., 2015, pp. 263–275) or automated handwriting identification and verification (Working Group on Human Factors in Handwriting Examination, 2020, pp. 68–71). Traditional biometric techniques, such as DNA (Lieberman et al., 2008), fingerprints (Nigam et al., 2015; Cole, 2004, p. 73), handwriting (Sulner, 2018) or voice identification (Morrison et al., 2016), also fail sometimes to meet standards of scientific validation, despite their long history of admissibility.

4 Conclusion

FRT has been promoted as the 'magic bullet' that will solve the problem of the real and urgent need to accurately identify people on the internet, especially since many financial crimes and other crimes of deception are committed online (Keenan, 2015). But, as shown in Sect. 2, the aura of infallibility sometimes associated with automated biometric technologies generates expectations that are often not met in the concrete reality of criminal investigations. Automated facial recognition is an inherently probabilistic endeavor, and hence inherently fallible. The probabilistic nature of the output, and the building of certain values into the tool, raise questions as to the justifiability of regarding the tool's output as 'objective' grounds for reasonable suspicion (Kotsoglou & Oswald, 2020, p. 86). Some of the obstacles to reliability of such methods have been considered here. Certainly, there is constant innovation in the area of facial biometric technologies that seek to overcome the difficulties of existing applications, such as the use of soft biometrics, but they still need some time to spread. Furthermore, as detailed in Sect. 3, there are also concerns about fundamental rights protection, function creep and social discrimination. To overcome them, transparency is an important tool. But biometric technologies are still ruled by proprietary solutions, kept secret and protected by patents. In many cases, that bars an independent evaluation of the device performances and of its real capabilities (Esposito, 2012, p. 9). If the right to a fair trial is to be upheld, the means by which the identification takes place must be disclosed to the defense, together with information regarding disregarded 'matches' and error rates and uncertainties of the system itself (Kotsoglou & Oswald, 2020, p. 88). The GDPR requires the explainability of decisions made by algorithms, but there is a gap with regard to tools and techniques that enable the forensic analysis of performance and failures in AI-enabled systems and the quantification of uncertainty (Baggili & Behzadan, 2019, p. 1; Champod & Tistarelli, 2017). FRT is no exception in this regard. This compromises the legal soundness of the results.

There are also other challenges that still prevent the large-scale adoption of facial biometric techniques within criminal investigations; most importantly, biometric data derived from the human body. From a legal perspective, there are understandably areas of resistance based upon individual, religious or socio-cultural factors (Tomova, 2009, p. 112). Fair processing of personal data requires that the data subject be informed of the storage of data. The data controller also has responsibility to establish a certain degree of accuracy of the system and to implement suitable measures to safeguard the data subject's rights and freedoms and legitimate interests, for instance by ensuring him or her the right to obtain human intervention on the part of the controller, to express his or her point of view, and to contest the decision, including the right of the data subject to receive meaningful information about the logic involved in automated processing. Hence there is a need within the various cultural, social and religious contexts for the right balance to be achieved between security needs for identification and verification and legal and ethical requirements for data protection. More uniform, comprehensive laws are also needed to fill the regulatory void, particularly evident at national level. These laws should provide the conditions that make acceptable the exceptional use of FRTs by LEAs. The setting of minimum accuracy standards across the industry can also reduce uncertainty of what defines an acceptable use of FRTs for law enforcement and forensic purposes.

Even with the present deficits, there are clear advantages of automated facial biometric approaches to criminal investigations. In particular, automated FRTs help in analyzing the evidence by overcoming the limitations of human cognitive abilities and thus increase both the efficiency and effectiveness of investigations. Moreover, these methods provide a solid scientific basis for the standardization of crime investigation procedure. They show a great potential as an instrument to help the experts to assess the strength of evidence and complement the human-based approach.

References

Abdurrahim, S. H., Samad, S. A., & Huddin, A. B. (2018). Review on the effects of age, gender, and race demographics on automatic face recognition. *The Visual Computer, 34*, 1617–1630. https://doi.org/10.1007/s00371-017-1428-z

Arigbabu, O. A., Ahmad, S. M. S., Adnan, W. A. W., & Yussof, S. (2015). Recent advances in facial soft biometrics. *The Visual Computer, 31*, 513–525. https://doi.org/10.1007/s00371-014-0990-x

Baggili, I., & Behzadan, V. (2019). Founding the domain of AI forensics. arXiv: 1912.06497v1.

Benzaoui, A., Adjabi, I., & Boukrouche, A. (2017). Experiments and improvements of ear recognition based on local texture descriptors. *Optical Engineering, 56*, 043109. https://doi.org/10.1117/1.OE.56.4.043109

Beveridge, J. R., Givens, G. H., Phillips, P. J., & Draper, B. A. (2009). Factors that influence algorithm performance in the face recognition grand challenge. *Computer Vision and Image Understanding, 113*(6), 750–762. https://doi.org/10.1016/j.cviu.2008.12.007

Bichard, M. (2004). *The Bichard Inquiry. Report* (No. HC 653). The Stationary Office.

Blackstone, W. (1893). *Commentaries on the laws of England* (p. 1769). J. B. Lippincott Co.

Bonastre, J.-F., Kahn, J., Rossato, S., & Ajili, M. (2015). Forensic speaker recognition: Mirages and reality. In S. Fuchs, D. Pape, C. Petrone, & P. Perrier (Eds.), *Individual Differences in Speech Production and Perception* (pp. 255–285). Peter Lang.

Bouchrika, I. (2016). Evidence Evaluation of Gait Biometrics for Forensic Investigation. In A. E. Hassanien, M. M. Fouad, A. A. Manaf, M. Zamani, R. Ahmad, & J. Kacprzyk (Eds.), *Multimedia Forensics and Security: Foundations, Innovations, and Applications* (pp. 307–326). Springer.

Browne, S. (2015). B®anding Blackness: Biometric Technology and the Surveillance of Blackness. In S. Browne (Ed.), *Dark Matters: On the Surveillance of Blackness* (pp. 89–130). Duke University Press.

Champod, C. & Tistarelli, M. (2017). Biometric Technologies for Forensic Science and Policing: State of the Art. In M. Tistarelli, M., & C. Champod (Eds.), *Handbook of Biometrics for Forensic Science* (pp. 1–15). Springer.

Chen, X., Liu, C., Li, B., Lu, K., & Song, D. (2017). Targeted backdoor attacks on deep learning systems using data poisoning. arXiv preprint arXiv: 1712.05526.

Cole, S. A. (2004). Fingerprint Identification and the Criminal Justice System. In D. Lazer (Ed.), *DNA and the Criminal Justice System. The Technology of Justice* (pp. 63–89). MIT Press.

Cooke, D. J., & Michie, C. (2013). Violence risk assessment: From prediction to understanding—or from what? To why? In C. Logan & L. Johnstone (Eds.), *Managing Clinical Risk* (pp. 22–44). Routledge.

Cummings, M. L. (2014). *Automation bias in intelligent time critical decision support systems*. American Institute of Aeronautics and Astronautics.

Dantcheva, A., Velardo, C., D'Angelo, A., & Dugelay, J.-L. (2011). Bag of soft biometrics for person identification. New trends and challenges. *Multimedia Tools and Applications, 51*, 739–777. https://doi.org/10.1007/s11042-010-0635-7

Dilek, S., Çakır, H., & Aydın, M. (2015). Applications of Artificial Intelligence Techniques to Combating Cyber Crimes: A Review. *International Journal of Artificial Intelligence and Applications, 6*(1), 21–39.

Esposito, A. (2012). Debunking some myths about biometric authentication. ArXiv abs/1203.03333.

Eubanks, V. (2018). *Automating Inequality. How high-tech tools profile, police, and punish the poor.* St. Martin's Press.

Fish, J. T., Miller, L. S., & Braswell, M. C. (2013). *Crime Scene Investigation.* Routledge.

FRA European Union Agency for Fundamental Rights. (2019). Facial recognition technology: Fundamental rights considerations in the context of law enforcement. Available at https://fra.europa.eu/sites/default/files/fra_upl oads/fra-2019-facial-recognition-technology-focus-paper-1_en.pdf

Freeman, K. (2016). Algorithmic injustice: how the Wisconsin Supreme Court failed to protect due process rights in state V. Loomis. *North Carolina Journal of Law and Technology, 18*(5), 75–106.

Galbally, J., Ferrara, P., Haraksim, R., Psyllos, A. I., & Beslay, L. (2019). *Study on Face Identification Technology for its Implementation in the Schengen Information System.* Publications Office of the European Union.

Garrett, B., & Mitchell, G. (2013). How Jurors Evaluate Fingerprint Evidence: The Relative Importance of Match Language, Method Information, and Error Acknowledgment. *Journal of Empirical Legal Studies, 10*(3), 484–511.

Howard, J. J., & Etter, D. (2013). The Effect of Ethnicity, Gender, Eye Color and Wavelength on the Biometric Menagerie. 2013 IEEE International Conference on Technologies for Homeland Security (HST), IEEE.

Jacquet, M., & Champod, C. (2020). Automated face recognition in forensic science: Review and perspectives. *Forensic Science International, 307*, 110124. https://doi.org/10.1016/j.forsciint.2019.110124

Keenan, T. P. (2015). Hidden Risks of Biometric Identifiers and How to Avoid Them. In Canadian Global Affairs Institute, *Black Hat USA 2015* (pp. 1–13). University of Calgary.

Kindt, E. J. (2013). *Privacy and Data Protection Issues of Biometric Applications.* Springer.

Kindt, E. J. (2018). Having yes, using no? About the new legal regime for biometric data. *Computer Law & Security Review, 34*, 523–538. https://doi.org/10.1016/j.clsr.2017.11.004

Kotsoglou, K. N., & Oswald, M. (2020). The long arm of the algorithm? Automated Facial Recognition as evidence and trigger for police intervention.

Forensic Science International: Synergy, 2, 86–89. https://doi.org/10.1016/j.fsisyn.2020.01.002

Lieberman, J. D., Carrell, C. A., Miethe, T. D., & Krauss, D. A. (2008). Gold versus platinum: Do jurors recognize the superiority and limitations of DNA evidence compared to other types of forensic evidence? *Psychology, Public Policy, and Law, 14*(1), 27–62. https://doi.org/10.1037/1076-8971.14.1.27

Maeder, E. M., Ewanation, L. A., & Monnink, J. (2017). Jurors' Perceptions of Evidence: The Relative Influence of DNA and Eyewitness Testimony when Presented by Opposing Parties. *Journal of Police and Criminal Psychology, 32*, 33–42. https://doi.org/10.1007/s11896-016-9194-9

Magnet, S. (2011). *When Biometrics Fail: Gender, Race, and the Technology of Identity*, Duke University Press.

Mordini, E., & Massari, S. (2008). Body, Biometrics and Identity. *Bioethics, 22*(9), 488–498.

Morrison, G. S., Sahito, F. H., Jardine, G., Djokic, D., Clavet, S., Berghs, S., & Goemans Dorny, C. (2016). INTERPOL Survey of the Use of Speaker Identification by Law Enforcement Agencies. *Forensic Science International, 263*, 92–100.

Murphy, E. (2007). The New Forensics: Criminal Justice, False Certainty, and the Second Generation of Scientific Evidence. *California Law Review, 95*(3), 721–797. https://doi.org/10.15779/Z38R404

New York City Bar Association (2020). Power, Pervasiveness and Potential: The Brave New World of Facial Recognition Through a Criminal Law Lens (and Beyond). Available at http://documents.nycbar.org.s3.amazonaws.com/files/2020662-BiometricsWhitePaper.pdf

National Research Council (2010). *Biometric Recognition: Challenges and Opportunities*. The National Academies Press. https://doi.org/10.17226/12720

Nigam, I., Vatsa, M., & Singh, R. (2015). Ocular biometrics: A survey of modalities and fusion approaches. *Information Fusion, 26*, 1–35. https://doi.org/10.1016/j.inffus.2015.03.005

Papernot, N., McDaniel, P., Sinha, A., & Wellman, M. P. (2018). SoK: Security and Privacy in Machine Learning. *2018 IEEE European Symposium on Security and Privacy (EuroS&P)* (pp. 399–414). Institute of Electrical and Electronics Engineers.

Riggan, B. S., Short, N. J., & Hu, S. (2018). Thermal to Visible Synthesis of Face Images using Multiple Regions. arXiv:1803.07599 [cs.CV].

Ross, A. A., Nandakumar, K., & Jain, A. K. (2006). *Handbook of Multibiometrics*. Springer.

Saini, M., & Kapoor, A. K. (2016). Biometrics in Forensic Identification: Applications and Challenges. *Journal of Forensic Medicine, 1*(2), 1–6. https://doi.org/10.4172/2472-1026.1000108

Sarangi, P. P., Mishra, B. S. P., & Dehuri, S. (2018). Fusion of PHOG and LDP local descriptors for kernel-based ear biometric recognition. *Multimedia Tools and Applications, 78*, 9595–9623. https://doi.org/10.1007/s11042-018-6489-0

Sharp, L. (2000). The Commodification of the Body and Its Parts. *Annual Review of Anthropology, 29*, 287–328.

Singh, S., & Prasad, S. V. A. V. (2018). Techniques and Challenges of Face Recognition: A Critical Review. *Procedia Computer Science, 143*, 536–543.

Sulner, S. (2018). Critical Issues Affecting the Reliability and Admissibility of Handwriting Identification Opinion Evidence. *Seton Hall Law Review, 48*(3), 631–717.

Sutrop, M. (2010). Ethical Issues in Governing Biometric Technologies. In *Proceedings of the Third International Conference on Ethics and Policy of Biometrics and International Data Sharing, ICEB'10* (pp. 102–114). Springer. https://doi.org/10.1007/978-3-642-12595-9_14

TELEFI. (2021). *Summary Report of the project "Towards the European Level Exchange of Facial Images".* https://www.telefi-project.eu/sites/default/files/TELEFI_SummaryReport.pdf

Thompson, E. (2018). Understanding the Strengths and Weaknesses of Biometrics [WWW Document]. Infosecurity Magazine. https://www.infosecurity-magazine.com:443/opinions/strengths-weaknesses-biometrics/. Accessed 26 September 2018.

Tistarelli, M., Grosso, E., & Meuwly, D. (2014). Biometrics in forensic science: Challenges, lessons and new technologies. In V. Cantoni, D. Dimov, & M. Tistarelli (Eds.), *Proceedings of the First International Workshop on Biometric Authentication (BIOMET 2014), Sofia, Bulgaria, June 23–24* (pp. 153–164). Springer. https://doi.org/10.1007/978-3-319-13386-7_12

Tome, P., Vera-Rodriguez, R., Fierrez, J., & Ortega-Garcia, J. (2015). Facial soft biometric features for forensic face recognition. *Forensic Science International, 257*, 271–284. https://doi.org/10.1016/j.forsciint.2015.09.002

Tomova, S. (2009). Ethical and Legal Aspects of Biometrics. In E. Mordini & M. Green (Eds.), *Identity, Security and Democracy: The Wider Social and Ethical Implications of Automated Systems for Human Identification* (pp. 111–114). IOS Press.

Wevers, R. (2018). Unmasking Biometrics' Biases: Facing Gender, Race, Class and Ability in Biometric Data Collection. *TMG Journal for Media History, 21*(2), 89–105.

Working Group for Human Factors in Handwriting Examination. (2020). *Forensic Handwriting Examination and Human Factors: Improving the Practice Through a Systems Approach.* U.S. Department of Commerce, National Institute of Standards and Technology. NISTIR 8282.

Završnik, A. (2020). Criminal justice, artificial intelligence systems, and human rights. *ERA Forum, 20*, 567–583.

Zeinstra, C. G., Meuwly, D., Ruifrok, A. C. C., Veldhuis, R. N. J., & Spreeuwers, L. J. (2018). Forensic face recognition as a means to determine strength of evidence: A survey. *Forensic Science Review, 30*(1), 21–32.

Zhou, S., & Xiao, S. (2018). 3D face recognition: A survey. *Human-Centric Computing and Information Sciences, 8*, 1–27. https://doi.org/10.1186/s13 673-018-0157-2

Part II

AI in Different Domains: Impacts of AI on Specific Rights

3

Artificial Intelligence, International Law and the Race for Killer Robots in Modern Warfare

Kristian Humble

1 Introduction

Artificial intelligence (AI) is now commonplace in all aspects of human life. McCarthy suggests that AI is 'the science and engineering of making intelligent machines' (McCarthy, 2007, p. 2). Over the past decade there has been a progressive escalation of the use of AI which in turn has led to our dependency on intelligence data gathering devices and the intrusion on our privacy by the state. AI is used in 'face recognition tools, autonomous vehicles, search engines, translation tools and within the context of modern warfare' (Kriebitz, 2020, p. 84).

The use of AI has had an impact on several wide-ranging legal and ethical concerns. However, there is a lack of a legal regulatory framework

K. Humble (✉)
School of Law and Criminology, Faculty of Liberal Arts and Sciences, University of Greenwich, London, UK
e-mail: K.P.Humble@greenwich.ac.uk

© The Author(s), under exclusive license to Springer Nature Switzerland AG 2023
A. Završnik and K. Simončič (eds.), *Artificial Intelligence, Social Harms and Human Rights*, Critical Criminological Perspectives,
https://doi.org/10.1007/978-3-031-19149-7_3

to address these concerns around the use of AI, particularly in the context of conflict. The only legal framework that exists in relation to AI is when it is linked to the right to privacy (International Covenant on Civil and Political Rights, 1966, Article 26).

The AI debate started to gain traction in 2012, with a series of documents on automated weapons. These documents included the policy directives by the US Department of Defense (DoD) on 'autonomy in weapons systems' (US Defense Directive, 2012) and a report from Human Rights Watch and the Harvard Law School's International Human Rights Clinic (HRW-IHRC Report, 2012) calling for an outright ban on automated weapons. The legal and ethical implications of the development and use of weapons that are capable of undertaking functions during conflict autonomously (without human intervention) are becoming increasingly focused on by governments and big tech companies. This issue was highlighted in 2017 with an open letter from the Future Life Institute to the United Nations (UN) signed by 126 CEOs and founders of 126 artificial intelligence and robotics companies who 'implored' states to prevent an arms race for autonomous weapons systems (AWS). The use of AI in conflict will shape modern warfare for years to come (West et al., 2019, p. 145).

This chapter will focus on the use of AI technology in AWS and in particular the use of drones during conflict and the threat posed to human rights without a legal regulatory framework on usage.

2   What Are Automated Weapons?

Within this chapter, the discussion will be centred around AWS, and in particular the use of drones in conflict situations. The advancement in AI has brought the debate around the usage of AWS into sharp focus. Therefore, in line with academic analysis on the legal implications of AWS, this chapter will focus first on the discussion around what constitutes an autonomous weapon. This discussion is needed because at the international level there is not an agreed definition of an AWS.

There are competing definitions of what constitutes an AWS. The debate is dominated by the definitions from the UK Ministry of Defence

(MoD) and the US Department of Defense (DoD). The UK MoD in 2011 issued the following definition of an AWS, as 'systems capable of understanding higher level intent and direction, namely of achieving the same level of situational understanding as a human and able to take appropriate action to bring about the desired state.' This UK stance is more in line with an AI-enabled system replacing a human operator. The US DoD proposes a different approach and bases the term autonomous and an AWS as being capable of 'once activated, to select and engage targets without further intervention from a human operator.' The 2012 HRW-IHRC report used similar language to the US DoD definition, stating 'fully autonomous weapons that could select and engage targets without human intervention.' However, the NATO Joint Air Power Competence Centre (JAPCC) includes similar language to the UK MoD definition of AWS and includes words such as 'consciousness' and 'self-determination.' This NATO JAPCC and the UK MoD definitions suggest a strong AI-enabled weapon system which is closely connected to human-like intelligence. However, weapons with such a high-level functioning AI do not currently exist.

AWS that do exist, fit more neatly into the definition offered by the US DoD and the wording contained in the HRW-IHRC report. These automated weapons include the anti-material defensive systems like the Israeli Iron Dome and the German MANTIS and the active protective vehicles like the Swedish LEDS-150 (Amoroso, 2017, p. 5). Such a definition would also include the robotic sentinels like the South Korean Super aEgis II which is used as a surveillance device along the South and North Korean border.

However, the real problem exists in a future proof definition of an AWS, one which encompasses the systems in place now, like for example in the South Korean Super aEgis which operates in a non-conflict environment and any AWS in the future that will be able to function autonomously without meaningful human control in the time of war. There must be an agreed definition within the international community which can encompass the AI human cognitive inputting algorithm which the Super aEgis possess and the future AWS which has human-like capabilities.

This chapter presupposes that an agreed international definition of an AWS should not be a barrier to an international legal doctrine governing the usage of AWS. To solve this problem the broader US DoD definition should be adopted. With a broader adoption, the argument of what constitutes an AWS will include the weaponry that is available here and now and will also cover the more sentient AI intelligent machines the UK MoD definition is predicting.

3 The Race for Killer Robots

The advancement of AI in modern warfare will forever alter the relationships between the US, China, Russia, and the private technological industry. China committed $150 billion dollars to becoming the AI technology world leader (Roberts et al., 2021, p. 59). In 2019, Chinese researchers published open-source code for AI missile systems which were ultimately controlled by deep reinforcement learning algorithms (Harvey, 2020, p. 61).

AI militarisation is no longer a futuristic, science fiction lead fantasy. The development of AI weaponry is already creating an arms race between competing states and private corporations. The development and reliance on the use of AI in warfare has the potential to not only transform strategic advantage but also shift the balance of power, as it did during the arms race in the Cold War era.

Therefore, AI is already a military reality. AI impacts on military logistics, intelligence and surveillance. AI weapons guidance systems make decisions that are free from human input and work independently. Governmental agencies can use algorithms to identify patterns that exist within datasets. Levine et al. (2016) has suggested that more troubling advances are being developed. This includes AI systems that will allow autonomous decision-making by networked computer agents. In a conflict situation, what is troubling is that autonomous decision-making, will enable instantaneous reactionary actions by drones without human input. Therefore, a drone reaction will be based on retaliatory violence and not peaceful negotiation.

Drones traditionally have been remotely piloted craft and were first used in the 1990s by the US for military surveillance (Chamayou, 2015). Advances in technology and the relatively low cost of manufacturing drones, now mean the cost is low enough for drones to be used for all kinds of purposes, from filming, monitoring conservation and delivering medicines or food supplies to remote areas.

Military technology in the use of drones has also advanced. The evolution of military drone technology is based on the same technology used to identify hidden Serbian strategic positions during the Kosovo war in 1999 (Black, 2014). Weapons within drones were first used in the immediate aftermath of the September 11 terrorist attacks in the US (Chamayou, 2015). Jane's (Sabbagh, 2019) analysts suggest that more than 80,000 surveillance drones and almost 2,000 attack drones will be purchased around the world in the next decade. Drones which are weaponised are, however, still expensive to purchase and expensive to train individuals to pilot them. This will inevitably lead to the more economically rich states to acquire drones and an increased economic disparity in modern warfare. The UK operates missile bearing drones and plans to spend £415 m (€520 m) on Protector drones by 2023 (Sabbagh, 2019). In 2020 Jane's (2021) suggested that the 10 biggest drone powers spent $8bn on drone units. Sabbagh (2019) states that the 'the wide variety in types of unmanned aerial vehicles (UAV) makes them suitable for both surveillance and conflict missions, with the low-cost models able to conduct surveillance operations.'

The current use of drones within conflict is dominated by the US, the UK and Israel. The US and the UK have used weaponised drones such as the Predator and the Reaper, both made by General Atomics, a US company based in California for over a decade. Israel has been developing its own weaponised drones. In the last five years, both Turkey and Pakistan have developed their own drone manufacturing programs (Bousquet, 2018). Since 2016, Turkey has used drones consistently against the separatist Kurdish PKK within its own territory, northern Iraq and in Syria (Bousquet, 2018). China is currently supplying several states with its Wing Loong and CH series drones, including the UAE, Egypt, Saudi Arabia, Nigeria and Iraq (Bowman et al., 2021). According to Drone Wars (2020) statistics, in four years of conflict in Syria from

2014 to 2018, Reaper drones were used more than 2,400 times during strategic missions, the equivalent of two a day. Drones account for 42% of all UK aerial missions against Isis and 23% of weapon-controlled strikes (Sabbagh, 2019).

There has been a change of perception of drones from merely being 'eyes' in the sky to being full realised offensive tools (Chamayou, 2015). At the start of the millennium the number of drones used by the US armed forces was only in the dozens, today these numbers add up to thousands. The Pentagon estimated that by 2035 remotely piloted aircraft will make up 70% of the United States Air Force. With the race for drones, analysts expect that at least 8,000 UAVs and 2,000 attack drones will be produced in the next decade (Sabbagh, 2019).

The US is not alone in believing that drones are the future of modern warfare. In 2005 about 40 states possessed drone capabilities, by 2012 that number had multiplied to about 76 states. By 2019, it was estimated that more than 90 states have drone capabilities and 63 also manufactured their own (Sabbagh, 2019). States as diverse as Syria to Pakistan, from Iran to North Korea as well as nearly every NATO member state now has the capability to use drones in conflict. Also, it is not just states which possess weaponised drone capabilities. For example, Hezbollah has used Iranian-built reconnaissance drones which have violated Israeli airspace (Grossman, 2018). Teheran has supplied Hamas with the needed technology to operate UAVs and Hamas has also been able to exploit Israeli drones captured in Gaza after they have been recovered from the ground (Rossiter, 2018). Also, ISIS has demonstrated the use of offensive drones which have been modified from models readily available on the civilian market (Schulte, 2019). The Houthi Movement has been able to carry out drone attacks in the Arabian Peninsula in 2020 by using both refitted commercial models and aircraft supplied by Iran (Muhsin, 2019). The Houthi Movement has also deployed drones for long-range actions, striking targets beyond Yemeni borders. In 2019, several Saudi Arabian airport infrastructures were targeted by drone attacks (Muhsin, 2019) and the heavy damage sustained in the Saudi Aramco Khurais oil installation in 2019 caused significant widespread concern amongst the international community (Hubbard et al., 2019).

The significance of Saudi Arabia as a newer entrant onto the drone marketplace cannot be underestimated because Saudi Arabia is a massive investor in military technology and hardware and invests nearly 9% of its GDP in military spending (Hubbard et al., 2019).

In 2017, the Stockholm International Peace Research Institute estimated that there were 381 different models of automated weaponry for military use, and approximately 175 of those have the capabilities of using lethal weaponry (Boulanin and Verbruggen, 2017). There are several different types of drones, some of which are the size of a backpack and are portable to the larger aircraft drones which are capable of remaining airborne for over 25 hours. The next step in technological advancement will be intelligent AWS capable of selecting targets and deciding autonomously whether to carry out an attack.

This rise of AI has also impacted state behaviour during the time of conflict (Krahenmann and Valadez, 2020). There has been an increased use of armed drones in warfare because of AI, particularly by the US in Afghanistan (Sharkey, 2015). AI has seen the rise in so-called 'killer robots' which raises ethical and legal questions (Docherty, 2012). Kallenborn (2020), also makes the case that, the use of automated drones in warfare comes with the risk that a drone may not be able to distinguish the difference between combatants and civilians.

4 The Ethical Concerns of the Use of Automated Weaponry

Many AI technologies are still in the developmental stages, leading to scepticism of whether conflict will be dominated by AI military advantage in the future. Unmanned aircraft can operate autonomously but are not at the stage of being able to undertake difficult missions in the same way human operators can. Simon (2015) suggests that AI functions well when it is used in a narrow-predetermined set of circumstances. We may, however, be on the brink of AI-automated machines being able to develop cognitive recognition to solve problems and make decisions much closer to those of humans.

There is an ethical concern of conflict being decided without or with limited human intervention or meaningful human control. The new normal of conflict and war may be a post human one, and the landscape of conflict and the rules which regulate them will need to be reconfigured (Mangiameli, 2012). This reconfiguring will be based around the notion of a more brutal, nihilistic AWS which will have less input by human operators. The basis of power within a conflict situation will be set by the instinct of a machine incapable of moral or ethical decisions and the ambiguity of victory. How the law will keep up or even stop such technological advances is impossible to predict. Chamayou (2015) expressed the conflict paradigm is no longer to oversee and punish but to oversee and annihilate.

Chamayou (2015) has expressed conflict by using the idea of war by Gentilis (1598) as two warring parties as duelists, formerly equal, bearing the same obligations and parallel objectives. Chamayou (2015) states that this fundamental expression of war is now changing and being shaped by the onset of the use of drones in conflict. The very basis of international law is based on war and conflict being based on some sort of parallel use of power and force. Grotius (2013) noted that the prohibition of the use of poison and assassination was to safeguard the need in wartime to keep safe the balance of duality, that each actor or combatant has the same means before them in the face of their opposing aggressor. These parallel objectives, and balance of duality within conflict, if not lost already, will be further eroded if one aggressor state has the capabilities of a more advanced automated drone weaponry, over another.

There is also the debate around the ethical justification of war and the arguments around *jus ad bellum* and *jus in bello* in relation to autonomy in weapons (Amoroso, 2017). The central issue here is around the initiation of hostilities. An AI-controlled weapon which is automated to make fast split-second decisions may by its very nature initiate hostilities quicker or even escalate conflict further without the built-in human response of contemplation and compromise. This very speed of judgement from AI decision-making threatens the foundations of *jus ad bellum* and *jus in bello* and the human ability to control strategic or tactical advantage.

Payne (2018) suggests ambiguity and error are inevitable and how would an automated machine make difficult philosophical and ethical choices that deal with the intrinsic value of life? Whose ultimate perspective would this be from? Would this perspective come from the leader in chief or the de facto leader of the state or some form of international standard of use? Making ethical considerations of the value of life made in a moment, relies on a human value system, and this ethical concern can often be retrospectively alerted to justify a judgement. Such notions could not be successfully part of an algorithm used in an automated weapon, as you could not successfully foresee every outcome that might occur during conflict.

The central ethical concern is when conflict is being driven by algorithms and machines without human intervention. Can this ever be solved? Ethical concerns within warfare are historically hard to solve. Drones, however, and their usage do pose some new ethical and consequently legal dilemmas. Their use does not fundamentally undermine the international legal standard imbedded in conflict. Drones are, however, the logical progression of weaponry in warfare that has seen in the last hundred years a move from hand combat to nuclear weapons to inter-continental ballistic missiles (ICBM).

There are, however, assumptions that there is a moral and ethical distance between the drone's operator and the target. Finn (2011) has rightly suggested that fully automated drones would bring with them ethical and legal dilemmas, but it's clear that the operation of drones is still, however, logistically controlled by a member of the military or intelligence agency of a state. Drone usage is still under the command responsibility and their usage must adhere to accountability measures, in the same way that other conflict missions are accountable. Aston (2010) suggested a decade ago, that the so-called 'PlayStation mentality' of targeted killings is unproven. However, in the study by O'Connell (2010), it was suggested that there was evidence that a drone operator was much more likely to dehumanise their targets.

5 The International Legal Accountability, Responsibility, and the Usage of Drones

A discussion of AWS and AI-enabled drones centres around the compliance with International Humanitarian Law (IHL). The problem area within IHL is how drone usage fits with the main principles of the laws of war and IHL, namely, distinction and proportionality within conflict. As Van den Boogaard (2015) suggested, an automated weapon should uphold the same principles of distinction at least as well as a competent and conscientious human soldier.

However, in practice the distinction between a combatant and noncombatant is not easily attained, an automated drone would have to have complex cognitive abilities to be able to be compliant with IHL. These capabilities are, for the moment some way off in the future. There is a fundamental concern that an automated drone will never be able to comply with the principles of distinction within the context of IHL. As Sparrow (2015) has suggested, the recognition of this IHL principle imbedded within the behaviour of an automated weapon will pose no less insurmountable challenges for AWS programmers and developers.

There is also the concern of proportionality or as Solis (2016, p. 293) has suggested the 'terrible and impossible problem of proportionality.' The complex nature of the proportionality principle concerns striking a balance between military gain from a specific action and the harm the action may produce to civilians. The use of autonomous drones will always have the unintended consequence of harm or death to civilians who are not taking part in the conflict. However, if this responsibility for the civilian is an unintentional consequence of using weapons which are imbued with AI, a state must seek to minimise the risk of a noncombatant victim. A state, therefore, has a legal and ethical imperative to anticipate this accidental harm when using drones. Byman (2013) suggests that the use of drones should be intwined with the ethical responsibility that comes with the need to adhere to proportionality and suggests that it may not be enough for the state to anticipate accidental civilian harm but also to proactively minimise it. This principle cannot be preset into an AI algorithm before a conflict is underway, such a principle is linked to a specific circumstance and the balancing of the action to be undertaken by the commanders involved in the plan and execution of attack. Therefore, elements such as the 'reasonable military commander,' as suggested by Sharkey (2012, p. 787) are simply an impossible algorithm to code.

The protection of human rights within the context of the use of drones during conflict and the wider general rules within the laws of war are complex. IHL is based on land combat and the control and possession of territory. These fundamental principles are seen within the regulations of the Hague Convention 1907 and the Geneva Convention 1949 and their additional protocols. Both these conventions set out a range of rules that govern armed conflict within state occupation and impose rules on the occupiers of that seized territorial land. The difficulty is in trying to adapt these rules on occupation and territory to fit with the use of drones. The usage of drones is primarily the battle for the airspace rather than land. Chamayou (2015) stated that the very understanding of the occupying territory is redundant and meaningless and the use of drones during warfare is based more on who controls the skies above.

This chapter asserts that for the control of AWS there needs to be a strict international legal regulatory framework for compliance of usage or a ban of weapons which have no meaningful human control or intervention.

There is, currently, only one international treaty which is focused on the control of and the acquisition of drones in conflict. In 2016, 45 states issued a Joint Declaration for the Export and Subsequent Use of Armed or Strike-Enabled Unmanned Aerial Vehicles (UAVs). The declaration's focus was aimed at the use of drones based on the ethical and legal protection of human rights in the increased use of unmanned weapons during conflict. The declaration contains questions of legality of usage, and responsibility within the context of IHL and international human rights law.

The Joint Declaration was conceived as a basis for a common international community approach to the use of armed drones. The agreement contains the following main principles; 'the applicability of international law, including both the law of armed conflict and international human rights law, as applicable, to the use of armed or strike enabled UAVs' and 'in light of the rapid development of UAV technology and the benefit of setting international standards for the export and subsequent use of such systems, we (the signatory states) are resolved to continue discussions on how these capabilities are transferred and used responsibly by all states.'

There has, however, been criticism of the Joint Declaration. The criticism has centred on the US leading the agenda setting of the Joint Declaration. The US is a state that uses drones and the acquisition of drones has been seen as the greatest concern for the international community regarding the use of drones during conflict. The US is expanding its use of drones within conflict and therefore, its 'responsible' use of drones (Stohl, 2018). Stohl (2018) also suggests the US is increasing the speed of drone strikes, expanding the geographic scope of where strikes can happen and delegating decision-making authority away from the President to military commanders.

The Joint Declaration's language itself has been criticised as being vague. The vagueness is centred around the use of the term 'responsible use,' without explanation of what responsible use means. The United Nations Institute for Disarmament Research highlighted the problematic nature of the meaning of responsible use and suggested that the term needed a succinct meaning. There is, however, no agreed approach of the understanding of responsible use, within the Joint Declaration, or the wider international community. Therefore, this limits the effectiveness of a declaration which pertains to set out rules on the control, and usage of an armed drone without a succinct definition on how to responsibly use an armed drone.

A state signing up to the Joint Declaration, might be under the impression, that by committing to the principles within the declaration (that armed drones must be used 'responsibly'), could legitimately claim to have adhered to an international standard for drone use. Without explicit details on what responsible use entails this 'responsible use' principle within the declaration is meaningless. The declaration itself, without succinct definitions on usage and responsibility, is therefore, merely a justification for the use of drones, rather than an internationally agreed set of principles restricting how drones are used. There is a call for states to sign up to the declaration but there doesn't seem to be much urgency to do so.

It's this chapter's assertion that a definition on responsible use must be narrow. A broader definition would see states use the wider or ambiguous element of a definition in much the same way as states do in the definition of self-defence. The narrow definition must be in line with the UN Charter and *jus as bello* principles. This would allow a solution to how drones are used if there is a clear criterion on how and when they can be deployed.

However, in this moment in time, there seems to be very little international recourse to punishment or limiting actions of the use or misuse of drones during warfare. Birdsall (2018) has suggested, that the US government has set out to blur the lines between the war or conflict and the enforcement of international rules. The US does this by suggesting that the use of drones during conflict involving terrorism must be seen as a domestic issue and therefore is outside the ordinary boundary of international law. This blurring of the lines could be used by any state to justify the use of drones in an aggressive manner and attach their usage to a domestic issue. The breaking of international legal norms or the normative effect of the laws of war is clear, the state can give its own justification for conflict use and drones because of this blurring of the narrative between the justification of war (especially on terrorist grounds) and the use of drones. Therefore, international law needs to have a clear set-out paradigm of when killing via drones is permissible and when it is not.

There is a more general international discussion on AWS (which includes drones) which has come within the international legal framework of the UN Convention on Conventional Weapons (CCW). The CCW informal meeting in 2013 of the High Contracting Parties gave the Group of Governmental Experts (GGE) an open-ended mandate to formulate an operative and normative framework for the usage of emerging technologies in the area of lethal autonomous weapons (LAWS). These meetings have culminated in the recommendation in 2019 by the GGE on LAWS that 11 guiding principles be adopted by the High Contracting Parties to the CCW. These guiding principles are:

(a) International humanitarian law continues to apply fully to all weapons systems, including the potential development and use of lethal autonomous weapons systems.

(b) Human responsibility for decisions on the use of weapons systems must be retained since accountability cannot be transferred to machines. This should be considered across the entire life cycle of the weapons system.

(c) Human-machine interaction, which may take various forms and be implemented at various stages of the life cycle of a weapon, should ensure that the potential use of weapons systems based on emerging technologies in lethal autonomous weapons systems is in compliance with applicable international law, in particular IHL. In determining the quality and extent of human-machine interaction, a range of factors should be considered including the operational context, and the characteristics and capabilities of the weapons system as a whole.

(d) Accountability for developing, deploying, and using any emerging weapons system in the framework of the CCW must be ensured in accordance with applicable international law, including through the operation of such systems within a responsible chain of human command and control.

(e) In accordance with States' obligations under international law, in the study, development, acquisition, or adoption of a new weapon, means or method of warfare, determination must be made whether its employment would, in some or all circumstances, be prohibited by international law.

(f) When developing or acquiring new weapons systems based on emerging technologies in the area of lethal autonomous weapons systems, physical security, appropriate non-physical safeguards (including cyber-security against hacking or data spoofing), the risk of acquisition by terrorist groups and the risk of proliferation should be considered.

(g) Risk assessments and mitigation measures should be part of the design, development, testing, and deployment cycle of emerging technologies in any weapons systems.

(h) Consideration should be given to the use of emerging technologies in the area of lethal autonomous weapons systems in upholding

3 Artificial Intelligence, International Law and the Race ...

compliance with IHL and other applicable international legal obligations.

(i) In crafting potential policy measures, emerging technologies in the area of lethal autonomous weapons systems should not be anthropomorphized.

(j) Discussions and any potential policy measures taken within the context of the CCW should not hamper progress in or access to peaceful uses of intelligent autonomous technologies.

(k) The CCW offers an appropriate framework for dealing with the issue of emerging technologies in the area of lethal autonomous weapons systems within the context of the objectives and purposes of the Convention, which seeks to strike a balance between military necessity and humanitarian considerations.

There was a further GGE meeting in August 2021 in which the GGE expressed four areas for discussion including the application of IHL, human responsibility, human and machine interaction, and weapons reviews. The areas for discussion will be presented with a report on LAWS at the Sixth Review Conference on Certain Conventional Weapons (CCW) held in December 2021, with expanded discussions held in March and July 2022. However, for supporters of the restriction, usage, or ban of AWS to be legally implemented within an agreed update of the CCW have been so far been disappointed.

The 11 guiding principles adopted by the GGE are not a legally binding normative framework of AWS and are merely a reemphasis of the principles of IHL and do not contain anything substantially new for the protection or regulation of the usage of autonomous weaponry. However, the principles can inform discussions and shows that the majority of CCW state parties agree on the need for a legal binding document to address the ethical, legal, and technical concerns raised by AWS. To be certain of a new treaty the state parties should at the very least agree at the CCW's Sixth Review Conference to a mandate to negotiate and timeously adopt a new legally binding document on AWS. If the Review Conference fails to approve such a legal binding mandate, then an internationally legal binding document must be found at a forum outside of the CCW and there must be an immediate agreement to prohibit AWS that select and engage targets in conflict without meaningful human control.

6 Conclusions

There is a move towards an increase in the use of AWS and AI-equipped drones in modern warfare. The use of drones and AWS brings with it problems which are both legal and ethical. It could be argued that the law on the usage and responsibility of drones is failing to keep up with technological advances. Drones have the effect of dehumanising conflict and have the capability to bring more lethal instantaneous force to a conflict situation. The distance between the operator and the drone could lead to a lack of ethical judgement between the operator and the combatant. With AWS able to make decisions based on their AI programming without direct human input in the decision-making, this problem becomes much more prevalent. These problems and concerns will only become greater as technological advances start to enable AWS with cognitive human-like decision-making.

The usage of drones and drone strikes often violate the principles of IHL. There is an added legal complexity in dealing with accountability issues when an AI drone used as a weapon performs an undesired deviant action. The international community or the state cannot hold an autonomous object responsible for their actions with legal sanctions. It would seem impossible to hold a programmer for the algorithm (unless the action involved gross negligence) if the drone has acted in an autonomous manner. It would also be difficult to find high-ranking officials liable for the actions of autonomous drones as to foresee all unpredictable actions would be remote at best.

There is beneficial usage of drones which does suggest a more trustworthy AI is being lost within the debate surrounding 'killer robots' and AWS. Whetham (2015) suggests that drones could play an important part in complex humanitarian emergencies as they are capable of surveillance in remote regions. Kennedy and Rodgers (2015) suggest that drones may be able to help the international community and the UN by replacing the need for peacekeepers in difficult conflict zones.

However, before the enlightened trustworthy use of AI drones can be fully embraced, international law must catch up with the advances in AI technology and regulate the usage of drones within conflict, non-conflict situations and the responsibility of using drones as killing machines. There must be a coherent, binding international legal framework on the usage of drones (and AWS) now and a framework which states that all AI-enabled drones must contain meaningful human control.

References

Amoroso, D., (2017). 'Jus in bello and jus ad bellum arguments against autonomy in weapons systems: a re-appraisal,' *Questions of International Law Journal*, 5.

Aston, A., (2010). 'Report of the Special Rapporteur on Extrajudicial, Summary or Arbitrary Executions,' *Human Rights Council*, A/HRC/14/24/Add.6.

Black, J., (2014). *War in the Modern World 1990–2014* (London: Routledge).

Birdsall, A., (2018). 'Drone Warfare in Counterterrorism and Normative Change: US Policy and the Politics of International Law,' *Global Society*, 32, 241–262.

Boulanin, V., & Verbruggen, M., (2017). 'Mapping the Development of Autonomous Weapons Systems,' *Solna Stockholm International Peace Research Institute*.

Bousquet, A., (2018). *The Eye of War: Military Perception from the Telescope to the Drone* (Minneapolis: University of Minneapolis Press).

Bowman B., et al., (2021). 'China's Surprising Drone Sales in the Middle East', Defence News, April 23.

Byman, D., (2013). 'Why Drones Work: The Case for Washington's Weapon of Choice,' *Foreign Affairs*, July/August, 32–43, 32.

Convention on Conventional Weapons (CCW) Meeting of High Contracting Parties, "Final Report," CCW/MSP/2019/CRP.2/Rev.1

Chamayou, G., (2015). *A Theory of the Drone* (New York Press).

Docherty, B., (2012). 'Losing Humanity, The Case Against Killer Robots,' *Human Rights Watch*, November 19.

Finn, P., (2011). 'A Future for Drones: Automated Killing,' *The Washington Post*, September 19.

Future of Life Institute, 'An Open Letter to the United Nations Convention on Certain Conventional Weapons' (21 August 2017). https://futureoflife.org/autonomous-weapons-open-letter-2017.

Gentilis, A., (1598). *De Jure Belli Libri Tres* (Hanoviae).

Grossman, N., (2018). *Drones and Terrorism: A Symmetric Warfare and the Threat to Global Security* (London and New York: I.B. Tauris).

Grotius, H., (2013). *On the Law of War and Peace* (Cambridge University Press).

Harvey, B. S., (2020). 'Applied Artificial Intelligence in Modern Warfare and National Security Policy,' *Hastings Science & Technology Law Journal*, 61.

Hubbard, B., Karasz, P., & Reed, S., (2019). 'Two Major Saudi Oil Installations Hit by Drone Strike and US Blames Iran,' *The New York Times*, 14 September.

Human Rights Council, 'Report of the Special Rapporteur on Extrajudicial, Summary or Arbitrary Executions, Philip Alston,' Fourteenth Session, 28 May 2010, para. 84.

Human Rights Watch (HRW) and Harvard Law School's International Human Rights Clinic (IHRC), 'Losing Humanity. The Case Against Killer Robots' (19 November 2012). www.hrw.org/report/2012/11/19/losing-humanity/case-against-killer-robots.

International Covenant on Civil and Political Rights, 16 December 1966, 999 UNTS 171 (ICCPR) Article 26.

Kallenborn, Z., (2020). 'Swarms of Mass Destruction: The Case for Declaring Armed and Fully Autonomous Drone Swarms as WMD,' *Modern War Institute*, May 28.

Kennedy, C., & Rodgers, J., (2015). 'The Legal and Ethical Implications of Drone Warfare,' *International Journal of Human Rights*, 19(2), 105–126

Krahenmann, S., & Valadez, G., (2020). 'Humanitarian Concerns Raised by the Use of Armed Drones,' *Geneva Call*, June 16.

Kriebitz, A. (2020). 'Artificial Intelligence and Human Rights: A Business Ethical Assessment,' *Business and Human Rights Journal*, 5, 84.

Levine, S., Lillicrap, T., & Kalakrishnan, M., (2016) 'How Robots Can Acquire New Skills from Their Shared Experience,' Google Research Blog, March 10. https://research.googleblog.com/2016/10/how-robots-can-acquire-new-skills-from.html.

Mangiameli, A., (2012). *Arte e/o Technica, Sfide Giuridiche*, Padova CEDAM.

McCarthy, J., (2007). 'What Is Artificial Intelligence,' *Stanford University.* http://www-formal.stanford.edu/jmc/whatisai.pdf, date accessed 3 March 2020.

Muhsin, D., (2019). 'Houthi Use of Drones Delivers Potent Message in Yemen War,' *The International Institute For Strategic Studies.*

NATO JAPCC, The Future Unmanned System Technologies Legal and Ethical Implications of Increasing Automation (Germany, November 2016).

O'Connell, M.E., (2010). 'Unlawful Killing with Combat Drones: A Case Study of Pakistan 2004–2009,' Notre Dame Law School, Legal Studies Research Paper No. 09-43, 8–10.

Payne, K., (2018). 'Artificial Intelligence: A Revolution in Strategic Affairs?' *Survival Global Politics & Strategy*, 7.

Roberts, H., Couls, J., Morley, J., Taddeo, M., Wang, V., & Floridi, L., (2021) 'The Chinese Approach to Artificial Intelligence: An Analysis of Policy, Ethics and Regulation,' *Artificial Intelligence & Society*, 59.

Rossiter, A., (2018). 'Drone Usage by Militant Groups: Exploring Variation in Adoption,' *Defense & Security Analysis*, 113.

Sabbagh, D., (2019). 'Killer Drones: How Many Are There and Who Do They Target,' *The Guardian*, November 18.

Schulte, P., (2019). *Future War: AI, Drones, Terrorism and Counter Terrorism Post 9/11* (Cheltenham: Elgar).

Sharkey, N., (2012). 'The Evitability of Autonomous Robot Warfare,' *International Review of the Red Cross*, 787.

Sharkey, N., (2015). 'The Automation and Proliferation of Military Drones and Protection of Civilians,' *Law, Innovation and Technology*, 3.

Simon, M., (2015). 'Stop Laughing at Those Clumsy Humanoid Robots,' *Wired*, 11 June. http://www.wired.com/2015/06/stop-laughing-clumsy-humanoid-robots/.

Solis, G.D., (2016). *The Law of Armed Conflict: International Humanitarian Law in War* (Cambridge University Press), 293.

Sparrow, R., (2015). 'Twenty Seconds to Comply: Autonomous Weapon Systems and the Recognition of Surrender,' *International Law Studies*, 699.

Stohl, R., (2018). *An Action Plan on U.S. Drone Policy: Recommendations for the Trump Administration* (Washington, DC: Stimson Centre), 5.

Universal Declaration of Human Rights, 10 December 1948 UNGA Res 217 A(III) (UDHR), International Covenant on Civil and Political Rights, 16 December 1966, 999 UNTS 171 (ICCPR).

UK Ministry of Defence, The UK Approach to Unmanned Aircraft Systems, Joint Doctrine Note 2/11 (30 March 2011).

US Department of Defense, 'Autonomy in Weapons Systems' Directive 3000.09 (21 November 2012).

Van den Boogaard, J., (2015). 'Proportionality and Autonomous Weapons Systems,' *Journal International Humanitarian Legal Studies*, 6.

West, M., Kraut, R., & Chew, H.E., (2019). 'I'd Blush if I Could, Closing the Gender Divides in Digital Skill Through Education,' *UNESCO and Equal Skills*, 145.

Whetham, D., (2015). 'Drones to Protect,' *International Journal of Human Rights*, 19(2), 105–126.

Willett, J., (2021). *Jane's Weapons Strategic Yearbook 19/20*, Jane's by HIS Markit.

4

Artificial Intelligence and the Prohibition of Discrimination in the EU: A Private Law Perspective

Karmen Lutman

1   Introduction

Although deeply rooted in the European legal heritage, human rights protection is facing new challenges brought about by the digital revolution. The use of new technologies and algorithms influences fundamental rights, the prohibition of discrimination being no exception. The risk of discrimination is particularly present where algorithms are used for decision-making (e.g. in the context of loan financing, education, marketing, employment, and insurance). For instance, in a hiring process an algorithm may help to choose candidates for a job interview. However, such decision-making can violate the prohibition of discrimination if a specific job requirement puts a certain group of candidates at a disadvantage (e.g. homosexuals). A potential algorithm that sorts jobs applications

---

K. Lutman (✉)
Faculty of Law, University of Ljubljana, Ljubljana, Slovenia
e-mail: karmen.lutman@pf.uni-lj.si

© The Author(s), under exclusive license to Springer Nature
Switzerland AG 2023
A. Završnik and K. Simončič (eds.), *Artificial Intelligence, Social Harms and Human Rights*, Critical Criminological Perspectives,
https://doi.org/10.1007/978-3-031-19149-7_4

according to this criterion should either be avoided or modified so as to omit such information from the selection procedure.

The discrimination is often difficult to discover due to the fact that a specific requirement is usually as such not discriminatory, but the algorithm is trained to include certain information that leads to a discriminatory result. This is usually done by including so-called proxy information in the decision-making process. Proxies stem from various datasets (e.g. social media data) and can be correlated with the prohibited grounds for discrimination. Such algorithmic profiling may result in social sorting and discrimination.

The aim of this chapter is to analyse the discriminatory effects of automated decision-making in the field of private law, more precisely in employment matters and in access to and the supply of goods and services. These are namely rare fields under EU law where anti-discrimination law applies to horizontal relationships (relationships between private individuals). By looking into selected practices of algorithmic selection and decision-making processes, this chapter strives to assess the lawfulness of such practices from the EU law perspective. While EU Member States might provide a higher level of protection against discrimination in their national laws, this chapter takes a supranational approach and focuses exclusively on the protection guaranteed by EU law.

The following text starts with a brief outline of EU anti-discrimination law applicable to horizontal relationships (Sect. 2). Then, the discriminatory practices caused by artificial intelligence (hereinafter also referred to as "AI") in the field of employment and general contract law (goods and services) are critically analysed from an EU law perspective (Sect. 3). The body of the chapter ends with a presentation of some mechanisms that could enhance trust in algorithmic activity and examples of good practices, where AI serves as a tool of positive discrimination (Sect. 4).

As will be shown, EU anti-discrimination law is far from capable of combating the new forms of discrimination brought by digital technologies and algorithms, which—at least temporarily—shifts the burden on to the Member States and their national laws. However, in the long term a uniform approach to preventing discrimination and social sorting is highly needed.

2 Non-discrimination in EU Law: The Legal Framework

The prohibition of discrimination is considered to be a specific formulation of the general principle of equality and is firmly rooted in EU law. It is embedded in several provisions of EU primary law and is reflected in secondary legislative acts as well. Article 18 of the Treaty on the Functioning of the European Union[1] (hereinafter referred to as "TFEU") prohibits any discrimination on grounds of nationality. Moreover, Article 157 of the TFEU requires the equal treatment of men and women in the field of employment. While these two provisions have a direct effect, Article 19 of the TFEU merely calls for legislative measures to combat discrimination based on sex, racial or ethnic origin, religion or belief, disability, age, or sexual orientation, and has no direct effect (Martin in: Kellerbauer et al. 2019, p. 426). Furthermore, the prohibition of discrimination laid down in Article 14 of the European Convention on Human Rights[2] (hereinafter referred to as the "ECHR") is—according to Article 6(3) of the Treaty on European Union[3] (hereinafter referred to as the "TEU")—a general principle of EU law. It can also be found in Article 21 of the Charter of Fundamental Rights of the European Union[4] (hereinafter referred to as "CFR").

Although the development of human rights and fundamental freedoms was originally driven by the need to protect the individual against the state, in more recent years a growing influence of these rights on private law can be observed. Since relationships between private individuals are usually less regulated in comparison to relationships between the state and individuals, the boundaries of the discriminatory practices of new technologies, including AI, are sometimes blurred and difficult to define. Unfortunately, the EU missed the opportunity to provide more

---

[1] The consolidated version of the Treaty on the Functioning of the European Union, OJ C 326 of 26 October 2012.

[2] The European Convention for the Protection of Human Rights and Fundamental Freedoms, as amended by Protocols Nos. 11 and 14, of 4 November 1950.

[3] The consolidated version of the Treaty on European Union, OJ C 326 of 26 October 2012.

[4] The Charter of Fundamental Rights of the European Union, OJ C 326 of 26 October 2012.

comprehensive protection against discrimination in horizontal relationships in 2008, when the European Commission's proposed Horizontal Directive[5] implementing the principle of equal treatment in horizontal relationships outside the labour market, irrespective of age, disability, sexual orientation, or religious belief, was not adopted. At present, there are several gaps in EU anti-discrimination law, particularly in the field of private law, where "algorithmic discrimination could potentially have its greatest and gravest impact" (Xenidis and Senden 2020). It is therefore (still) up to the anti-discrimination laws of the Member States to provide more comprehensive protection in the field of private law in order to prevent discriminatory practices caused by algorithmic decision-making.

In the field of EU primary law, Article 18 (the prohibition of discrimination on grounds of nationality) and Article 157 (the prohibition of discrimination on grounds of sex in the field of employment) of the TFEU are considered to be applicable also to horizontal relationships, which is—although disputed (Leible in: Schulze 2011, p. 35)—also the case with Article 21 of the CFR (Martin in: Kellerbauer et al. 2019, pp. 2165, 2166).

A number of grounds listed in EU primary law are also reproduced in secondary legislation. Four EU directives are dedicated to protection against discrimination:

- Directive 2000/43/EC on equal treatment between persons irrespective of racial or ethnic origin[6] (the "Race Equality Directive"),
- Directive 2000/78/EC[7] on equal treatment in employment and occupation (the "Employment Equality Directive"),

---

[5] The Proposal for a Council Directive on implementing the principle of equal treatment between persons irrespective of religion or belief, disability, age, or sexual orientation of 2 July 2008.

[6] Council Directive 2000/43/EC of 29 June 2000 implementing the principle of equal treatment between persons irrespective of racial or ethnic origin, OJ L 180 of 19 July 2000.

[7] Council Directive 2000/78/EC of 27 November 2000 establishing a general framework for equal treatment in employment and occupation, OJ L 303 of 2 December 2000.

- Directive 2004/113/EC on equal treatment between men and women in the access to and supply of goods and services[8] (the "Goods and Services Directive"), and
- Directive 2006/54/EC on equal opportunities and equal treatment of men and women in matters of employment and occupation[9] (the "Gender Equality Directive").

These directives address discriminatory practices in relationships between private individuals, which is—as explained above—rather atypical in the field of human rights and fundamental freedoms. However, as we can see, EU protection against discrimination in private law is very limited (the reasons for this are explained below in Sect. 3): it applies to employment matters and to a limited part of general contract law that deals with access to and the supply of good and services. Below, the focus is placed on discriminatory practices of AI in these two fields of private law where the prohibition of discrimination is addressed by EU law.

3 The Prohibition of Discrimination in Horizontal Relationships: Combating Discriminatory Practices of AI in Relationships Between Private Individuals

In recent years, new business strategies based on mass data collection and other AI activities have made private individuals vulnerable as never before. The profiling, targeting, nudging, and manipulation of citizens and consumers have become daily practices (Ebers and Navas 2020, p. 71 see also Wagner and Eidenmüller, 2019). These techniques driven by AI systems are used to find and select job candidates, to advertise and

---

[8] Council Directive 2004/113/EC of 13 December 2004 implementing the principle of equal treatment between men and women in the access to and supply of goods and services, OJ L 373 of 21 December 2004.

[9] Directive 2006/54/EC of the European Parliament and of the Council of 5 July 2006 on the implementation of the principle of equal opportunities and equal treatment of men and women in matters of employment and occupation (recast), OJ L 204 of 26 July 2006.

82 K. Lutman

sell products, etcetera. However, practice has shown that algorithmic profiling, selection, and decision-making sometimes brings discriminatory results. Most problematic are those cases where the results are not *prima facie* discriminatory. In such cases, individuals are usually not aware of being treated unlawfully. However, an algorithm may have been (in a training process) fed with biased data from an incorrect database or a correct database which is distorted due to statistical long-standing inequality in a certain field.[10] The discrimination may also occur due to the use of protected grounds (sex, race, age, etc.) as a decisive factor in a selection process (Ebers and Navas 2020, p. 78).

In contract law, the EU traditionally provides generally adequate protection against discrimination only in employment matters. The reason for this is explained below (Sect. 3.1). General contract law, on the other hand, lacks sufficient protections against discrimination. This is problematic since the majority of discriminatory practices such as profiling, targeting, price discrimination, etcetera, nowadays occur particularly in this area. Companies offer their products and set prices specifically to a consumer's profile, which leads to discrimination and social sorting.

Below, a short discourse on the reasons for such weak protection against discrimination in the field of contract law (Sect. 3.1) is followed by an analysis of AI's discriminatory practices in employment matters (Sect. 3.2) and in access to and the supply of goods and services (Sect. 3.3).

3.1 The Prohibition of Discrimination V. The Freedom of Contract

It has already been acknowledged that although it is sometimes considered to be highly beneficial to allow fundamental rights to play a role in relationships between private parties, it also opens the door to several issues and concerns (Trstenjak et al. 2016, p. 7). In the field of contract law, the prohibition of discrimination may come into collision with the

---

[10] For more, see: Ebers and Navas (2020, p. 77).

4 Artificial Intelligence and the Prohibition of Discrimination ... 83

freedom of contract. Namely, private law and more precisely the freedom of contract, being a cornerstone of contract law, is a priori based on discrimination (Leible in: Schulze 2011, p. 28), since private parties are in principle almost entirely free in choosing their contracting partner.[11] However, this freedom has been to a certain degree curtailed by the abovementioned provisions of EU primary law and the EU directives that can be invoked in horizontal relationships.

As mentioned above, there are two main areas of contract law where discrimination is forbidden on the EU level in various stages of the contract life cycle: employment contracts and contracts for the supply of goods and services. Labour law is one of those areas of private law where discrimination has traditionally been prohibited. The reason for this lies in the nature of employment contracts, where the employer has a superior role in relation to the employee, which is close to the vertical relationship between the state and an individual (Basedow in: Trstenjak et al. 2016, p. v). For this reason, party autonomy is much narrower than in general contract law.

In employment and occupation matters, discrimination is prohibited under EU law on grounds of sex, racial or ethnic origin, religion or belief, disability, age, and sexual orientation (according to the Race Equality Directive, Employment Equality Directive, and Gender Equality Directive). Regarding access to and the supply of goods and services, it is prohibited to discriminate on grounds of sex and racial or ethnic origin (according to the Goods and Services Directive and the Race Equality Directive).

However, EU Member States can introduce a regulatory framework that provides a higher level of protection against discrimination, that is, by introducing other prohibited grounds for discrimination, and several of them indeed provide better protection against discrimination in horizontal relationships. Slovenia, for example, took advantage of this opportunity and introduced a much more generous legal framework

---

[11] However, there are certain rules or general concepts of private law limiting the freedom of contract, such as the principle of protecting the economically weaker party, the principle of good faith, etc. For more, see: Trstenjak et al. (2016, pp. 11, 12).

in this regard. The Slovenian Protection against Discrimination Act[12] lists sex, nationality, race or ethnic origin, language, religion or belief, disability, age, sexual orientation, gender identity, and gender expression, social position, financial status, education, or *any other personal circumstance* as prohibited grounds for discrimination also in horizontal relationships, including employment and occupation matters and access to and the supply of goods and services.[13] However, Slovenian courts have not yet been given an occasion to rule on the compatibility of such a broad interpretation of the principle of non-discrimination with the fundamental concepts of contract law, such as party autonomy, which encompasses the freedom to choose a contracting partner. In German law, which is traditionally rather reluctant to limit party autonomy for this reason (Freedland and Lehmann 2013, p. 165), such an open catalogue of prohibited grounds in private law without any further limitations would probably be considered to be problematic (also in the light of the German *Allgemeines Gleichbehandlungsgesetz*[14]). It has also been stressed in private law theory that the instruments of private law might not be the most appropriate for changing or eliminating discriminatory practices (Vandenberghe in: Schulze 2011, p. 13).

3.2 Employment and Occupation Matters

Although the use of algorithms has brought several advantages in terms of time- and cost-efficiency in the recruitment and hiring process, discriminatory practices have also been detected. While instances of direct discrimination are rather rare in practice, algorithms are often inclined toward indirect discrimination. However, the most problematic are discriminatory practices conducted by self-learning AI systems, since they make autonomous, unpredictable decisions, which are often difficult to trace (Thüsing 2021, para. 34). In these cases, it is often

---

[12] *Zakon o varstvu pred diskriminacijo* (ZVarD), Official Gazette of the Republic of Slovenia, Nos. 33/16 and 21/18.

[13] For details, see: Articles 1 and 2 of the Protection against Discrimination Act. See also: Štajnpihler (2016).

[14] BGBl. I S. 1897 of 14 August 2006, last amendment in 2022 (BGBl. I S. 768).

4 Artificial Intelligence and the Prohibition of Discrimination ... 85

impossible to discover for which reasons and on the basis of which differentiation criteria the programme made the final decision, making the AI a "black box" (Kischel in: Epping and Hillgruber 2022, para. 218c). It has been suggested that in cases where the final result is discriminatory and—at the same time—it cannot be explained how the AI came to this result, the presumption should apply that the decision-making process was based on discriminatory grounds and is thus prohibited (Kischel in: Epping and Hillgruber 2022, para. 218c).

However, most problematic decisions made by algorithms are not those that have an apparently discriminatory result, but those were (usually hidden) discrimination follows from a decision that has been made due to the use of an unsuitable criterion or set of criteria, the problematic selection of facts made available to the programme, etcetera, for instance, residing in a notorious part of a city and/or having a foreign name should not be a reason to be rated worse than other job candidates. It is thus important to ascertain how and why the employment decisions were made and whether prohibited grounds for discrimination such as nationality, sex, racial or ethnic origin, religion or belief, disability, age, or sexual orientation played a role.

It has been disputed whether an employer can relieve itself of liability for damages arising from the discrimination of candidates or employees by stating that the selection process was (mainly) done by means of AI.[15] However, in the EU the entire procedure cannot be pursued solely by means of AI, since Article 22 of the General Data Protection Regulation[16] (hereinafter referred to as the "GDPR") prohibits automated individual decision-making. Despite the fact that self-learning AI systems act autonomously, they have no will of their own and lack legal capacity. For this reason, their conduct is to be attributed to the employer, which bears the risk of using discriminatory practices in such cases. Namely, if the employer could relieve itself of liability solely by claiming that it did not have control over the AI's decision-making process, such protection

---

[15] See, e.g., Sheard (2022).

[16] Regulation (EU) 2016/679 of the European Parliament and of the Council of 27 April 2016 on the protection of natural persons with regard to the processing of personal data and on the free movement of such data, and repealing Directive 95/46/EC, OJ L 119 of 4 May 2016.

86   K. Lutman

would be inadequate (this view is also supported by Thüsing 2021, para. 34).

3.2.1 Candidate Sourcing

Candidate sourcing is usually the first step in the recruitment process where discrimination might occur, mainly by means of targeted advertising of vacant positions. Algorithms are used to spread such advertisements usually via social media platforms for ad delivery such as Facebook or LinkedIn. The personalisation of online ads based on collected data enables some ads are only visible to certain groups of potential candidates, with the selection being made by AI systems. If the selection criteria are—directly or indirectly—based on prohibited grounds such as sex, racial or ethnic origin, religion or belief, disability, age, or sexual orientation, this is a cause for concern since EU directives explicitly prohibit discrimination in relation to "conditions for access to employment, to self-employment and to occupation, including selection criteria and recruitment conditions, whatever the branch of activity and at all levels of the professional hierarchy, including promotion".[17]

The biggest employers, such as Verizon, Amazon, Goldman Sachs, Target, and Facebook, have allegedly placed job advertisements limited to particular age groups on platforms such as Facebook, LinkedIn, and Seek (Angwin et al. 2017; Sheard 2022). Candidates have been targeted on grounds of detailed profiles created by algorithms from data "provided" by potential job candidates themselves, inferred from their online activity (also generated by liking and commenting on things on social platforms). For instance, Verizon placed an advertisement on Facebook targeted 25–36 years old who lived in the US capital, or had recently visited there, and had a demonstrated interest in finance (Angwin et al. 2017).

Such practices may discriminate against those job seekers who are excluded from being targeted and consequently from viewing particular

---

[17] Article 3(1) (a) of Directive 2000/43/EC; Article 3(1) (a) of Directive 2000/78/EC, and similar in Article 1 (a) of Directive 2006/54/EC.

job advertisements.[18] The problem arises when such differentiation is made on prohibited grounds, for example, age, as was the case in Verizon, unless such differentiation is objectively and reasonably justified (in EU law, such justification should meet the conditions laid down in Article 6 of the Employment Equality Directive).

However, in the abovementioned cases, the discrimination was a result of human conduct—the input of information regarding the targeting criteria was determined by the employer. Nevertheless, from a legal point of view, the same conclusion could be reached in cases where such criteria for targeted advertising would be set by an AI's self-learning activity.

3.2.2 Selection Processes and Conditions for the Promotion

Discriminatory practices might also occur at a later stage, in the process of selecting job seekers or of employee promotion. One of the most famous examples of discriminatory algorithmic decision-making in the stage of candidate selection is the Amazon AI recruitment tool. The company developed an experimental hiring tool using machine learning algorithms to rate job candidates. However, it showed bias against women and was thus allegedly not used in practice. The programme was trained to examine applicants by observing patterns in resumes submitted to the company over a 10-year period (Dastin 2018). Since most came from men, the system taught itself that male candidates were preferable and thus discriminated against female applicants.

Another tool that might lead to discrimination is a video interviewing system. It can be used by employers to pre-interview, screen, or automate interviews with candidates. The service is offered by several platforms, such as Spark Hire, 1alview, Hire Vue, Jobma, Modern Hire, etcetera. Such "one-way video interviews" require job seekers to record themselves answering a set of questions, while machine learning algorithms make the selection of candidates according to data gathered from the video: tone and facial expressions, eye contact, word selection, emotions, etcetera (Sheard 2022). However, several discriminatory practices have

---

[18] For more, see: Sheard (2022).

been detected when using such technology, since candidates with non-native accents, people of colour, and autistic persons were rated worse than others (Sheard 2022). Analyses have shown that self-learning algorithms choose nationality, racial or ethnic origin, and disability as criteria for such differentiation.

The problem regarding such discriminatory decision-making usually lies in the database where the algorithms derive their decisions from. The database used might be unsuitable due to a long-standing inequality, which could also be taste-based (i.e. where unequal treatment is based on the personal, prejudiced dislikes or preferences of the decision-makers regarding a certain group of people or on dislikes or preferences for certain products [Orwat 2020, p. 25]). A machine learning system that would teach itself that white salespeople are preferred by the employer's customers and that thus would give preference to white applicants, is unlawful under EU law. Namely, customers' preferences (or prejudices) are not a valid justification for discrimination under EU law. The position in cases of statistics-based discrimination is similar. If a system were to teach itself that (according to the statistics) women change jobs more often than men and would consequently prefer male applicants, this is unlawful discrimination based on apparently neutral criteria (indirect discrimination).

Problems might also arise through the use of customer ratings and evaluations in the hiring or promotion process, the latter being protected by EU non-discrimination law as well. It is well known that biases have been found to shape customers' behaviour, including their ratings and evaluations. If any of the prohibited grounds significantly correlates with employee evaluations and algorithms rely on such biased input data, which consequently harms individuals' career opportunities, this would constitute unlawful discrimination under EU law.[19]

---

[19] For more, see: Ducato et al. (2018) and Rosenblat et al. (2017) and Xenidis and Senden (2020).

3.3 Access to and the Supply of Goods and Services

While the prohibition of discrimination in labour law is usually explained by the nature of the relationship between an employee and employer, which is close to the vertical relationship between the state and citizens, non-discrimination in the field of access to and the supply of goods and services touches the core of general contract law. As mentioned above, the scope of protection in this area is very limited since EU law prohibits discrimination only on grounds of sex, race, and ethnic origin, and extends merely to goods and services available to the public. Many EU Member States provide wider protection in such cases, including Slovenian law, which makes arguments against broadening the range of prohibited grounds in private law due to party autonomy being rather weak. However, numerous problematic practices have a cross-border dimension and for this reason a uniform approach to combating discrimination is highly needed. Below, we will examine the two selected practices, targeted advertising and algorithmic pricing, more closely.

3.3.1 Targeted Advertising

Online marketing is based on targeted advertising. Social media platforms use a number of approaches to select the audience for an ad. A company might target users via social media with specific ads based on collected data, such as age group and interests, or they might target users who like particular websites. Another option is to target an audience with ads based on websites and posts that their friends have liked. While offers to specific persons have always existed, the mass targeting of a specific audience has become possible with machine learning algorithms.

However, such selective advertising might be discriminatory and lead to social sorting. As mentioned above, in the US several claims have been filed against Facebook complaining of discriminatory practices in sending ads for employment opportunities. In addition, such practices have also been reported when advertising particular products, accommodation, housing, and services.[20] Facebook's micro-targeting tools allegedly excluded its users from being sent ads based on the users' sex, race, colour, religion, ancestry, national origin, marital status, citizenship, primary language, immigration status, or other personal characteristics added by the courts to those characteristics protected by US legislation.[21] These cases have not been decided by the judiciary since Facebook decided to pay compensation to settle the claims and agreed to take measures against targeted advertising in the field of housing, employment, and credit ads, based on age, gender, and other grounds prohibited by US anti-discrimination law.[22]

Viewed from an EU perspective, it is not entirely clear whether such online targeted advertising in the field of goods and services available to the public is illegal. While the Gender Equality Directive explicitly excludes advertising from its scope (Article 3[3]), the Race Equality Directive remains silent on this issue. However, in its Resolution of 3 September 2008,[23] the European Parliament called on the Member States "to ensure by appropriate means that marketing and advertising guarantee respect for human dignity and the integrity of the person, are neither directly nor indirectly discriminatory nor contain any incitement to hatred based on sex, racial or ethnic origin, religion or belief, disability, age or sexual orientation, and do not contain material which, judged in its context, sanctions, promotes or glamorises violence against women" (Paragraph 19). It seems that the EU legal framework is rather ill-equipped to address discriminatory practices when offering ads for goods and services (see also: Wachter 2020, p. 29; Corrêa 2021; Xenidis and Senden 2020) and leaves this task to the Member States.

In the Member States, targeted ads have usually been litigated by referring to the legal framework of data protection due to privacy concerns. For instance, it has been reported that in 2017 the French data protection authority imposed a fine on Facebook for collecting personal data and

---

[20] Riddick and others v. Facebook, Case 3:18-cv-04529-LB.

[21] Ibid.

[22] For more, see: Gillum and Tobin (2019) and Griffin (2022).

[23] European Parliament Resolution of 3 September 2008 on how marketing and advertising affect equality between women and men, OJ C 295E of 4 December 2009.

4 Artificial Intelligence and the Prohibition of Discrimination ...

displaying targeted ads without a legal basis (Corrêa 2021). Two years later, the same authority imposed a fine on Google for breaching the GDPR since it lacked transparency and valid consent regarding its advertisement personalisation. In the Netherlands, the Dutch data protection authority revealed that Facebook used the personal data of 9.6 million Dutch citizens for targeted ads without having their explicit consent while the platform enabled advertisers to select "men who are interested in other men" for targeted advertising purposes (Corrêa 2021). However, all these cases focus rather on data protection, while none of them has dealt with the issue of discrimination. It therefore seems that more should be done on the EU level in order to protect consumers against such discriminatory practices.

3.3.2 Algorithmic Pricing

Algorithmic pricing is commonly understood as a practice of calculating the price for traded products via an algorithm that makes use of data to identify market conditions and the behaviour of individual consumers. While dynamic pricing is the practice of calculating the price in response to market conditions, such as changes in supply and demand or the behaviour of competitors, price discrimination differs from dynamic pricing in that it calculates the price on the basis of individual consumer's characteristics, rather than on market conditions affecting all consumers equally (Grochowski et al. 2022). Such personalised pricing uses AI tools to target individual consumers (or a group of consumers) with a price that matches their personal buying threshold. Prices may vary depending on objective (e.g. the type of browser, the type of device) or subjective criteria (e.g. age, gender, zip code, previous consumer behaviour). One of the first publicly revealed examples of such personalised pricing was the hotel website Orbitz. The company relies on data such as postal code, type of browser, and type of device to calculate prices for each user depending on their digital footprint. By searching for accommodation on this website, Mac users can expect to see higher prices than their PC-using counterparts (Baldwin 2018). Similar practices can also be found at the Booking.com website and many others.

While offering different prices to students or retirees is a well-established practice in most legal systems, it is—as a measure of positive discrimination—generally not considered to be problematic. As has been stressed by scholars, price setting is an important aspect of freedom of enterprise and contract, while its limits are not extensive (Möllers 2018, p. 114). However, the expansion of big data and artificial intelligence has opened a Pandora's box of controversial practices that may be harmful to consumers. Namely, consumers are usually unaware that they are being subjected to differential treatment and—in contrast to businesses that dispose of their digital footprints—do not have access to equivalent information about their contractual partner. Algorithmic pricing is thus problematic from different viewpoints: (price) fairness under private law, competition law, anti-discrimination law, and data protection.[24]

EU anti-discrimination law explicitly requires gender-neutral pricing in insurance contracts (Article 5[1] of the Gender Equality Directive). This requirement was set by the CJEU in the Test-Achats case,[25] where the Court held that differences in insurance pricing based purely on a person's sex are discriminatory. However, it is not explicitly written in the Goods and Services Directive whether—outside of insurance law—it provides protection against price discrimination. However, it seems inherent in the term "access to goods and services" that it also includes the pricing of products, since financial accessibility is an important aspect of access to goods and services. Therefore, it would be unlawful to calculate different prices based on gender and race or ethnic origin. However, there are no other prohibited grounds for price discrimination in horizontal relationships in EU anti-discrimination law, which makes protection in this area inadequate. It would be very difficult to argue that such a narrow scope of protection omitting grounds such as sexual orientation is objectively justified by private autonomy.

---

[24] For more, see, e.g.: Grochowski et al. (2022) and Paal (2019).

[25] *Association Belge des Consommateurs Test-Achats ASBL and Others v Conseil des ministres* (Case C-236/09), Judgment of the Court (Grand Chamber) of 1 March 2011.

4 Algorithms *Against* Discrimination: Algorithmic Audits and Examples of Good Practice

Despite the several threats that algorithms may pose to anti-discrimination law, they also have great potential to eliminate human biases and make decision-making processes more transparent. One of the tools that can help achieve this goal and build trust in algorithmic decision-making is algorithmic auditing. This procedure is carried out by an independent party and aims to test an algorithmic system for biases, accuracy, robustness, interpretability, privacy characteristics, and other unintended consequences (Engler 2021). There are firms that offer such services,[26] while companies can also develop an internal self-auditing system.[27] However, since EU law does not impose obligatory auditing in the field, domestic sanctions such as civil liability and administrative fines in case of discrimination might serve as an incentive to test algorithmic systems for biases. While auditing is usually intended to verify the requirements set by an AI system in a decision-making stage, controlling the design stage of AI systems is another way to cope with this problem (Ebers and Navas 2020, p. 80).

These mechanisms are highly needed since private enforcement of anti-discrimination law in such cases is very difficult due to the lack of awareness of private individuals that they were victims of discriminatory algorithmic practices. In addition, since AI tools are usually considered to be a "black box", for a private individual to prove even *prima facie* discrimination seems *probatio diabolica*.

However, algorithms can also serve as a tool of positive discrimination where such measures are needed. An example is Entelo's search tool that helps recruiters identify job candidates who are women, of particular races or ethnicities, or who have served in the military.[28] In doing so, it targets candidates from traditionally underrepresented groups.

---

[26] E.g. O'Neil Risk Consulting & Algorithmic Auditing (ORCAA), Parity AI.

[27] For instance, Siemens has developed such an internal self-auditing system (Hempel 2018).

[28] https://www.recruiter.com/recruiting/entelo-diversity-isnt-racist-its-just-the-opposite/. Accessed on 5 August 2022.

5 Concluding Remarks

The aim of this chapter was to analyse the existing threats of artificial intelligence and algorithmic decision-making regarding the prohibition of discrimination in employment matters and in access to and the supply of goods and services under EU law. It was established that while the current legal framework can—more or less successfully—combat discriminatory practices in recruitment, hiring, and promotion processes, the situation is far from satisfactory in general contract law, where discrimination is only prohibited on grounds of sex, race, and ethnic origin, and only regarding access to and the supply of goods and services available to the public. In this regard, two selected practices were examined more closely: targeted advertising and algorithmic pricing. While the former is not covered by EU anti-discrimination directives, protection against algorithmic pricing is insufficient, since it protects consumers only against unequal treatment based on sex, race, and ethnic origin. This can lead to discrimination on other grounds that deserve protection, for example, sexual orientation, and promotes consumer exploitation and social sorting.

Unfortunately, the EU missed an opportunity to ensure better protection against discrimination in horizontal relationships in 2008, when the European Commission's proposed Horizontal Directive was not adopted. Since then, a comprehensive approach to combating discrimination in horizontal relationships is still awaited. Hopefully, the controversial practices of AI systems will be a sufficiently strong incentive to provide a higher level of protection under EU law.

Acknowledgements The research leading to this chapter has received funding from the Slovenian Research Agency, under the research project "Human Rights and Regulation of Trustworthy Artificial Intelligence" (No. V5-1930).

References

Angwin, Julia et al. 2017. Dozens of Companies Are Using Facebook to Exclude Older Workers from Job Ads. https://www.propublica.org/article/facebook-ads-age-discrimination-targeting#:~:text=Series%3A%20Machine%20Bias-,Dozens%20of%20Companies%20Are%20Using%20Facebook%20to%20Exclude%20Older%20Workers,said%20one%20employment%20law%20expert. Accessed on 5 August 2022.

Baldwin, Grace. 2018. What's the Difference Between Dynamic and Personalized Pricing? https://www.omniaretail.com/blog/difference-dynamic-and-personalized-pricing. Accessed on 5 August 2022.

Buchholtz, Gabriele; Scheffel-Kain, Martin. 2022. Algorithmen und Proxy Discrimination in der Verwaltung: Vorschläge zur Wahrung digitaler Gleichheit. Neue Zeitschrift für Verwaltungsrecht (NVwZ), pp. 612–617.

Corrêa, Ana Maria. 2021. Addressing discrimination in data-driven advertising: Regulatory opportunities and failures within the EU. https://www.diplomacy.edu/blog/addressing-discrimination-in-data-driven-advertising-regulatory-opportunities-and-failures-within-the-eu/. Accessed on 5 August 2022.

Dastin, Jeffrey. 2018. Amazon scraps secret AI recruiting tool that showed bias against women. https://www.reuters.com/article/us-amazon-com-jobs-automation-insight-idUSKCN1MK08G. Accessed on 5 August 2022.

Ducato, Rossana; Kullman, Miriam; Rocca, Marco. 2018. Customer ratings as a vector for discrimination in employment relations? Pathways and pitfalls for legal remedies. https://orbi.uliege.be/bitstream/2268/222031/1/RD%20MK%20MR%20-%20Customer%20ratings%20as%20a%20vector%20for%20discrimination.pdf. Accessed on 5 August 2022.

Ebers, Martin; Navas, Susana (eds.). 2020. *Algorithms and Law.* Cambridge: Cambridge University Press.

Engler, Alex. 2021. Auditing employment algorithms for discrimination. https://www.brookings.edu/research/auditing-employment-algorithms-for-discrimination/. Accessed on 5 August 2022.

Epping, Volker; Hillgruber, Christian (eds.). 2022. *BeckOK Grundgesetz.* 51st Edition. Munich: Beck.

Freedland, Mark; Lehmann, Matthias. 2013. Non-discrimination and the "Constitutionalization of Contract Law". In: Dannemann, Gerhard et al. (eds.). *The Common European Sales Law in Context.* Oxford: Oxford University Press, pp. 160–189.

96   K. Lutman

Gillum, Jack; Tobin, Ariana. 2019. Facebook Won't Let Employers, Landlords or Lenders Discriminate in Ads Anymore. https://www.propublica.org/art icle/facebook-ads-discrimination-settlement-housing-employment-credit#: ~:text=Series%3A%20Machine%20Bias-,Facebook%20Won't%20Let% 20Employers%2C%20Landlords%20or%20Lenders%20Discriminate%20i n,sparked%20lawsuits%20and%20widespread%20outrage. Accessed on 5 August 2022.

Griffin, Rachel. 2022. Tackling Discrimination in Targeted Advertising: US Regulators Take Very Small Steps in the Right Direction—But Where Is the EU? https://verfassungsblog.de/targeted-ad/. Accessed on 5 August 2022.

Grochowski, Mateusz; Jabłonowska, Agnieszka et. al. 2022. Algorithmic Price Discrimination and Consumer Protection. *A Digital Arms Race? Technology and Regulation, Special Issue: Should Data Drive Private Law?* pp. 36–47.

Hempel, Jessi. 2018. Want to Prove Your Business Is Fair? Audit Your Algorithm. https://www.wired.com/story/want-to-prove-your-business-is-fair-audit-your-algorithm/. Accessed on 5 August 2022.

Kellerbauer, Manuel et al. (eds.). 2019. *The EU Treaties and the Charter of Fundamental Rights: A Commentary.* Oxford: Oxford University Press.

Möllers, Thomas M.J. 2018. Working with Legal Principles–Demonstrated Using Private Autonomy and Freedom of Contract as Examples. *European Review of Contract Law* (14), pp. 101–114.

Orwat, Carsten. 2020. *Risks of Discrimination through the Use of Algorithms.* Berlin: Federal Anti-Discrimination Agency.

Paal, Boris. 2019. Missbrauchstatbestand und Algorithmic Pricing - dynamische und individualisierte Preise im virtuellen Wettbewerb. Gewerblicher Rechtsschutz und Urheberrecht (GRUR), pp. 43–53.

Rosenblat, Alex et al. 2017. Discriminating Tastes: Uber's Customer Ratings as Vehicles for Workplace Discrimination: Customer Ratings and Workplace Discrimination. *Policy and Internet*, Vol. 9 (4).

Schulze, Reiner (ed.). 2011. *Non-discrimination in European Private Law.* Tübingen: Mohr Siebeck.

Sheard, Natalie. 2022. Employment Discrimination by Algorithm: Can Anyone Be Held Accountable? *University of New South Wales Law Journal*, Vol. 45(2).

Štajnpihler, Tilen. 2016. Prepoved diskriminacije v pravu varstva potrošnikov. In: Vlahek, Ana et al. (eds.). *Pravo in politika sodobnega varstva potrošnikov.* Ljubljana: GV Založba, pp. 67–110.

4 Artificial Intelligence and the Prohibition of Discrimination ... 97

Thüsing, Gregor. 2021. Allgemeines Gleichbehandlungsgesetz (AGG). In: Jürgen Säcker, Franz et al. (eds.). *Münchener Kommentar zum BGB*, 9th Edition. Munich: Beck.

Trstenjak, Verica et al. (eds.). 2016. *The Influence of Human Rights and Basic Rights in Private Law*. Cham, Heidelberg, New York, Dordrecht, London: Springer.

Wachter, Sandra. 2020. Affinity Profiling and Discrimination by Association in online Behavioural Advertising. *Berkley Technology Law Journal*, Vol. 35 (2).

Wagner, Gerhard; Eidenmüller, Horst. 2019. Down by Algorithms? Siphoning Rents, Exploiting Biases, and Shaping Preferences: Regulating the Dark Side of Personalized Transactions. *The University of Chicago Law Review*, Vol. 86, pp. 581–609.

Xenidis, Raphaele; Senden, Linda. 2020. EU non-discrimination law in the era of artificial intelligence: Mapping the challenges of algorithmic discrimination. In: Bernitz, Ulf et al. (eds.). *General Principles of EU Law and the EU Digital Order*. Kluwer Law International, pp. 151–182.

Part III
Policy, Regulation, Governance: AI and Ethics

5

In Defence of Ethics *and* the Law in AI Governance: The Case of Computer Vision

Aleš Završnik

1 Introduction

An ethics assessment encapsulates the idea that Artificial Intelligence (hereafter: AI) systems may cause individual or societal harm and that the way to prevent harm is through *ex-ante* review and *ex post* monitoring. This includes ensuring that AI systems reflect human values, can explain the logic behind their decisions and learn without harming people. While the early phase of AI governance focused on the "ethics of AI" and "ethical AI", in the later stages, scholars and NGOs warned that the term "ethics" may be overly "soft", vague and contingent on the interests of "big tech" and that it should be substituted or at least decisively complemented by the "law" (such as international human rights

---

A. Završnik (✉)
Institute of Criminology at the Faculty of Law, Ljubljana, Slovenia
e-mail: ales.zavrsnik@pf.uni-lj.si

© The Author(s), under exclusive license to Springer Nature
Switzerland AG 2023
A. Završnik and K. Simončič (eds.), *Artificial Intelligence, Social Harms and Human Rights*, Critical Criminological Perspectives,
https://doi.org/10.1007/978-3-031-19149-7_5

law and European law) since the law is universally agreed upon and its results are legally binding.

The main concern about the role of ethics in the governance of AI is that it is self-imposed regulation, which has been historically relatively weak in curbing the interests of powerful actors (e.g. in curbing environmental pollution). Moreover, the idea that ethics should be replaced with human rights law is even more compelling since the law is, at least at the abstract level, clear. In contrast, ethics is more fluid, flexible and contingent on culture, place and time, as demonstrated by experimental ethics (e.g. Awad et al., 2018). Also, the non-binding ethical guidelines lack mechanisms to ensure that they are respected and that principles are translated into binding provisions. The idea that ethics is "not sufficient" hence rests on several deficiencies of ethics itself (e.g. what do we talk about when we talk about "ethics governance" as there are several strands of ethics, which offer varied, if not contradictory, guidance on how to act ethically) and reflects the struggle for power and prestige of those that seek and offer ethical and legal expertise.

However, prioritising, if not glorifying the law, also has several flaws. The law is not a clear monolith that does not serve the particular interests of powerful groups. "The law" is not floating in a societal, cultural vacuum and is clear at the abstract level only. It is often expressed in the form of standards that do not offer sufficiently specific guidance for building AI systems. It contains legal principles and open-ended concepts that need to be built upon in the specific case. The longitudinal and indirect impacts of technologies such as AI on individuals, society and the environment quite often fall through the "normative net" as the study of social harms in criminology (referred to as zemiology) has persuasively unveiled on many occasions, for example by creating specific theoretical concepts (and showing their empirical counterparts) such as "crimes of the powerful" and "state crimes", which were not *stricto* sensu crimes or recognised as civil damages. Critical criminology offers an abundance of theoretical tools and practical examples that reflect the "permeable" and biased nature of "law in books" and even more contingent adjudication of the law in specific cases ("law in action"). This chapter is informed by these critical voices about the law and ethics.

This chapter shows how the standard approach to the *ex-ante* ethics assessment of AI systems in research and development (R&D) has often encapsulated the core ideas and concepts of human rights law, and that the division between ethics and the law has not been as clear as many scholars of both camps have implied. This does not denigrate the relevance of drawing sharp lines between the law and ethics in conceptualising the various modes of AI governance and its deficiencies, but should help to shed some light on the power of the law and ethics to jointly curb the negative effects of AI technologies—which have been clearly demonstrated, as this chapter summarises.

The ethics assessment of AI systems in R&D has been especially focused on data protection and discrimination laws. What if the fundaments of ethical assessment in R&D are already well aligned with human rights law? If we do not ground ethical judgements on the universally accepted human rights law, where should we ground them then? Moreover, ethics and international human rights law are already "on the same page" if we speak generally. But in specific cases, when we delve into details, we can observe how ethics assessment can complement the human rights law and offer guidance on specific challenges that can only be dealt with by combining the two—the law and ethics.[1]

This chapter examines the intersection of the legal and ethical compliance of AI systems in the R&D domain. It aims to fill the gap in understanding the complementarity of the law and ethics to help researchers evaluate *ex-ante* the ethical and legal risks related to the development/deployment of the AI systems/techniques and how to mitigate the potential negative social impacts of AI. The central question of this chapter is whether there is a place for ethics "beyond" the law when *ex-ante* assessing AI systems in R&D. *Firstly*, this chapter offers some insights into the various forms of harm of AI and the awareness of the engineering community about these harms. *Secondly*, it offers some

---

[1] To ease the discussion, I compare the "law" and "ethics" in the field of AI governance, albeit I am aware that the "law" is taken here as a monolith, which makes some injustice to the law. A more nuanced discussion on international human rights law, European law, Personal data protection law and Discrimination law is needed. Similarly, "ethics" is taken as a moonlight and discussions of deontological ethics, utilitarian ethics and so forth would be more nuanced. I remedy this simplification by delving into an example of computer vision and processing of personal data.

insight into "AI governance" as a specific field of governance of ICT, in which ethics has obtained a prominent policy role (similarly to bioethics from the 1970s onwards). The trend has gone from the "race to AI" to the rush to "AI ethics" and onwards and upwards to the "race for the governance of AI" (e.g. Wagner, 2018; Koulu, 2020; Smuha, 2021; Dijk et al., 2021; Koniakou, 2022). *Thirdly*, this chapter then delves deeper into the relationship between ethics and law by narrowing down the analysis to the example of legal and ethical assessments of access, collection and another type of processing of personal data (aka "new oil") for the purposes of computer vision applications. This example shows how the tensions between ethics and the law exist more at a surface and abstract level, while they are complementary in mitigating the potential negative societal and individual harms of AI applications (e.g. Senden, 2005; Sartor, 2020).

2 AI Harm: Why an *Ex-ante* Assessment of AI Is Needed?

Researchers have documented the societal and ethical implications of many AI tools in several domains, such as banking (O'Hara and Mason, 2012), payment sectors (Gefferie, 2018) and the financial industry (McGee, 2016), in insurance (Ambasna-Jones, 2015), education (Ekowo and Palmer, 2016) and employment (O'Neil, 2016) as well as in armed conflicts and criminal justice (Završnik, 2018). The domains in which AI is used are growing daily, and their societal, ethical and legal implications vary significantly between different domains. While the implications of some AI tools, such as a tool which predicts the structure of all scientifically known proteins (DeepMind's AlphaFold, Heikkilä, 2022a) or the uses of AI by pharmaceutical companies to streamline the discovery of new medicines (Knight, 2017), are not problematic for the legal position of individuals, the gravest negative implications of AI have been identified in the following four broadly defined domains:

(1) When AI is used in *automated decision-making (ADM) systems* implemented in public administration, including policing, the criminal

justice system and social welfare. Extensive reports, such as the Automating Society Reports by AlgorithmWatch (Chiusi et al., 2020) and alGOVrithms by ePanstvo (Škop et al., 2019), show the dangers of rushing the implementation of AI tools into decision-making procedures in which individual rights and duties are defined, recognised, imposed or enforced. From the tax administration fiasco in the social welfare domain for the automated childcare benefit fraud detection in the Netherlands (Amnesty International, 2021) that led to the resignation of the Dutch government in 2021, the racially biased probation algorithms in the USA (Angwin et al., 2016) and the UK exams debacle with a standardisation algorithm to combat grade inflation in 2020 (Quinn, 2020), to hiring processes in companies to pre-screen candidates and filter out desired candidates (Wall and Schellmann, 2021) and so forth, the examples of harmful (and unintended) effects of ADM systems are burgeoning.

(2) The *computer vision domain* and image processing applications (including biometric technology), which form the foundation for AI-based technology products is another domain at the forefront of legally and socially significant implications that warrant *ex-ante* assessment. The AI techniques that can spot skin cancer (Takiddin et al., 2021) and outperform doctors at detecting breast cancer (McKinney et al., 2020) and tumour growth (Gregory, 2022) may have immense potential for the prevention of personal harm, but the same technology used for identification and authentication purposes was found to be extremely risky, especially discriminatory (Crockford, 2020) facial recognition-fuelled surveillance (Buolamwini and Gebru, 2018; Raji and Buolamwini, 2019). AI tools have been used to detect people's emotional states (Kaye, 2022a) and there was the problematic scraping of personal data from social media platforms for the purpose of machine learning, among other occurrences.

(3) The growth of *natural language processing tools*, which include powerful Large Language Models (LLMs) (e.g. OpenAI's GPT-3; Google's LaMDA, or BLOOM—BigScience Large Open-science Open-access Multilingual Language Model) (Heikkilä, 2022b) that scrape data from the internet and learn the structures of languages,

outpace a critical reflection on the ethical concerns related to misrepresentations and the misleading of users, the lack of adequate policies on data governance and privacy and the algorithms' tendency to spew toxic content. The data scraped from the internet must be properly selected and these data also inevitably merge personal data, biased data and fake data.[2] The LLMs are proprietary, secret and exclusive to those that can afford them. Similarly, the ease of creating false images (deepfakes) increases with simple-to-use tools, such as the image-making program DALL-E2 (https://openai.com), whose ethical implications are yet to be grasped (with notable exceptions, e.g. Bender et al., 2021).

(4) Lastly, ethically sensitive uses of AI relate to *targeted advertising*, i.e. for profiling by networks and recommender systems on the internet, which shape our digital world, moderate the content we consume and facilitate disinformation-spreading content and deepfakes (Vaccari and Chadwick, 2020). As users receive specific ads and miss information about offers that they would potentially be interested in, they become locked in "filter bubbles" or "echo chambers". The creation and reinforcement of "filter bubbles" weaken critical thinking and lead to the manipulation of consumers and citizens. Since engagement is often prioritised in the social media landscape,[3] the moderation with the help of AI results in the dissemination of offensive content, replication of social stereotypes and reinforcement of "confirmation bias". These uses of AI clearly have implications on the quality of democracy, such as meddling with elections.[4]

---

[2] BLOOM is one of the exceptions as the researchers developed a data governance model for LLMs and developing a specific licence (referred to as Responsible AI Licence) designed to deter use of BLOOM in high risk sectors, such as law enforcement or to deceive or harm people. BLOOM also has its own Ethical Charter. More in Heikkilä (2022b).

[3] According to Frances Haugen on Facebook: "…machine-learning algorithms create a much more powerful feedback loop. Not only can they personalize what each user sees, they will also continue to evolve with a user's shifting preferences, perpetually showing each person what will keep them most engaged" (Hao, 2021b).

[4] Detailed accounts of harms of AI see O'Neil (2016) and Noble (2018).

5 In Defence of Ethics *and* the Law ...   107

Despite the above-mentioned concerns about some of the uses of AI tools and the abundance of documented harms, the ethical awareness of the AI community is low. The computer vision community has been reluctant to recognise the connections between the research advancements and awe-inspiring math problem-solving achievements on the one hand and the possible uses for that tech once it is baked into apps and software products on the other hand. "AI researchers building surveillance tech and deepfakes resist ethical concerns" (Kaye, 2022b). For instance, at one of the computer vision community's most prestigious annual conferences, the Computer Vision and Pattern Recognition (CVPR) Conference—a global event with around 10,000 attendees, researchers experience "a general disregard for ethical considerations and the human rights impacts of computer vision-based technologies used for border surveillance, autonomous and drone warfare and law enforcement" (Kaye, 2022b). Only in 2022 did the attitudes change slightly, as the organisers of the CVPR Conference encouraged researchers to include a discussion about the potential negative societal impacts of their research. However, the vast majority of tutorials, workshops and research papers presented at CVPR made little or no mention of ethical considerations, while the obligation for researchers was small as they were only asked to tell reviewers whether or not their work might have a social impact (Kaye, 2022b).

How can such a discrepancy between the documented harms of the AI uses briefly outlined above and the computer community's (lack of) action to prevent and mitigate such harm, be understood?

The computer community's arguments against the in-depth assessment of the societal impacts of their research have merits. They think it is not their job to consider the applications of their research since they were not trained to think about possible futures regarding the techniques that are in very early stages of development and years away from product viability (Kaye, 2022b). Moreover, computer science training does not have a sufficient and systematic ethics component; hence computer scientists are stepping into an unknown field. They often ask "what is ethics?", a hard question to answer, even for social scientists. Various ethical theories could serve as a valuable substrate for the legal governance of AI, from virtue ethics to deontological ethics, such as Kant's ethics, Pufendorf's or Lock's ethics, consequentialist ethics and so forth. Selecting one of these ethical directions leads to various outcomes, and the exercise of *ex-ante* assessment may be very complex for philosophers versed in "classical" ethics. Moreover, the social acceptability of the outcomes of different ethical theories changes in place and time, as cross-cultural studies of moral preferences in sacrificial dilemmas have persuasively demonstrated. The MIT Moral Machine experiment (Awad et al., 2018), for instance, clarified that in traditional countries such as Japan, participants would rather sacrifice younger than older pedestrians in the classical "trolley problem" compared to the theoretical sacrifices in more liberal countries. More specifically, the quantitative acceptability of each sacrifice showed substantial country-level variations.[5] Ethics should hence be operationalised in a manner of an "ethics tuning button", for example, in automated vehicles, to reflect the regional, country-specific preferences. Since computer scientists are not versed in these subtle philosophical dilemmas, which are complex on their own, it is not surprising that they are reluctant to think through the ethical and societal implications of their work.

Despite such complex ethical dilemmas, computer science ethics has become an emerging field in the last decade. Embedding ethics in the computer science curriculum, however, is a relatively new development with, for instance, the Harvard initiative from 2019 being "seen as a national model" (Karoff, 2019). While the early studies in ethics attitudes among computer scientists in the 1990s delved into students' perceptions (Lorents et al., 2006), more recent studies have been focusing on offensive hacking, ethics and automated vehicles, algorithmic bias, the need for empathy in engineering education and practice (Afroogh et al., 2021), data collection and data sharing,[6] ethics of AI in human resources

---

[5] In contrast, in every scrutinised country, the analysed sacrificial dilemmas displayed the same qualitative ordering of sacrifice acceptability, suggesting that this ordering is best explained by basic cognitive processes rather than cultural norms. See Awad et al. (2020).

[6] On ethical challenges related to big social data research projects (in the context of migration) see Mahoney (2022). On the ethical issues related to social media and online platforms research and online data collection see Bamdad et al. (2022).

(HR),[7] addictive design and questionable personal data ownership, diversity in tech development,[8] and with the Covid-19 pandemic, also on ethical aspects of digital tracing technologies (Afroogh et al., 2022).

Computer scientists often perceive themselves as being "super aware" of the potential impacts of their research on the real world; however, they cherish their academic freedom. Asking them to predict future applications for research that could be in the very early stages of development and years away from viability in products is perceived as something that restricts their independence (Kaye, 2022b). This is especially true if the development team is evaluated on their production rate of feature developments and capabilities in software releases and not the impact and ethics that a given implementation might have either at the design or the implementation phase. However, the empirical studies on computer scientists' perceptions still show reluctance to assess the ethical implications of their products. In 2020, the data science platform Anaconda (2020) found that 27% of data practitioners thought the biggest problem to tackle in AI was the social impact of bias in data and models. Concerns about bias and privacy are on the minds of data professionals, with nearly half of the respondents citing one of these two topics as the "biggest problem to tackle in the AI/ML arena today". But, concerningly, only 15% of respondents said that their team is currently actively addressing the issue of bias, and only 15% of universities include courses in ethics (Anaconda, 2020).

Finally, computer scientists also evoke the argument about technology being neutral, that is, it is not the AI techniques that are "bad" or "good", but the way we use them: Nuclear power can be used for positive and negative purposes, and fire can be used with good and bad intentions. According to this "neutrality of technology" argument, the research into neural networks is perceived as pure math with no direct links to negative (or positive) social impact. However, the interdisciplinary field

---

[7] See, e.g., special issue of Ethics and Information Technology on the Ethical Uses of AI in Human Resources at: https://resource-cms.springernature.com/springer-cms/rest/v1/content/189 61356/data/v1.

[8] Benjamin (2019) raised concerns about a case where developers failed to include Black people's voices in training AI speech recognition algorithms, under the belief that fewer Black people would use the app.

of Science and Technology Studies (STS) has convincingly shown that science and technology are socially embedded enterprises (Bijker et al., 2012). Technology is a product of culture and social norms, for example, what counts as a "proper", "adequate" and "socially acceptable" way of responding to environmental and societal challenges, such as crime or pandemics, is socially and culturally defined and embedded. Scientific answers stemming from socially framed questions are, therefore, always social constructions.

Discrepancies between the harms of AI use on the one hand, and the computer community (in)action to prevent and mitigate such harms, on the other, are still significant and need to be tackled in a more meaningful way. The curricula for the education of legal professionals and ethicists, on the one hand, and computer software developers, on the other, must be fundamentally revived and mutually adulated. But to achieve the desired influence on the development of technology, ex-ante ethics *and* legal assessment of AI from the lens of potential harms need to be applied. Floridi (2018: 7) rightly claims: "Ethics in general and digital ethics, in particular, cannot be a mere add-on, an afterthought, a late-comer, and owl of Minerva that takes its flight only when the shades of night are gathering, only once digital innovation has taken place". The best way "to catch the technology train is not to chase it, but to be at the next station" (Floridi, 2018: 6). But how should digital ethics jump to this "next station" without it being merely a vision and opinion of self-proclaimed ethicists and how should existing legal provisions be respected? To complement and extend Floridi's point on digital ethics' political relevance (Floridi, 2018: 7), I claim that ethics *and* the law must sit at the table of policy-making and decision-making procedures from day one. How else shall we steer the desired AI technology development (positive end) and anticipate and avoid possible harms (negative end)?

3 AI Governance: Assessing the Ethical and Fundamental Rights Impacts of AI

The idea of AI governance is that the societal, ethical and environmental impacts of AI applications are recognised as early as possible and mitigated as soon as they occur. Existing governance frameworks on how to assess and anticipate impacts of specific AI tools include hard and soft law instruments, for instance recommendations, and practical tools, such as guidelines and checklists. Floridi (2018) maps the governance of digital, that is, how to shape and guide the development of the digital, as encompassing three normative approaches. While *digital governance* is the practice of establishing and implementing policies, procedures and standards for the proper development, use and management of the infosphere (e.g. with guidelines and recommendations), *digital regulation* is a system of rules elaborated and enforced through social or governmental institutions to regulate the behaviour of the relevant agents in the infosphere. *Digital ethics*, the third normative approach to governing the digital, is a branch of ethics that studies and evaluates moral problems relating to data and information, algorithms and corresponding practices and infrastructures in order to formulate and support morally good solutions. Digital ethics only partly overlaps with digital governance and digital regulation (Floridi, 2018). The question is, why do we need all three normative approaches? Why not resort only to digital regulation (laws), ethics or governance?

The existing instruments that shape and guide the development of AI reflect a telling evolution of how to address the harms (deterrence from negative impacts) and how to steer the development of AI towards the desired outcomes (the pursuit to the desired ends). The urge to regulate the use of AI in the public and private sectors came first in the form of a "race to ethical AI", which lead to an "ethification" of ICT Governance (Dijk et al., 2021). The first stage of shaping and guiding the development of AI began in the middle of the second decade of the twenty-first century[9] with increased reliance on ethics in governing

---

[9] The German interdisciplinary study "Assessing Big Data" (2015) was one of the first studies to reflect upon ethics and AI. The ABIDA (Assessing Big Data) project, funded by the German

the use of AI and earlier precursors of "turn to ethics" from legal regulation were observed in the field of information privacy protection in 2016.[10] The relatively stronger political role of ethics in regulating AI technology can be compared to the similar recourse to ethics in biotechnology governance in the form of bioethics in the second half of the twentieth century.[11]

The impetus for "ethical AI" came from practically all international organisations that produced normative documents identifying the potential benefits, harms and associated recommendations related to AI (Schiff et al., 2022). A 2019 study, considered state of the art in shaping and guiding the development of the digital, identified 84 different documents with ethical principles for AI (Jobin et al., 2019). The EU Agency for Fundamental Rights (FRA), which kept an updated record of ethics guidance and policy initiatives in the field of AI governance, identified 183 initiatives in 2019 (15 October) and 351 initiatives in 2020.[12] The comparative analysis conducted by Jobin et al. (2019) analysed the corpus of principles and guidelines on ethical AI adopted by private companies, research institutions and public sector organisations and found that there is a global convergence emerging around five ethical principles (transparency, justice and fairness, non-maleficence, responsibility and privacy), but with substantive divergence in relation to how these principles are interpreted, why they are deemed important, what issue, domain or actors they pertain to, and how they should be implemented. The divergence is not particularly surprising as reaching a consensus about abstractly defined values and principles is only the

---

federal Department of Science and Research, focused on the societal opportunities and risks of producing, integrating and analysing big data, and on developing opportunities for policy activism, research and development. Available at: https://www.abida.de/.

[10] Raab (2016) speaks of "a noticeable 'turn' from reliance on legal regulation to an emphasis on ethics", and accountability and transparency as well, in the field of processing of information.

[11] For instance, the European Commission established in 1991 the Group of Advisers on the Ethical Implications of Biotechnology (GAEIB).

[12] The last update from 1 December 2020. The study defined a "policy initiative" to include a range of initiatives that could contribute to policy making and standard setting in the field of AI. These could include, but are not limited to, actual (or draft) legislation, soft law, guidelines and recommendations on the use of AI, or reports that include conclusions relevant to AI governance or AI-related policy (European Union Agency for Fundamental Rights [FRA], 2020).

5 In Defence of Ethics *and* the Law ... 113

first step of ensuring "ethical AI", and consensus quickly vanishes when specific interests of individual stakeholders step in to "fill" a principle. Critical unanswered questions hence still remain around representation and power and *the translation of principles to practices* (Schiff et al., 2022).

3.1 Positive Role of Ethics

The positive role of ethics can be discerned into four categories: *first*, arguments based on ethics were among the first to voice concerns over the potential negative effects and implications of AI due to unclear regulation. For instance, the "persuasive design" of apps and internet services that have started to shift from benevolent to persuasion tools and to manipulative "dark patterns" (these are features of interface design crafted to trick users and lead to "addiction") (Wu, 2018; Luguri and Strahilevitz, 2021) could be tackled with consumer protection law or contract law; however, details of such protection still remain to be seen. It is not clear "where to draw the line" between beneficial and harmful engagement. The architecture of internet services as a whole is based on recommender systems that inevitably shape our digital world and are an inherent part of the "free" internet services. Another reoccurring issue in AI governance is the collusion between big tech companies and the elite academic institutions that feed them, which is "one of the root causes of unethical AI solutions" (Gebru, 2021). A former co-lead of Google's Ethical AI team observes how big tech leaders are also the leaders who control big philanthropy and the government's agenda for the future of AI research. The role of researchers who uncover challenges related to the use of AI and AI-based social media is also important not only from their labour protection and the future ability for fundraising points of view but also from how they communicate problems (Spohr, 2017). Sætra et al. (2022) emphasise that the way how the researchers choose avenues to communicate problems only using the technologies and tools the "big tech" provides can even be counter-productive. These (and similar) questions of power imbalances and the problems of AI "surveillance capitalism" (Zuboff, 2015) are often (if not always) "beyond" the law and legality since the law is part of a problem rather than a solution, for example when big tech companies strategically employ the law to serve their interests (e.g. hire larger teams of lawyers than the regulators can afford).

Second, AI developers themselves adopted "ethics codes" (ethics "principles" or "guidelines") in a bottom-up approach that should always complement top-down regulation. Tech players were very quick in responding to public concerns, for example, IBM adopted "*Everyday Ethics for Artificial Intelligence*" (IBM, 2018) and "*Advancing AI ethics beyond compliance*" (Goehring et al., 2020); Google adopted "*AI Principles*" (Google, 2019), and Microsoft, "*The Future Computed*" (Microsoft, 2018). The bottom-up approach to regulation is of key importance since the expertise of the AI engineering communities lies closest to the problems, for example, engineering-out the negative societal and ethical impacts of AI is a way to ensure the "by design" solutions (e.g. privacy-by-design, ethics-by-design or "compliance-by-design"). The creators of harmful AI tools should also act as the "first responders" in mitigating its harms. The AI tech's reaction should not be judged less favourably than not acting at all. The AI tech was at least attempting to address the growing public concerns in the light of sensationalist press-induced fears that AI is coming for "your jobs and souls".[13]

Third, several conceptual innovations in governing the development and use of technology, such as the use of algorithmic impact assessment (AIA), showed that some thought has been invested into considering the impacts of the emerging AI tech "in the nub" of the issues (at the same time, voices emerged about drawbacks of AIA in the absence of effective accountability).[14] In defence of ethics, Floridi (2018: 4–5) explained how he sees the relationship between law and ethics:

---

[13] Such as a roundtable "Be Afraid, Be Very Afraid: The Robots Are Coming and They Will Steal Our Livelihoods", Intelligence Squared (2015).

[14] About AIA and the history of impact assessment in other domains see Metcalf et al. (2021). About mandatory Algorithmic Impact Assessment in Canada see https://www.canada.ca/en/government/system/digital-government/digital-government-innovations/responsible-use-ai/algorithmic-impact-assessment.html. For an example of AIA in healthcare see Ada Lovelace Institite (2022).

It [legislation] does not cover everything (nor should it), and agents should leverage digital ethics in order to assess and decide what role they wish to play in the infosphere, when regulations provide no simple or straightforward answer, when competing values and interests need to be balanced (or indeed when regulations provide no guidance) and when there is more that can be done over and above what the law strictly requires.

The breakdown of ethics into "hard" and "soft" ethics seems far-fetched, but enables Floridi to advocate the "soft ethics" to offer answers to what ought and what ought not to be done "over" and "above" the existing regulation, not against it, and so forth.[15] But the part of the argument on the density of the legal "normative net" ("legislation does not cover everything (nor it should)" opens up a legitimate place for ethics.

However, scholars reflected upon such an "ethificated" AI governance model, where ethics was supposed to "sit by table with policymakers" (Floridi, 2018: 7), and clearly pointed to its downsides: the risk of "ethics washing", that is the practice of camouflaging practices and tools to appear more ethical than they really are, and warnings against "ethics shopping", a practice of "mixing and matching" ethical principles from various sources to avoid a real change of behaviour (Wagner, 2018; Amram and Comandé, 2020), were just some of the more blatant downsides of the "turn to ethics" in AI governance.

3.2 Critique of Ethics

Critique of ethics in AI governance has been fierce. Wagner (2018) warned that the "turn to ethics" is side-lining the role of states and emphasises the role of the private sector, which was an opportunity not just to provide a way to go beyond existing legal frameworks but an

---

[15] Floridi does not offer sufficiently clear examples of "hard" ethics and is implying that "hard" ethics is the one that "crushes" the law and "soft" ethics "goes beyond" the law. For instance, an example on the use of "hard" ethics to criticise apartheid is about a political use (or use case) of ethics and does not denote a substantively different form of ethics from the so-called "soft" ethics.

opportunity to ignore them. Ethics as self-regulation is used as a form of escape from regulation or a way to delay the debate and work on law for AI. Moreover, states were portrayed as a problem rather than a solution (Wagner, 2018). NGOs, for example Access Now and European Digital Rights warned the EU regulators that what is needed in the EU AI debate is a bold, bright-line approach that prioritises fundamental rights (Chander et al., 2020).

The "codes of ethics" were used to a great extent as a smokescreen, claimed Metzinger (2019), a member of the AI HLEG group, who lamented how the industry organises ethical debates to delay effective regulation and policymaking by "including lots of conceptual smoke screens and mirrors, highly paid industrial philosophers, self-invented quality seals and non-validated certificates for 'Ethical AI made in Europe'". Similarly, the UN Special rapporteur on extreme poverty and human rights, Alston (2019, point 40) claimed that in the context of raising a "digital welfare state" "[t]he industry has gone into high gear in producing, influencing and embracing 'codes of ethics' and other non-binding standards purporting to 'regulate' digital technologies and their developers". The industry convinced the public that "the pilot is still in the cockpit", but given the substantive emptiness of the "ethical commitments" Alston critically asserted:

> These codes contain a reference to human rights, but the substance of human rights law is invariably lacking. Instead, the token reference to human rights serves only to enhance claims to legitimacy and universality. Meanwhile, the relevant discussions of ethics are based on almost entirely open-ended notions that are not necessarily grounded in legal or even philosophical arguments and can be shaped to suit the needs of the industry.

The vague references to "ethics" shed a bad light on the self-regulatory instruments. The references to ethics were shallow in their own terms as it was not clear what type of ethics the drafters had considered. Moreover, the use of open-ended "human rights" concepts was more a superficial "verbiage" that could serve any end goal that the developers wanted to pursue. Since the very essence of governmental regulation is *per definitionem* to curb private interest—the interests of AI developers in our case—camouflaging private interests under universal "ethics" and "human rights" turned into "the race to AI regulation" (Smuha, 2021).

The first set of criticism of ethics in AI governance assemblage concerns the nature of ethics. Ethics as a branch of philosophy developed in several schools of ethics, such as virtue ethics or deontological ethics, such as Kant's ethics, Pufendorf's or Lock's ethics, consequentialist ethics and so forth. The growing role of ethics in AI governance does not correspond to elaborated discussions specifying the ethics in a "classical ethics" sense. Dijk et al. (2021) express this concern by pointing to a lack of content in ethical principles, as there is "no authoritative 'home-base'", a lack of discipline standards, no checks and balances systems (e.g. clear accountability and enforcement mechanisms) and no sufficient public legitimacy of ethical work, which lacks the credentials of democratic representativity and deliberative mechanisms, and so forth. Albeit diverse ethical directions exist, "classical" ethics is rarely debated in the "ethics" analyses of AI (the notable exception being Bringas Colmenarejo et al., 2022). The "ethics" as understood by governing and policy bodies, such as the European Commission, is not the same type of ethics compared to "classical" ethics. These bodies (co-)create and operationalise ethics and Dijk et al. (2021) call it "ethics produced in institutional settings", where it has acquired a different form intertwined with policy, regulation and research integrity or—more generally—politics. Such "institutional" ethics differs between institutions, as Dijk et al. (2021) identify at the level of the European research programme Horizon 2020: "Research Ethics" is tied to the co-production excellence of EU science in the first pillar of H2020, "Innovation Governance Ethics" to "societal challenges" in the second pillar of H2020. The consequences of the flexibility of ethics are not limited to expertise and representativeness. Ethics as a means for regulation often also lacks the checks and balances and processual quality guarantees, thus constituting "rule-making beyond the rule of law" (Dijk et al., 2021). Furthermore, there are no quality control mechanisms such as setting up the norms of who is an ethicist and who can speak in the name of ethics. As the ethics codes are not legally binding, they are used merely as authoritative sources "to be taken into account" and as "much as possible", according to Dijk et al. (2021).

The second set of criticism concerns the relationship between law and ethics. Where does the law "stop" and ethics "begin"? Where does ethics fill the normative net "beyond" the law? Is ethics "before" the law—as it is more "flexible" and "quick" to adapt to new technological realities, or is ethics a "substrate" of the law which helps to steer the law from the start? Or does ethics come "after" the law to "enhance" the law "beyond compliance"?

To sum up, advocates of the law (e.g. human rights law or European law) claim that the "rush to ethics" in AI governance has resulted in conceptual incoherence, conflicts among norms; meaningful input is rarely sought from stakeholders and accountability mechanisms are absent. The key for them is to regulate relevant actors, such as companies producing AI tools, with (binding) legal rules based on established human rights legal doctrine, or at least on established philosophical conceptualisations of human rights (Alston, 2019). The governance of AI needs to prioritise fundamental rights. The legal corpus has clear substance (substantive rules) and clear procedural safeguards (e.g. the roles of actors are clearly defined, the quality control and accountability mechanisms are clear). The law is, moreover, vested with democratic representativeness, for example it was adopted in *a priory-defined* procedure by the mandate of the representatives of the public. NGO stated: "We support human rights impact assessments and red lines around the use of these technologies, rather than an ethics, risk-based, or sandboxing approach" (Access Now, 2020).

3.3 Critique of the Law

The advocates of prioritising "the law" in AI governance have pointed to relevant deficiencies of ethics governance and expected too much from ethics. Similarly to asking for a specific school of the "classic" ethics, the same can be argued for the law—which law, human rights law, European law or its specific national transpositions and so forth? The legal norms have never been "transparent". The norms have to be interpreted all over again and creatively used in specific cases. "The law" seems coherent and with effective procedural safeguards on the surface level only. The painting of "the law" by lawyers is ideological insofar as it implies "democratic" (representing all groups) and clear substantive content, and flawlessness in its procedures. Moreover, it is always more comfortable to list shortcomings (of ethics) than to list irrefutable characteristics (of the law) itself. Legal regulation offers powerful players hard-to-dispute advantages. For instance, enforcing GDPR rights has become a huge endeavour in itself, as attested by NGOs and individuals fighting for their rights (e.g. see Max Schrems' legal actions and the Noyb ("None of Your Business") strategic court cases to achieve compliance of big tech). As the example from the computer vision domain below will show, straightforward legal answers offer workable solutions only in very limited cases. Moreover, employing the line of "law" or "ethics" in "hard cases" can lead to very similar results.

4 A Case Study: Computer Vision and GDPR's Exception for Research Purposes

A legal perspective on fairness in AI can be narrowed down to several legal regimes: (1) legal framework on the prohibition of discrimination, (2) personal data protection law and (3) the protection of intellectual property rights.[16]

In regard to the prohibition of discrimination, European anti-discrimination law is designed to prevent discrimination against particular groups of people that share one or more characteristics (the so-called "protected attributes"), from which the group acquires the category of a protected group.[17] In a general sense, indirect discrimination occurs when seemingly neutral provisions, criteria or practices put members

---

[16] From a broader perspective, AI has implications for several other fields of law, e.g. criminal law (e.g. predictive policing tools), labour law (e.g. AI surveillance of workers), contract law (e.g. AI use in preparing, executing contracts), election law (e.g. the use of AI for microtargeting or digital gerrymandering) etc. However, these three legal regimes are relevant for data processing and compiling datasets, which are needed for computer vision applications.

[17] For instance, sex, race or ethnic origin, colour, ethnic or social origin, genetic features and so forth, according to Article 21 of the Charter of Fundamental Rights of the European Union.

of a protected category in a disadvantaged position compared to other persons (and such provisions, criteria or practices are not justifiable by a legitimate aim, and the means of achieving that aim are appropriate and necessary). In the context of AI, one of the key insights is that the AI tool may not be directly discriminatory but may still be (unintentionally) indirectly discriminatory. The AI tool may be neutral towards a protected attribute but still offers a less favourable output to individuals from a protected group. While the abstract definition of indirect discrimination is clear, it is not obvious in which specific cases members of a protected category are in a disadvantaged position compared to others. According to Zuiderveen Borgesius (2018), this means that the prohibition of indirect discrimination should be considered closer to a standard than to a rule. It must be proven that a seemingly neutral rule, practice or decision disproportionately affects a protected group. As is often the case with AI, it is impossible to discover for which reasons and based on which differentiation criteria the AI tool made the discriminatory decision due to AI's "black box" effect. Indirect discrimination hence, concerns neutral models, which are blinded to protected attributes and do not operate based on those protective attributes (Bringas Colmenarejo et al., 2022: 110) but still "calculate" protective attributes indirectly through proxies (Caliskan et al., 2017).

Data collected for AI training purposes is often protected as *personal data*, i.e. data relating to a specific or identifiable individual and, therefore, a specially protected category of data, and as data protected *by intellectual property rights*. Despite the legal protection of data by these two legal regimes—the personal data protection law and intellectual property rights (IPR) law—both regimes also provide for exceptions to the protection. The European data protection regime provides for exceptions of processing of personal data for *scientific research* (and archival, statistical) purposes (Article 89 GDPR), while the IPR protection is loosened by the new Directive 2019/790 on Copyright in the Digital Single Market, which introduces two new copyright exceptions for the field of data analytics or text and data mining, providing a legal basis for such mining and facilitating legally permissible access to data for Machine Learning (hereinafter: ML) purposes.[18]

In regard to personal data protection, AI-related processing of personal data must be lawful, fair, and transparent. The principle of fairness entails the processing of personal information that is not in any way unduly detrimental, unexpected or misleading to the individuals concerned (Bringas Colmenarejo et al., 2022: 110). Despite several provisions in GDPR, such as on data accuracy or the need to prevent the risks to the rights and freedom of natural persons, which could lead to physical, material or non-material damage (e.g. the Recital 71 and 75 of GDPR), Bringas Colmenarejo et al. (2022: 110) rightly conclude that "ensuring fairness is still quite a subjective matter as it requires that the data processing shall not exceed reasonable expectations nor provoke unjustified adverse effects on the individuals". The meaning of "reasonable expectations" and "justifiable effects" is open to interpretation, leaving the notion of fair processing undefined (Bringas Colmenarejo et al., 2022: 110). The standard of "fair processing" hence opens the door to ethics and the following case detailing the processing of personal data for computer vision applications shows how "ethics" can complement "the law".

4.1   What Is Computer Vision?

Computer vision is a field of data science which has entered many domains, significantly revolutionising the scientific method and enabling new insights in many scientific disciplines.[19] Some of the computer

---

[18] I put aside a more in-depth discussion about AI and the prohibition of discrimination and AI and intellectual property rights, and instead focus on the case of personal data protection law and frictions occurring in the field of data processing in the computer vision domain. For in-depth analysis of the prohibition of discrimination and AI see Chapter 4 of this volume (by Karmen Lutman).

[19] For instance, computer vision in: (a) digital humanities: used for comparing images or illustrations; (b) zoology, to tag animal specimens when studying their behaviour; (c) archaeology, to measure excavated items; (d) market research, e.g. theft prevention; (e) medical research, e.g. for automated cell counting; (f) anthropology, e.g. to match different group members in pictorial material; (g) material sciences, e.g. to measure crystallisation; (h) the analysis of sport, e.g. to analyse football players; (i) monitoring traffic flow or (j) for damage analysis of buildings.

vision applications recognise *objects* (which, in principle, do not have legal or ethical implications) and some *individuals*, where the engineering work may collide with (legal and ethical) obligations related to personal data processing.

Highly content-rich databases were the key to developing computer vision and ML.[20] ML needs large amounts of learning data of sufficient quality in the chosen learning domain. Quality of training data means that the data are relevant, accurate and representative of the purpose and context of their intended use. Several such databases for the training of computer vision algorithms were created by computer scientists in good faith with the aim of training algorithms. Scientists compiled databases for their research needs and made the most valuable ones available to the (global) scientific community for the public good. *The Labelled Faces in the Wild* database,[21] for instance, a database of facial photographs compiled to study issues related to the unlimited identification of celebrities and public figures, received the highest professional award, the *Mark Everingham Award*, for serving the scientific community in the field of computer vision. *ImageNet*, one of the first databases for developing computer programs for visual recognition, is a benchmark for comparing image recognition models. It contains 14 million manually annotated images obtained from internet sources and is available for free. The images are annotated with more than 20,000 categories (a category in this context means, for example, "balloon", "apple", etc.), and the database contains several hundred photographs, images and illustrations for each category.

However, *ImageNet*, which enabled the explosive development of automated image recognition and paved the way for the development of computer vision, has also been widely criticised for embodying prejudices and biases (e.g. Steed and Caliskan, 2021). It is unclear what kind of policy is behind the categorisation of images and which taggers' values are reflected in the tagging of photos. For instance, the collection contains many bizarre and offensive categories such as a young man with a beer

---

[20] The relationship between AI (Artificial Intelligence) and ML (Machine Learning) can be defined as AI using ML to implement predictive actions based on context-specific data.

[21] Labeled Faces in the Wild is available at: http://vis-www.cs.umass.edu/lfw/.

labelled "alcoholic" and a smiling girl in a swimsuit labelled "promiscuous" (Crawford and Trevor, 2019). Moreover, databases designed with noble intentions may not have been collected following personal data protection regulations or ethics requirements (such as stipulated in the GDRP; or ethics codes of universities). In fact, there is a "wild west" in several areas of (personal) data sharing for machine learning (Hao, 2021a), even in the medical context (May, 2018).

The critical questions hence remain: where did all these data in the database come from and how are they exchanged and processed? Was the consent of the persons depicted obtained and were the principles of personal data processing in force in Europe respected? In sum: were the databases created in legally permissible ways?

4.2 The Tensions Between Scientific Ends and the Data Subject's Rights

The computer scientists' position is that data on the web, accessible without significant effort, without hacking into IT systems and user accounts, that is without removing specific barriers, is considered "freely available", "in the public domain" and may be used without restrictions to advance science, such as for the development of computer vision in our case. According to Williams et al. (2017), most researchers today do not obtain explicit consent from the users whose visual images they analyse, relying instead on the implicit consent of having accessed the material in a public or semi-public space. Arguments of computer scientists can be summarised in the following way:

First, it is reasonable to assume that data were voluntarily placed on the web, that is by web users (data subjects) themselves, at least until the contrary is alleged (e.g. until the user claims that the material was stolen). Data subject's consent is, therefore, implicitly presumed, for example, by uploading the photographs to an open profile on a social networking site, the user has clearly expressed their willingness to make the material publicly available to anyone from anywhere, or consent is not even necessary because of a legitimate third-party interest (e.g. because the photographs were taken at a public event in a public place). The photographs (material) may also have been taken in the course of legitimate activity, such as that of journalists, in a place of public interest where the individual has no reasonable expectation of privacy.

Second, material from the internet is not intended to be used to recognise, identify, track, trace or perhaps control a data subject depicted in the material. On the contrary, the aim is to train ML models and neural networks or, more generally, to improve computer programs. For instance, identifiable data, such as the face of a data subject, cannot be reconstructed from the spinal neural network model as the degree of abstraction in such a model is very high. The images are used only to enable "calculations", such as the relationships between individual pixels, which do not differ, for example, between dogs of different breeds. Computer scientists are not interested in an "identifiable" individual. On the contrary, the person's identity is irrelevant to the pursued goal. Their interest lies in the abstraction of images, correlations between pixels, learning the laws of the natural world to conceptualise it as accurately as possible and teaching systems of autonomous AI recognition and prediction on new datasets.

Third, while the misuse of statistical models cannot be completely ruled out in advance (e.g. to create deepfakes), misuse is not the result of the malicious work of computer scientists. The statistical models are generic and value-neutral because the training of neural networks is about finding "natural" regularities, patterns and correlations between parts of the image (e.g. pixels). Computer scientists admit that misuse of AI technology is possible, insofar as any human tool can be misused, but as with the abuse of many tools, we do not automatically attribute liability for the misuse to their creators, because we consider the causal link to be broken (e.g. in a typical case, the maker of a knife is not liable for a murder).

The above-mentioned views on the importance of scientific development are reflected in the European personal data protection regulation, as GDPR provides for a particularly privileged regime for the processing of personal data for scientific research purposes. Such a regime is based on

5 In Defence of Ethics *and* the Law ...

a specific conception of science as an activity which primarily serves the interest of society "as a whole", that is the interest of increasing "collective knowledge" and the "common good" (as opposed to serving primarily private interests). But what is the "scientific research" that should benefit from this privileged regime of GDPR (Article 89)? Where should law focus on to define "science research" to facilitate "fair" processing of personal data, if not the field of ethics?

4.3 Scientific Research as a Privileged Case of Personal Data Processing

Several existing computer vision databases represent public research database benchmarks that were key to developing the field of computer vision—but are collections created in legally permissible ways?

To be used in Europe, the collections should be created according to the European legal order, which contains "European values". These values are difficult to define, but at a minimum, they are the values of human rights, the rule of law and democracy.[22] Indeed, in developing AI technologies, Europe wants to distinguish itself from, for example, the Chinese and American models[23] by reflecting upon the societal and ethical impacts of these technologies, such as on the principle of equality and non-discrimination, and impacts on the economy and the political system.[24] Reliability of the technology, fairness and transparency are fundamental European principles in developing AI technology to ensure trust in the technology and its social acceptance. The more difficult question, however, is what these values mean and require in specific terms, for

---

[22] Council of Europe's ad hoc body CAHAI structured impacts of AI as impacts on human rights, democracy and the rule of law (Council of Europe, 2020).

[23] According to Policy and Investment Recommendations for Trustworthy AI (European Commission, High-Level Expert Group on Artificial Intelligence [HLEG], 2019).

[24] See the Council of Europe's Study on the use of internet in electoral campaigns (MSI-MED, 2018) and Declaration by the Committee of Ministers on the Manipulative capabilities of algorithmic processes (Committee of Ministers, 2019).

126   A. Završnik

example, when does a specific technology comply with the principles of explainability,[25] transparency and reliability?[26]

In contrast to the above-mentioned computer scientists' views, the legality of personal data protection in the EU is, in principle, clear (Article 6 GDRP): the processing of personal data, such as photos of an individual, for computer vision purposes, is lawful in seven (alternatively) situations.[27] Given the nature of R&D activity, the data processing for the purposes of computer vision will be lawful on the basis of (a) consent of the data subject or (b) in the case of a *legitimate interest* of the data controller.

Scientific research activity is given a special position in data protection regulation: the European Union's objective under Article 179(1) of the Treaty on the Functioning of the EU (TFEU) is to create a *European Research Area* (similarly recital 159 GDPR), which can be achieved through broadly defined scientific (including historical), statistical and archival purposes. According to the established interpretation of Article 29 Working Party and the European Data Protection Supervisor (EDPS), scientific research purposes include: technological development, demonstration activities, fundamental research, applied research and privately funded research.[28] Scientific research purposes are defined broadly: they cover studies carried out in the public interest in the field of public health; the integration of information from registers to gain new insights and knowledge on prevalent diseases (e.g. cardiovascular diseases, cancer

---

[25] See discussion on "Explainable AI" (XAI) and the level of "adequate" explainability in Liao et al. (2020).

[26] Reliability raises the issue of "socially acceptable risk": a concept used in the criminal regulation of autonomous vehicles, whereby it is a foregone conclusion that autonomous vehicles will cause harm, but their benefits nevertheless outweigh these harms, as there will be fewer human-caused accidents at an aggregate level. More on the concept of "socially acceptable risk" can be found in Gless et al. (2016).

[27] According to Article 6 of GDPR these are: (a) the explicit and informed consent of the data subject depicted in the photograph was given; (b) processing is necessary for the performance of a contract with a data subject; (c) the processing is necessary for compliance with a legal obligation of the controller (e.g. a statutory health insurer); (d) the processing is necessary for the protection of the vital interests of the data subject; (e) the processing is necessary for the performance of a task carried out in the public interest (or in the exercise of official authority) or (e) where the processing is necessary for the purposes of the legitimate interests of the controller or of a third party.

[28] See also recital 159 of GDPR.

and depression) and in the social sciences, they cover studies using data from registers to gain insights into "the long-term correlation of a number of social conditions such as unemployment and education with other life conditions" (recital 157 GDPR). Research results obtained through registries are welcomed by the GDPR because they offer "robust, high-quality knowledge that can inform the design and implementation of knowledge-based policy and can improve the quality of life of many people and the effectiveness of social services" (recital 157 GDPR).

The main question from the point of view of personal data processing is, therefore, not whether to enable research based on personal data but how to ensure adequate safeguards ("technical and organisational measures") for the rights and freedoms of the individual when processing data for scientific research purposes.[29]

GDPR, therefore, provides a specific provision on the exceptions from the stringent rules in the form of exceptions for scientific research (and also statistical and archival) purposes. It is legally relevant that Article 89 GDPR does not constitute a legal basis for the processing of personal data, the potential legal basis being *legitimate interest* ((6)(1)(f) GDPR). The restriction on further processing also does not apply to further processing for scientific research purposes referred to in Article 89, as this is always considered compatible with the original purposes of the processing (according to (5)(1)(b) GDPR).

However, GDPR does not offer sufficiently nuanced details on legitimate scientific research. Due to digitisation, which has made it easier and cheaper to obtain and disseminate personal data, the division between research activities in the private sector and traditional academic institutions has become increasingly blurred: "Corporate secrecy, particularly in the tech sector, which controls the most valuable data for understanding the impact of digitisation and specific phenomena like the dissimilation of misinformation, is a major barrier to social science research" (European Data Protection Supervisor—EDPS, 2020). Scientific research is more than ever before conducted by private corporations or data mastodons, which own both the data and the scientific talent.

---

[29] Examples are offered in Article 89(1) of GDPR.

128 A. Završnik

Such science primarily supports the particular interests of data companies and is far from being designed to enhance the well-being of all humanity and the common knowledge as we understand it to be the case of traditional science.

For the privileged case of personal data processing under Article 89 of the GDPR, a greater degree of flexibility for *original* research is offered only to research that takes place within the *ethical framework* of the research activity, which includes, for example, universities' ethical rules, rules of scientific national or European research funders, with an aim of enhancing the *common social* knowledge and well-being (EDPS, 2020: 2). For the purposes of data protection regulation, a scientific study is, therefore, only a research project conducted following sectorally relevant methodological and ethical principles (Article 29 Working Party, 2018). In the context of data protection rules, scientific research work is always (or at least partly) in the public interest and contributes to the general knowledge and well-being of all humanity. Merely labelling the processing of personal data as a (part of) "scientific research activity" hence is not sufficient as the "research" is not *carte blanche* for increased risks for data subjects (EDPS, 2020: 11). According to EDPS (2020: 12), scientific research activity is an activity that meets the following cumulative criteria: (1) personal data are processed in the survey; (2) the research is subject to appropriate sectoral standards of methodology and ethics, including the obligation of informed consent, the responsibilities of the processor are clear and the research is independently supervised; (3) the research is carried out to increase collective knowledge and social welfare and does not primarily serve one or more private interests.

5 Ethics and the Law in AI Governance Assemblage

Extensive discussions have taken place in the last decade on the appropriate AI governance assemblage: "'soft' ethics or 'hard' law"; digital "soft" ethics and digital "hard" ethics and so forth. This chapter examines the role of ethics and law in AI governance, which has often been presented in terms of a dichotomy between ethics and human rights and as "fluid" ethics and "solid" law. While ethics is conceived as non-compulsory, human rights are enforceable, at least in principle, as they constitute the international human rights corpus of law. While there are several fields of ethics, such as virtue ethics, deontological ethics, Pufendorf's or Lock's ethics and so forth, human rights are based on consensus. Ethics also includes a variety of principles, while human rights are based on universal principles.

This chapter presents an evolution from the "rush to ethics in AI" and subsequent reluctance, if not fierce resistance, to ethics in AI governance and the calls to provide legal regulations of AI to avoid risks of "ethics washing" (Amram and Comandé, 2020) and "ethics shopping" (Wagner, 2018): ethics must not be an alternative to regulation and not a substitute for fundamental rights (Wagner, 2018). The contemporary speed of developing binding rules for the governance of AI seems to prioritise hard law and no longer "soft" ethical principles. Some authors claim that human rights offer a more robust and effective framework for the governance of AI compared to ethics (e.g. Dijk et al., 2021; Koniakov, 2022). Others claim that ethics should not be toothless (Rességuier and Rodrigues, 2020) and can have a great value in complementing the law (e.g. Sartor, 2020). Along the latter line of thought, this chapter advocates that although the division between law and ethics is key for offering a sufficiently dense "normative net" to prevent or mitigate harmful societal or environmental impacts of AI, the division is often not as sharp as critics of ethics (or law) have claimed. Despite the contemporary "race to AI regulation" (Smuha, 2021) and the "race for governance" in AI (Koniakou, 2022), the key questions that have not yet been answered continue to relate to the translation of principles to practices (Schiff et al., 2022). This chapter hence narrows down to the case of personal data processing in the *computer vision domain* in order to show how "translation" of the GDRP principles of lawfulness, fairness and transparency into operational practice is inevitably supplemented with ethics.

More specifically, the question of what is "indirect discrimination" in AI should be considered closer to a standard than a rule (cf. Zuiderveen Borgesius, 2018). Similarly, the issue of "fair" personal data processing

130   **A. Završnik**

requires that the data processing shall not exceed "reasonable expectations" nor provoke "unjustified adverse effects" on the individuals, which opens the door to ethics to complement the law. The case of personal data processing for computer vision applications also exemplifies how scientifically valuable methods that enable new insights in many scientific disciplines are now conducted in the "grey" area, if not illegally, from the perspective of personal data protection regulation. However, these new scientific ML techniques can be, under certain circumstances, conducted legally and according to the scientific research exception envisaged in the law (Art. 89 GDRP) if ethics is used to interpret and "extend" the law. The dialectic between legal and ethical consideration may often be circular, which can be problematic as Dijk et al. (2021) have clearly pointed out. Authors have been forcefully against such "circular ethics" in AI governance, that is when the ethics has "no authoritative 'home-base'" and lacks sufficient discipline standards and, more perversely, calls upon human rights and law as "*the* authoritative source" and the point of reference for ethical principles so forth (Dijk et al. 2021).

However, as pointed out by Sartor (2020), ethical considerations may influence legal interpretation, which is not problematic as long as this preserves the connection to legal sources and accepted modes of interpretation. Since AI enters into a legally regulated space, its pervasive and sometimes destructive social impacts are not always met with adequate responses (Sartor, 2020). The need for a law change may also be argued through ethical considerations. The example of computer vision shows how ethical arguments can support a specific legal interpretation of scientific research exception in the field of personal data processing and how ethics can complement law.

While ethics entering the field of AI governance references the law (e.g. human rights), this chapter shows that the opposite is also the case—the law makes "references" to ethics to support law. Only research conducted within an established *ethical framework*, as this chapter discussed, can qualify for a more flexible personal data protection regime under GDPR's scientific research exception. Interpretation of the exception stipulated in Article 89 GDPR refers to ethics through the conception of "established frameworks of research activity". In EDPB opinion, the definition of "scientific research" clearly shows the difficulties of where to draw the line

5 In Defence of Ethics *and* the Law ... 131

between research activities in the private sector and traditional academic institutions as the latter enhances the well-being of humanity and the "common knowledge" and does not primarily serve only private interests. The research "deserving" the *legal* scientific research exception is hence only activity that takes place incorporating the appropriate standards of methodology and *ethics*.

Both ethics and law exist in parallel and can contribute to positively influencing human behaviour. Sartor (2020) argues that human/fundamental rights and social values are central to both ethics and law and outlines how they can jointly provide a useful normative reference in addressing the normative issues arising in connection with AI. Moreover, both—law and ethics—can be framed in different ways and may pull in different directions or overlap, but can (and should) be coordinated, while remaining in a productive dialectical tension (Sartor, 2020).

Ethical principles can have a valuable role either as a policy framework that leads to the adoption of binding legal obligations or as non-binding recommendations that complement the legal obligations (Senden, 2005). It might be logical to make ethical imperatives legally binding, so that they are more readily complied with by the relevant actors, but on the other hand, Sartor (2020) rightly warns that law and ethics are not "functionally equivalent": when only coercive public response can counter misuses of AI, then the law is needed to curb them; but when the law would interfere into individual liberties by meticulously codifying desired activities (as everything that is unethical should also not be prohibited and punished), ethics can provide more suitable "soft" guidance, for example, in the development of AI tools in the R&D domain. Both law and ethics protect important human interests and the overlapping and sometime dialectic (or even circular) moral and legal duties can provide a firmer "normative net" for the *ex-ante* prevention and *ex post* mitigation of the negative societal, individual and environmental impacts of AI.

Acknowledgements The research leading to this chapter and book has received funding from the European Union's Horizon 2020 research and innovation programme under the Marie-Sklodowska-Curie grant agreement

132   A. Završnik

for project "Transmaking" project (no. 734855), and the Slovenian Research Agency, research project "Human Rights and Regulation of Trustworthy Artificial Intelligence" (no. V5-1930, led by Aleš Završnik).

References

Access Now. (2020, October 13). Access Now Resigns from the Partnership on AI. Available at: www.accessnow.org/access-now-resignation-partnership-on-ai/

Ada Lovelace Institite. (2022). Algorithmic Impact Assessment: A Case Study in Healthcare. Available at: www.adalovelaceinstitute.org/wp-content/upl oads/2022/02/Algorithmic-impact-assessment-a-case-study-in-healthcare. pdf

Afroogh, S., Esmalian, A., Donaldson, J. P., Mostafavi, A. (2021). Empathic Design in Engineering Education and Practice: An Approach for Achieving Inclusive and Effective Community Resilience. *Sustainability 13*(7): 4060. https://doi.org/10.3390/su13074060

Afroogh, S., Esmalian, A., Mostafavi, A. et al. (2022). Tracing App Technology: An Ethical Review in the COVID-19 Era and Directions for Post-COVID-19. *Ethics and Information Technology 24*: 30. https://doi.org/10.1007/s10 676-022-09659-6

Alston, P. (2019). Report of the Special Rapporteur on Extreme Poverty and Human Rights. Available at: www.ohchr.org/Documents/Issues/Pov erty/A_74_48037_AdvanceUneditedVersion.docx

Ambasna-Jones, M. (2015, August 3). The Smart Home and a Data Underclass. *The Guardian.*

Amnesty International. (2021, October 25). Dutch Childcare Benefit Scandal an Urgent Wake-Up Call to Ban Racist Algorithms. Available at: www.amnesty.org/en/latest/news/2021/10/xenophobic-machines-dutch-child-benefit-scandal/

Amram, D., Comandé, G. (2020, September 10). Feedback for the EU Commission Inception Impact Assessment Towards a "Proposal for a Regulation of the European Parliament and the Council Laying Down

Requirements for Artificial Intelligence". Available at: https://ec.europa.eu/info/law/better-regulation/have-your-say/initiatives/12527-Requirements-for-Artificial-Intelligence/F551050

Anaconda. (2020). The State of Data Science 2020. Moving from Hype Toward Maturity. Available at: www.anaconda.com/state-of-data-science-2020

Angwin, J., Larson, J., Mattu, S., Kirchner, L. (2016, May 23). Machine Bias: There's Software Used Across the Country to Predict Future Criminals. And It's Biased Against Blacks. *ProPublica.* Available at: www.propublica.org/article/machine-bias-risk-assessments-in-criminal-sentencing

Article 29 Working Party. (2018). *Guidelines on Consent Under Regulation 2016/679.* WP259 rev.01. Available at: https://ec.europa.eu/newsroom/article29/items/623051/en

Awad, E., Dsouza, S., Kim, R. et al. (2018). The Moral Machine Experiment. *Nature 563*: 59–64. https://doi.org/10.1038/s41586-018-0637-6

Awad, E., Dsouza, S., Shariff, A., Rahwan, I., Bonnefon, J.-F. (2020). Universals and Variations in Moral Decisions Made in 42 Countries by 70,000 Participants. *PNAS 117*(5): 2332–2337. https://doi.org/10.1073/pnas.1911517117

Bamdad, S., Finaughty, D. A., Johns, S. E. (2022). 'Grey Areas': Ethical Challenges Posed by Social Media-Enabled Recruitment and Online Data Collection in Cross-Border, Social Science Research. *Research Ethics 18*(1): 24–38. https://doi.org/10.1177/17470161211045557

Bender, E. M., McMillan-Major, A., Gebru, T., Shmitchell, S. (2021, March). On the Dangers of Stochastic Parrots: Can Language Models Be Too Big? FAccT '21: Proceedings of the 2021 ACM Conference on Fairness, Accountability, and Transparency: 610–623. https://doi.org/10.1145/3442188.3445922

Benjamin, R. (2019). *Race After Technology.* Polity Press.

Bijker, W. E., Hughes, T. P., Pinch, T., Douglas, D. G. (2012). *The Social Construction of Technological Systems: New Directions in the Sociology and History of Technology.* Cambridge: MIT Press.

Bringas Colmenarejo, A., Nannini, L., Rieger, A., Scott M. K., Zhao, X., Patro, K. G., Kasneci, G., Kinder-Kurlanda, K. (2022, August 1–3). Fairness in Agreement With European Values: An Interdisciplinary Perspective on AI Regulation. In: *Proceedings of the 2022 AAAI/ACM Conference on AI, Ethics, and Society (AIES'22).* Oxford, UK; New York, NY: ACM. https://doi.org/10.1145/3514094.3534158

Buolamwini, J., Gebru, T. (2018). Gender Shades: Intersectional Accuracy Disparities in Commercial Gender Classification. Conference on Fairness, Accountability, and Transparency. *Proceedings of Machine Learning Research 81*: 1–15. Available at: https://proceedings.mlr.press/v81/buolamwini18a/buolamwini18a.pdf

Caliskan, A., Bryson, J. J., Narayanan, A. (2017). Semantics Derived Automatically from Language Corpora Contain Human-Like Biases. *Science 356* (6334): 183–186.

Chander, S., Jakubowska, E., Leufer, D. (2020, October 21). Attention EU Regulators: We Need More Than AI "Ethics" to Keep Us Safe. *Access Now and European Digital Rights (EDRi)*. Available at: https://edri.org/our-work/attention-eu-regulators-we-need-more-than-ai-ethics-to-keep-us-safe/

Chiusi, F., Fischer, S., Kayser-Bril, N., Spielkamp, M. (2020). Automating Society Report 2020. *AlgorithWatch*. Available at: https://automatingsociety.algorithmwatch.org

Council of Europe, Ad hoc Committee on Artificial Intelligence (CAHAI). (2020). *Feasibility Study.* CAHAI(2020)23. Available at: https://rm.coe.int/cahai-2020-23-final-eng-feasibility-study-/1680a0c6da

Council of Europe, Committee of Experts on Media Pluralism and Transparency of Media Ownership (MSI-MED). (2018). *Internet and Electoral Campaigns—Study on the Use of the Internet in Electoral Campaigns.* DGI(2017)11. Available at: https://edoc.coe.int/en/internet/7614-internet-and-electoral-campaigns-study-on-the-use-of-internet-in-electoral-campaigns.html

Council of Europe, Committee of Ministers. (2019). *Declaration by the Committee of Ministers on the Manipulative Capabilities of Algorithmic Processes.* Decl(13/02/2019)1. Available at: https://rm.coe.int/090000168092dd4b

Crawford, K., Trevor, P. (2019). *Excavating AI: The Politics of Training Sets for Machine Learning.* Available at: https://excavating.ai/

Crockford, K. (2020, June 16). How Is Face Recognition Surveillance Technology Racist? *ACLU.* Available at: https://www.aclu.org/news/privacy-technology/how-is-face-recognition-surveillance-technology-racist

Ekowo, M., Palmer I. (2016, October 24). The Promise and Peril of Predictive Analytics in Higher Education. *New America, Policy Paper.*

European Commission, High-Level Expert Group on Artificial Intelligence (HLEG). (2019). *Policy and Investment Recommendations for Trustworthy AI.* Available at: https://digital-strategy.ec.europa.eu/en/library/policy-and-investment-recommendations-trustworthy-artificial-intelligence

European Data Protection Supervisor (EDPS). (2020). *A Preliminary Opinion on Data Protection and Scientific Research.* Available at: https://edps.europa.eu/sites/edp/files/publication/20-01-06_opinion_research_en.pdf

European Union Agency for Fundamental Rights (FRA). (2020). *AI Policy Initiatives (2016–2020).* Available at: https://fra.europa.eu/en/project/2018/artificial-intelligence-big-data-and-fundamental-rights/ai-policy-initiatives

Floridi, L. (2018). Soft Ethics and the Governance of the Digital. *Philosophy & Technology 31*: 1–8. https://doi.org/10.1007/s13347-018-0303-9

Gebru, T. (2021, December 6). For Truly Ethical AI, Its Research Must Be Independent from Big Tech. *The Guardian.*

Gefferie, D. (2018, February 27). The Algorithmization of Payments. *Towards Data Science.* Available at: https://towardsdatascience.com/the-algorithmization-of-pay-ments-how-algorithms-are-going-to-change-the-payments-industry-5dd3f266d4c3

Gless, S., Silverman, E. in Weigend, T. (2016). If Robots Cause Harm, Who Is to Blame? Self-Driving Cars and Criminal Liability. *New Criminal Law Review 19*(3): 412–436. https://doi.org/10.1525/nclr.2016.19.3.412

Goehring, B., Rossi, F. in Zaharchuk, D. (2020). Advancing AI Ethics Beyond Compliance. *IBM.* Available at: www.ibm.com/downloads/cas/J2LAYLOZ

Google. (2019). AI Principles 1-Year Progress Update. *Google.* Available at: https://ai.google/static/documents/ai-principles-2019-progress-update.pdf

Gregory, A. (2022, April 23). AI Tool Accurately Predicts Tumour Regrowth in Cancer Patients. *The Guardian.*

Hagendorff, T. (2020). The Ethics of AI Ethics: An Evaluation of Guidelines. *Minds & Machines 30*: 99–120. https://doi.org/10.1007/s11023-020-09517-8

Hao, K. (2021a, August 13). Deleting Unethical Data Sets Isn't Good Enough. *MIT Technology Review.* Available at: www.technologyreview.com/2021a/08/13/1031836/ai-ethics-responsible-data-stewardship/

Hao, K. (2021b, October 5). The Facebook Whistleblower Says Its Algorithms Are Dangerous. Here's Why. *MIT Technology Review.* Available at: www.technologyreview.com/2021b/10/05/1036519/facebook-whistleblower-frances-haugen-algorithms/

Heikkilä, M. (2022a, July 28). DeepMind Has Predicated the Structure of Almost Every Protein Known to Science. *MIT Technology Review.* Available at: www.technologyreview.com/2022a/07/28/1056510/deepmind-predicted-the-structure-of-almost-every-protein-known-to-science/

136   A. Završnik

Heikkilä, M. (2022b, July 12). Inside a Radical New Project to Democratise AI. *MIT Technology Review*. Available at: www.technologyreview.com/ 2022b/07/12/1055817/inside-a-radical-new-project-to-democratize-ai/

IBM. (2018). Everyday Ethics for Artificial Intelligence. *IBM*. Available at: https://www.ibm.com/watson/assets/duo/pdf/everydayethics.pdf

Intelligence Squared. (2015, March 13). Be Afraid, Be Very Afraid: The Robots Are Coming and They Will Steal Our Livelihoods. Available at: www.intelligencesquared.com/events/the-robots-are-coming-and-they-will-destroy-our-livelihoods/

Jobin, A., Ienca, M., Vayena, E. (2019). The Global Landscape of AI Ethics Guidelines. *Nature Machine Intelligence 1*: 389–399. https://doi.org/10. 1038/s42256-019-0088-2

Karoff, P. (2019, January 25). Embedding Ethics in a Computer Science Curriculum. The *Harvard Gazette*. Available at: https://news.harvard.edu/ gazette/story/2019/01/harvard-works-to-embed-ethics-in-computer-science-curriculum/

Kaye, K. (2022a, April 13). Companies Are Using AI to Monitor Your Mood During Sales Calls. Zoom Might Be Next. *Protocol*. Available at: www.pro tocol.com/enterprise/emotion-ai-sales-virtual-zoom

Kaye, K. (2022b, July 11). Not My Job: AI Researchers Building Surveillance Tech and Deepfakes Resist Ethical Concerns. *Protocol*. Available at: www. protocol.com/enterprise/ai-computer-vision-cvpr-ethics

Knight, S. (2017, July 3). Pharmaceutical Companies Are Turning to AI To Streamline Drug Discovery Process. *Techspot*. Available at: www.techspot. com/news/69969-pharmaceutical-companies-turning-ai-streamline-drug-dis covery-process.html

Koniakou, V. (2022). From the "Rush to Ethics" to the "Race for Governance" in Artificial Intelligence. *Information Systems Frontiers*. https://doi.org/10. 1007/s10796-022-10300-6

Koulu, R. (2020). Proceduralizing Control and Discretion: Human Oversight in Artificial Intelligence Policy. *Maastricht Journal of European and Comparative Law 27*(6): 720–735. https://doi.org/10.1177/1023263X2097 8649

Liao, Q. V., Gruen, D., Miller, S. (2020). Questioning the AI: Informing Design Practices for Explainable AI User Experiences. In: *Proceedings of the 2020 CHI Conference on Human Factors in Computing Systems* (str. 1–15). Association for Computing Machinery. https://doi.org/10.1145/3313831. 3376590

Lorents, A. C., Maris, J. M., Morgan, J. N., Neal, G. L. (2006, March). *Ethics of Computer Use: A Survey of Student Attitudes*. Working Paper Series 06-02. Available at: http://openknowledge.nau.edu/id/eprint/1555/7/Lorents_AC_etal_2006_FrankeWPS_06-02(1).pdf

Luguri, J., Strahilevitz, L. J. (2021). Shining a Light on Dark Patterns. *Journal of Legal Analysis 13*(1): 43–109.

Mahoney, J., Le Louvier, K., Lawson, S., Bertel, D., Ambrosetti, E. (2022). Ethical Considerations in Social Media Analytics in the Context of Migration: Lessons Learned from a Horizon 2020 Project. *Research Ethics 18*(3): 226–240. https://doi.org/10.1177/17470161221087542

May, T. (2018). Sociogenetic Risks—Ancestry DNA Testing, Third-Party Identity, and Protection of Privacy. *New England Journal of Medicine 379*(5): 410–412. https://doi.org/10.1056/NEJMp1805870

McGee, S. (2016, May 15). Rise of the Billionaire Robots: How Algorithms Have Redefined Hedge Funds. *The Guardian.*

McKinney, S. M., Sieniek, M., Godbole, V., Godwin, J., Antropova, N., Ashrafian, H., Back, T., Chesus, M., Corrado, G. S., Darzi, A., Etemadi, M., Garcia-Vicente, F., Gilbert, F. J., Halling-Brown, M., Hassabis, D., Jansen, S., Karthikesalingam, A., Kelly, C. J., King, D., … Shetty, S. (2020). International Evaluation of an AI System for Breast Cancer Screening. *Nature 577*(7788): 89–94. https://doi.org/10.1038/s41586-019-1799-6

Metcalf, J., Moss, E., Watkins, E. A., Singh, R., Elish, M. C. (2021, March 3–10). Algorithmic Impact Assessments and Accountability: The Co-construction of Impacts. In: *ACM Conference on Fairness, Accountability, and Transparency (FAccT '21)*. Virtual Event, Canada. Available at: https://papers.ssrn.com/sol3/papers.cfm?abstract_id=3736261

Metzinger, T. (2019, April 8). Ethics Washing Made in Europe. *Der Tegesspiegel*. Available at: www.tagesspiegel.de/politik/eu-guidelines-ethics-washing-made-in-europe/24195496.html

Microsoft. (2018). The Future Computed. *Micorsoft*. Available at: https://news.microsoft.com/cloudforgood/_media/downloads/the-future-computed-english.pdf

Noble, S. U. (2018). *Algorithms of Oppression: How Search Engines Reinforce Racism*. New York: NYU Press.

O'Hara. D., Mason L. R. (2012, March 30). How Bots Are Taking over the World. *The Guardian.*

O'Neil, C. (2016). *Weapons of Math Destruction: How Big Data Increases Inequality and Threatens Democracy*. New York: Crown.

138   A. Završnik

Quinn, B. (2020, August 17). UK Exams Debacle: How Did This Year's Results End Up in Chaos? *The Guardian.*

Raab, Charles D. (2016). Information Privacy: Ethics and Accountability. Available at: https://ssrn.com/abstract=3057469

Raji, I., Buolamwini, J. (2019). Actionable Auditing: Investigating the Impact of Publicly Naming Biased Performance Results of Commercial AI Products. Conference on Artificial Intelligence, Ethics, and Society. Available at: www.media.mit.edu/publications/actionable-auditing-investigating-the-impact-of-publicly-naming-biased-performance-results-of-commercial-ai-products/

Rességuier, A., Rodrigues, R. (2020, July–December). AI Ethics Should Not Remain Toothless! A Call to Bring Back the Teeth of Ethics: 1–5. Available at: https://doi.org/10.1177/2053951720942541

Sætra et al. (2022). The AI Ethicist's Dilemma: Fighting Big Tech by Supporting Big Tech. *AI and Ethics 2*: 15–27.

Sartor, G. (2020). Artificial Intelligence and Human Rights: Between Law and Ethics. *Maastricht Journal of European and Comparative Law 27*(6): 705–719. https://doi.org/10.1177/1023263X20981566

Schiff, D. S., Laas, K., Biddle, J. B., Borenstein, J. (2022). Global AI Ethics Documents: What They Reveal About Motivations, Practices, and Policies. In: Laas, K., Davis, M., Hildt, E. (eds.), *Codes of Ethics and Ethical Guidelines.* The International Library of Ethics, Law and Technology, 23. Cham: Springer. https://doi.org/10.1007/978-3-030-86201-5_7

Senden, L. (2005). Soft Law, Self-Regulation and Co-regulation in European law: Where Do They Meet? *Electronic Journal of Comparative Law 9*: 23–24.

Smuha, N. A. (2021). From a 'Race to AI' to a 'Race to AI Regulation': Regulatory Competition for Artificial Intelligence. *Law, Innovation and Technology 13*(1): 57–84. https://doi.org/10.1080/17579961.2021.1898300

Spohr, D. (2017). Fake News and Ideological Polarization: Filter Bubbles and Selective Exposure on Social Media. *Business Information Review 34*(3): 150–160.

Škop, M., Merényi, M., Turashvili, T., Izdebski, K., Kerekeš, D., Ilić, V. (2019). *alGOVrithms—State of Play: Report on Algorithms Usage in Government-Citizens Relations in Czechia, Georgia, Hungary, Poland, Serbia and Slovakia.* Fundacja ePanstvo.

Steed, R. in Caliskan, A. (2021). Image Representations Learned With Unsupervised Pre-Training Contain Humanlike Biases. *Proceedings of the 2021 ACM Conference on Fairness, Accountability, and Transparency*, 701–713. https://doi.org/10.1145/3442188.3445932

Takiddin, A., Schneider, J., Yang, Y., Abd-Alrazaq, A., & Househ, M. (2021). Artificial Intelligence for Skin Cancer Detection: Scoping Review. *Journal of Medical Internet Research 23*(11): e22934. https://doi.org/10.2196/22934

Vaccari, C., Chadwick, A. (2020). Deepfakes and Disinformation: Exploring the Impact of Synthetic Political Video on Deception, Uncertainty, and Trust in News. *Social Media + Society.* https://doi.org/10.1177/205630512 0903408

Van Dijk, N., Casiraghi, S., Gutwirth, S. (2021). The 'Ethification' of ICT Governance. Artificial Intelligence and Data Protection in the European Union. *Computer Law & Security Review 43.* https://doi.org/10.1016/j.clsr. 2021.105597

Wagner, B. (2018). Ethics as an Escape from Regulation: From Ethics-Washing to Ethics-Shopping. In: Hildebrandt, M. (ed.), *Being Profiled: Cogitas Ergo Sum.* Amsterdam University Press, 86–90.

Wall, S., Schellmann, H. (2021, August 4). Looking for Work? Here's How to Write Résumé That an AI Will Love. *MIT Technology Review.* Available at: www.technologyreview.com/2021/08/04/1030509/job-search-how-write-resume-ai-artificial-intelligence/

Williams, M. L., Burnap, P. in Sloan, L. (2017). Towards an Ethical Framework for Publishing Twitter Data in Social Research: Taking into Account Users' Views, Online Context and Algorithmic Estimation. *Sociology 51*(6): 1149–1168. https://doi.org/10.1177/0038038517708140

Wu, T. (2018). Blind Spot: The Attention Economy and the Law. *Antitrust Law Journal 82*: 771.

Završnik, A. (2018). Big Data: What Is It, and Why Does It Matter for Crime and Social Control? In: Završnik, A. (ed.), *Big Data, Crime and Social Control.* Abingdon and New York: Routledge, 3–28.

Zuboff, S. (2015). Big Other: Surveillance Capitalism and the Prospects of an Information Civilization. *Journal of Information Technology 30*(1): 75–89.

Zuiderveen Borgesius, F. (2018). *Discrimination, Artificial Intelligence, and Algorithmic Decision-Making. Technical Report.* Strasbourg: Council of Europe.

6

What Role for Ethics in the Law of AI?

Mariavittoria Catanzariti

1 Introduction

In April 2019 the Independent High-Level Expert Group on AI (AI HLEG) presented the Ethics Guidelines for Trustworthy Artificial Intelligence (AI).[1] This document was originally entrusted by the European Commission and then opened to consultation with more than 500 participants. It was the result of a composite regulatory process, which began with the Resolution of the European Parliament of 2017 that aimed to establish a European Agency for Robotics and AI, which would have had the duty of offering technical, regulatory, and ethical support

---

M. Catanzariti (✉)
Robert Schuman Centre for Advanced Studies, European
University Institute, Fiesole, Italy
e-mail: Mariavittoria.Catanzariti@eui.eu

[1] Ethics Guidelines for Trustworthy AI, https://op.europa.eu/it/publication-detail/-/publication/d3988569-0434-11ea-8c1f-01aa75ed71a1.

© The Author(s), under exclusive license to Springer Nature
Switzerland AG 2023
A. Završnik and K. Simončič (eds.), *Artificial Intelligence, Social Harms and Human Rights*, Critical Criminological Perspectives,
https://doi.org/10.1007/978-3-031-19149-7_6

to institutions and Member States and private and public stakeholders involved. This process is still ongoing and so far, it has led to the adoption of various tools, including the White Paper on Artificial Intelligence of February 2020 with the aim of supporting a regulatory and investment-oriented approach,[2] up to the recent Guidelines for the military and non-military use of intelligence artificial as well as the Proposal for AI Regulation.[3] The ultimate goal of the European legislator is to bring together the different regulatory initiatives in the field of AI into a regulation to collect the results of the public consultation on policy options that need to be consistent with the model of fundamental rights and European values.[4] The clear choice to support regulatory instruments based on primary and secondary European sources as well as on international treaties on human rights with a variety of soft law instruments,[5] highlights an approach particularly aimed at creating a broad institutional sharing of the European Union reference framework in the context of technological development. It has the purpose of bringing ethics back to the analysis of the impact of artificial intelligence on society, on individual psychology, on the legal system, on finance, on the environment, and on trust in technology.[6] However, it is not perfectly clear how the ongoing Proposal for AI Regulation (Artificial Intelligence Act) integrates the ethical guidelines, and what is the purpose of this dual approach.

---

[2] White Paper on Artificial Intelligence. A European Approach to Excellence and Trust, https://ec.europa.eu/info/sites/info/files/commission-white-paper-artificial-intelligencefeb2020en.pdf.

[3] Guidelines for Military and Non-military Use of Artificial Intelligence, https://www.europarl.europa.eu/news/en/press-room/20210114IPR95627/guidelines-for-military-and-nonmilitary-use-of-artificial-intelligence.

[4] See the Proposal for a Regulation of the European Parliament and of the Council laying down harmonized rules on artificial intelligence (Artificial Intelligence Act) and amending certain union legislative acts, https://eur-lex.europa.eu/legal-content/EN/TXT/PDF/?uri=CELEX:520 21PC0206&from=EN.

[5] On global regulatory models, see Yeung and Lodge (2019) and Bignami (2018).

[6] European Framework on Ethical Aspects of Artificial Intelligence, Robotics and Related Technologies, https://www.europarl.europa.eu/RegData/etudes/STUD/2020/654179/EPRSSTU(202 0)654179EN.pdf; The Ethics of Artificial Intelligence: Issues and Initiatives, https://www.europarl.europa.eu/RegData/etudes/STUD/2020/634452/EPRSSTU(2020)634452EN.pdf; Artificial Intelligence: From Ethics to Policy, https://www.europarl.europa.eu/RegData/etudes/STUD/2020/641507/EPRSSTU(2020)641507EN.pdf.

This chapter explores the reasons and implications of an ethical approach to artificial intelligence that nurtures the aspiration to be "reliable" (trustworthy) in order to guarantee "responsible competitiveness" (§ 17). In particular, the chapter reflects upon the adequacy of the ethical approach regarding the issue of algorithmic inferences about people and society, as well as the relationships between ethical and legal precepts. For the sake of accuracy, the chapter does not tackle the description of the relevant artificial intelligence systems deployed in the legal field and the impact of artificial intelligence on the law.[7] However, the ethical approach to artificial intelligence systems, as outlined in the European context, reflects some of them that will be analyzed, such as the legal rationales as compared to the ethical ones and the ethical and legal implications of inferences. Finally, the reflection will address the possible relationships between the ethical guidelines and the proposal for AI regulation.

2 Ethics and Fundamental Rights

The EU ethical approach to artificial intelligence is programmatically based on the safeguard of fundamental rights, whose common core is represented by the concept of human dignity, upon which the anthropocentric European architecture is grounded (§ 38).[8] More generally, although this is an increasingly recurring paradigm in various regulatory segments and in various fields of application, from nutritional genomics to sustainable finance and climate change, in the context of the ethical guidelines the integration of the two components of AI, legality and ethics, is justified in the light of the pervasiveness of artificial intelligence systems in daily life.

---

[7] On these aspects see Catanzariti (2020a, 239–255; 2020b, 149–165).

[8] Cath et al. (2018, 525): "This approach to human dignity provides the much-needed grounding in a well-established, ethical, legal, political, and social concept, which can help to ensure that tolerant care and fostering respect for people (both as individuals and as groups), their cultures and their environments, play a steering role in the assessments and planning for the future of an AI-driven world. By relying on human dignity as the pivotal concept, it should become less difficult to develop a comprehensive vision of how responsibility, cooperation, and sharable values can guide the design a 'good AI society'". See also McCrudden (2013, 1–58).

144 M. Catanzariti

The reason for this institutional choice is given by the transposition into the AI field of a traditional dichotomy between fundamental rights and human rights.[9] While the first would rely on the legality of AI, the second are inherent to the individual (§ 39). Furthermore, the ethical guidelines specifically refer to respect for fundamental rights in the framework of democracy and the rule of law, stating that

> These rights are described in the EU Charter by reference to dignity, freedoms, equality and solidarity, citizens' rights and justice. The common foundation that unites these rights can be understood as rooted in respect for human dignity – thereby reflecting what we describe as a "human-centric approach" in which the human being enjoys a unique and inalienable moral status of primacy in the civil, political, economic and social fields. (§ 38)

The paragraph, with the generic and ambiguous title "From fundamental rights to ethical principles" (§§ 40–45), includes five benchmarks: respect for human dignity, according to which people must be treated as subjects moral and not as objects to be classified and manipulated (§ 41); freedom of the individual by virtue of which human beings must be free to take decisions about oneself and not be manipulated by applying this in a broad sense to the freedom of enterprise, to the freedom of the arts, to the freedom of expression, assembly, and association, the right to respect privacy and confidentiality (§ 42); democracy, justice, and the rule of law, understood as a triad, which legitimizes the powers authorized by law and constitutes the framework within which the AI systems must contribute to democratic processes and ensure their foundations, such as due process (§ 43); equality and the principles of non-discrimination and solidarity (including the rights of people at risk of exclusion), which is based on equal respect for the moral value and dignity of all human beings, according to which AI cannot generate discrimination nor unfairly biased results (for example, the data used to educate AI systems should be as inclusive as possible and represent different population groups); finally, the one related to citizens' rights,

---

[9] Pariotti (2013, 31).

6 What Role for Ethics in the Law of AI?   145

whose access to goods and services must be promoted by AI systems (§ 45). In fact, it seems that there is not any substantial difference in the contents of the ethical guidelines and in that of the fundamental values of the EU enshrined in Art. 2 TEU such as human dignity, freedom, democracy, equality, the rule of law, and the respect for human rights, including rights of persons belonging to minorities.

What raises interpretative doubts is rather the fact that while the non-observance of an ethical rule does not imply a sanction, the risk, or the existence of a serious violation of the fundamental values of the EU involves the activation of the procedure referred to in Art. 7 TEU, a sort of political sanction in presence of serious risks of violation or breaches of EU values. However, as Sheppele pointed out, the procedures laid down by Art. 2 and Art. 7 TEU (replicated by Art. 49 TEU as a requirement for the membership in the EU) involve a political mechanism, not a legal one, since the unanimous political will of the Member States is needed to start a sanctioning mechanism and only based on a case-by-case deci-sion.[10] The principle of mutual trust on which the European Union is built represents the intrinsic content of the rule of law. It is therefore clear that the introduction of a mechanism based on values significantly fades the basic idea of enforcement, as it depends on the related cultural context and may well have different premises.[11] In the case of artificial intelligence, ethical rules "are not necessarily legally binding yet crucial to ensure trustworthiness" (§ 39). But what is the reason that led a group of experts to deploy a term such as "ethical orientation" and not "value" what in the substance can be considered the quintessential core of fundamental rights? The choice of AI HLEG, first of all, raises some epis-temological perplexities as it would seem to suggest that AI is based on fundamental rights in a double sense: on the one hand, as binding tools, fundamental rights are inherent in legality, on the other hand, as intrinsic values of humanity, they can be subsumed in the ethical paradigm (§ 39). The confusion derives from the fact that an attempt would thus be made to base the integrated theory of human rights, which does not

---

[10] Sheppele (2018), https://verfassungsblog.de/rule-of-law-retail-and-rule-of-law-wholesale-the-ecjs-alarming-celmer-decision/.

[11] Rawls in the edition of 1999 of A Theory of Justice revisited the concept of overlapping consensus, exploring the issue of its possible effects on ethics (Rawls, 1999, 340 ss.).

reduce its scope to a mere moral or juridical dimension, on a contradictory premise, namely that ethics is based on the protection of rights. Affirming that ethics is based on the law means reversing the order of the legitimacy process and identifying in other words which is the right that legitimizes and authorizes ethics. The integrated vision, which recognizes the presence of the moral and legal dimensions in human rights considering them as strong moral claims, supported and expressed by legal norms, is indeed based on a completely different premise, which excludes the possibility to base ethics on the law.[12] Unless believing that the use of ethics in such a context is nothing more than a communication strategy between the Member States acting as a facilitator of an institutional process to be perfected,[13] it is problematic for lawyers to accept that ethics acts as an additional element to the normative framework in order to build trust in artificial intelligence,[14] and that it is also based on fundamental rights.

Going into the merits, the ethical guidelines contain four ethical principles and seven AI trustworthiness requirements, but it is not clear what is the relationship between them. The first include: (1) the principle of respect for human autonomy, which is based on self-determination such that AI systems should not manipulate human beings (§ 50); (2) the principle of damage prevention, which is based on the robustness of the systems that should prevent damages for humans, including respect for the environment (§ 51); the principle of equity, according to which the development, the distribution and the use of AI systems should not only

---

[12] Pariotti's conceptualization on this is convincing in the sense that human rights are a resting notion with respect to ethics, not the contrary, as rights are derivative concepts. See Pariotti (2013, 204). See also Eisler (1987, 287).

[13] Artificial Intelligence. From Ethics to Policy, https://www.europarl.europa.eu/RegData/etudes/STUD/2020/641507/EPRSSTU(2020)641507EN.pdf, p. 24; see also Yeung et al. (2020, 81–82).

[14] See Ethics Guidelines, parr. 36 and 46. See also cfr. Mantelero (2018, 29): "the effect of the social and ethical values on the interpretation of these human rights. These values represent the societal factors that influence the way the balance is achieved between the different human rights and freedoms, in different contexts and in different periods. Moreover, social and ethical values concur in defining the extension of rights and freedoms, making possible broader forms of protection when the regulatory framework does not provide adequate answers to emerging issues". See also White Paper, p. 36, on the lack of legal basis of concepts such as transparency, traceability and human intervention, https://ec.europa.eu/info/publications/white-paper-artificial-intelligence-european-approachexcellence-and-trusten.

6 What Role for Ethics in the Law of AI? 147

not produce unfair distortions but it must also increase the possibilities of access to goods and services (§ 52); the principle of explicability, on which the framework of trustworthy AI systems is based, that means transparency and access to algorithmic decision-making at each stage of the process (§ 53). Besides the principles, the guidelines also draw seven requirements for the realization of a trustworthy artificial intelligence: (1) human intervention and oversight, aimed at avoiding a negative impact on fundamental rights, preserving the human autonomy with respect to AI systems, being able to modulate their intensity depending on whether human intervention is required in each cycle, granting human supervision during the design and the monitoring of operation or human control as a whole (§ 62–65); (2) technical robustness and security, implemented through a risk prevention approach aimed at avoiding that unintentional damages can be caused and enabling systems to operate according to forecasts and be resilient against external attacks, accurate, reliable, and reproducible (§ 66–70); (3) data confidentiality and governance, which require confidentiality and data protection throughout the entire collection process and use, the high quality and integrity of the data in order to reduce the margin of inaccuracy and error of AI systems, and also rules on access to personal data (§ 71–74); (4) Transparency, whose meaning is expressed in the traceability of data sets and processes, explainability of technical and decision-making processes and identification of them as non-human systems with the possibility to always prefer human interaction (§ 75–78); (5) diversity, non-discrimination, and fairness, which place the inclusion and the pluralism as bases of the starting cycle of the AI process in order to avoid unfair distortions and to ensure access to a wider spectrum of subjects (§ 79–82); (6) social and environmental well-being, which aim at the use of AI for the benefit of future generations in a context of sustainability and ecological responsibility and to ensure that the human perception of social intervention as well as of social and affective relationships is not altered, also evaluating the social impact on institutional and political processes and on voting rights (§§ 83–86); (7) accountability, exemplified by the verifiability of algorithms as well as of data used and design processes, from the minimization of potential negative effects and related reporting, identification of ethically acceptable compromises between conflicting solutions finally, the possibility of appealing against violations that cause unjustified negatives effects (§§ 87–91). Among the potential risks reported by AI, HLEG deserves particular attention to the risk of assessing the ethical integrity of citizens by scoring them to the detriment of their freedom and autonomy (§§ 132–133). This prohibition has been included into the AI Act only regarding public authorities' scoring. The ban on citizen scoring is in stark contrast to the cultural option of the Chinese Government's initiative related to the Social Credit System, which provides for the ethical scoring of citizens based on the reliability of their private and public habits and which affects the totality of the dimensions of the daily life and actions not only legally illicit but also morally and professionally considered undeserving: from financial history to contractual capacity and daily habits, from social relations to personal qualities.[15] This risk raises alarming concern, beyond the analysis of the Chinese project, if we consider that social credit represents an example of an ethical approach based on the law. It builds on a notion of civic virtue where the glue of the political community is represented by the conformity to social norms to the detriment of the possibility of expressing dissent.[16]

3 Artificial Ethics or Artificial Reason?

On closer inspection, if, on the one hand, one can agree that the ethical approach to artificial intelligence has its foundations in the culture of fundamental rights by and large, found ethics on the rights makes it vague both in terms of its contents, as they are in fact duplicated, but also in terms of its purposes, as they question the concept of secularization of democratic societies.[17] After all, the criticism of the mixture

---

[15] Orgad and Reijers (2020, 2–3), https://cadmus.eui.eu/bitstream/handle/1814/66910/RSCAS%20202028.pdf.

[16] Síthigh and Siems (2019, 17), https://cadmus.eui.eu/bitstream/handle/1814/60424/LAW201901.pdf.

[17] See § 40 of the Ethics Guidelines: "Among the comprehensive set of indivisible rights set out in international human rights law, the EU Treaties and the EU Charter, the below families of fundamental rights are particularly apt to cover AI systems. Many of these rights are, in specified circumstances, legally enforceable in the EU so that compliance with their terms is legally obligatory. But even after compliance with legally enforceable fundamental rights has

6 What Role for Ethics in the Law of AI?   149

between ethics and secularism also comes from the Catholic philosophical thought, in the well-known paradox by Ernst-Wolfgang Böckenförde dating back to the famous 1967 essay on the secularization:

> the secularized liberal state thrives on assumptions that cannot guarantee: on the one hand it can exist only if freedom is regulated from within, that is, starting from the moral substance of the individual; on the other hand, however, if the state tries to guarantee for itself these internal regulatory carachter, it gives up its own liberal character and falls back - on a secularized level - in that same instance of totality from which he had taken off with the confessional civil.[18]

It is therefore undeniable that precisely in the context of innovation an ethical approach evokes the idea of a confessional state, by posing a problem of generalized acceptance of some principles and values that they are based on normative prescriptions. Nor is the reason for having reaffirmed compliance with the already positivized fundamental rights from an ethical point of view. The ontological justification provided by the experts, that is, related to the ethical nature of fundamental rights appears frankly weak, revealing instead a problem in their applicability and effectiveness. Now, if such weakness derives from the impossibility of enforcement or from a necessity to strengthen the existing legal framework, which can represent a vademecum for the trustworthiness of the operators in the AI sector, it is not entirely clear. However, the non-binding nature of the ethical guidelines is perceived as a gap to be filled by duplicating legal contents and anchoring European secondary legislation to fundamental rights. From the first point of view, the operation also appears superfluous on the merits; from the second perspective, it is also conceptually wrong, in that in this sense there is not an authorizing law However, it seems probably more convincing to go beyond this reading and grope for a type of interpretation of the European policy that considers the choice for the ethical approach in another perspective,

---

been achieved, ethical reflection can help us understand how the development, deployment and use of AI systems may implicate fundamental rights and their underlying values, and can help provide more fine-grained guidance when seeking to identify what we *should* do rather than what we (currently) *can* do with technology".

[18] Author's translation from the Italian edition, see Böckenforde (1967, 68–69).

namely as a transposition of an Anglo-Saxon model that in a context other than the European one means something different. This understanding can look interesting and plausible because it is in line with the European trend toward innovation on the one hand and with the concept of digital sustainability on the other. If on the one hand, ethics can replace the American-style self-regulation which often involves the derogation to the rights, on the other hand a sort of global ethical reach of the European model, a sort of ethical Brussels Effect valid for ethics,[19] could be more effective than a legal global reach. In a regulatory context where Europe has often been positioned as a "regulatory standard-setter",[20] compliance with ethical principles through mechanisms of self-certification prevents what is usually overseas delegated to self-regulation and which in Europe would encounter some resistance. As highlighted by Chiti and Marchetti, the impact of artificial intelligence as a "crisis" also explains the type of interventions developed by the European Union: on the one hand, funding; on the other, regulation; finally, the ethical guidelines. The recognized aim of the combination of these interventions is to soften the harshness of the regulatory intervention to stabilize the behavior of private individuals and promoting innovation.[21] As for the ethical guidelines it would not be clear whether they should foster a sort of social ethics, which the community, as a whole, can conform to, or an individual ethics,[22] and what is their relationship with the law. These authors define ethical guidelines as non-binding legal norms that have an open moral content[23] as it is not always easy to distinguish whether these guidelines respond to questions related to rights and duties or to moral imperatives. On such a premise, it can be better framed what the term "ethics" refers to: a body of principles that has a regulatory ambition without having a legislative standing and yet it claims legitimacy.[24] Ethics is therefore everything that goes beyond

---

[19] Bradford (2019, 7, 142, 147).

[20] Cremona and Scott (2019, 11), Bradford (2015, 158), and Ebers and Cantero Gamito (2021, 8).

[21] Chiti and Marchetti (2020, 39).

[22] Ibidem, 40 and 41.

[23] Ibidem, 48.

[24] Waldman (2020, 107).

6 What Role for Ethics in the Law of AI? 151

the law either in the sense that it is not covered by the legal remit or it exceeds the scope of the law - and not exactly what is based on the protection of fundamental rights. To pursue this ambition instead, moral suasion is needed, through composite and heterogeneous techniques: sometimes ethics replicates the content of the rights, so there are no structural or content differences between legal and ethical obligations; other times it expands the scope of the applicability of the rights (thinking for example of the applicability of the European Charter of Fundamental Rights only in the matters covered by the European Union law), while other times it places ethical obligations and legal obligations on the same level. In essence, ethical principles would avoid the use of self-regulation by companies that in the European environment would be regarded with suspect, as it would imply a blank delegation from the regulation toward private negotiation autonomy. Concepts such as social impact and sustainability are hardly binding in the short term and when they do not have legal coverage, nor is an express derogation needed. For this reason, ethics can be better understood in practice as a kind of soft self-certification system that acts as a trustworthy 'business card': this also in consideration of the fact that the presence of an ethical committee within each individual company would be discretionary and expensive, while the checklist for the compliance with the seven requirements of trustworthy artificial intelligence certainly represents a more accessible and user-friendly mechanism.

With the new Proposal for AI Regulation (AI Act), the EU legislator has clearly marked the line between ethics and the law that lays on the acceptability/non-acceptability threshold. Depending on the identification of the artificial intelligence practices shall be prohibited (Art. 5 AI Act). Among these practices, those that are particularly relevant are related to AI systems that: deploy "subliminal techniques beyond a person's consciousness in order to materially distort a person's behavior"; "exploit any of the vulnerabilities of a social group in order to distort their behavior"; are based on the evaluation of social behavior (social scoring) or on predictions of personal or personality characteristics aimed at assessing the trustworthiness of individuals, leading to a detrimental or unfavorable treatment; make use of real-time remote biometric identification systems in public spaces for law enforcement purposes (except for those targeted to identify victims of crimes, to prevent threats to life and public safety or execute a European Arrest Warrant). These practices are considered unacceptable because they contravene EU values and fundamental rights. As pointed out in this chapter, EU values and fundamental rights have been identified as the basis of the ethical guidelines for a trustworthy AI.

Besides the unclear relationship between the ethical guidelines and the AI Act, the issue at stake is the relationship between law and ethics and how each of these systems places itself towardthe other. The idea to create a common core of values on a non-mandatory basis (ethical guidelines) that acts as a common field of reference to establish legal rules but also as a trigger to enhance good practices, appears as a cultural compromise between self-regulation and legal compliance. While the former is allowed in those areas that are not particularly sensitive regarding the impact on human oversight, strict legal rules of compliance are instead laid down for high-risk AI systems, such as for example AI systems used for migration, asylum, and border control management, for the management and operation of critical infrastructures, those used in education and vocational training. Among these rules, the AI Act requires providers of high-risk AI systems to set up risk and quality management systems; data governance and management measures involving relevant design choices on data collection, assumptions, preparation processing operations, possible biases; technical documentation; automatic records of events; transparent information to users; appropriate human–machine interfaces (Art. 8–29).

4 The Morality of Inferences

From another point of view, the ethical claim of machines' functioning is newfangled, meaning that machines can be potentially moral.[25] Compared to the question that opens Alan Turing's famous essay of

---

[25] Renda (2021, 667) and Punzi (2003, 1–428).

6 What Role for Ethics in the Law of AI? 153

1950,[26] that is whether machines can think, ethics lies outside the *imitation game*, because its verification process is not necessarily concurrent. From the point of view of philosophical-legal analysis, ethical principles can be valid as an *ex post* justification of an intervention that has already been implemented, in a twofold manner: trying to combine two different logics, that of law and that of ethics, and to make them as homogeneous as possible in their mandatory character, or by referring a space of freedom that leaves the actors and in particular the companies free to operate in a non-enforceable field, in other words free of mandatory rules, such as that of ethics. In the first case, the problem arises to assess to what extent ethics and the law are functionally complementary and what this complementarity means in practice, or perhaps, striking a balance in essence, which of the two logics prevails.[27] In the second case, the delegation of regulatory choices to ethics is already in itself grounded on a basic value choice that somehow preorders preferences starting from the value level (but not binding) and playing on ambiguity. The knot to be solved, for which neither the intervention of the law as the legal design of the algorithms nor the flattened ethical approach on fundamental rights seems to be adequate,[28] is that relating to algorithmic inferences which, creating logical connections between the data elaborated by algorithms, especially in those of machine learning, perform on the cognitive level of the representation of reality.[29] On the one hand, the changes in the cognitive process resulting from the interaction of causality and correlation rules are autonomous with respect to the effects. In other words, when algorithms affect the lives of individuals, they become hegemonic processes and are hard from being neutral for the sole fact of being the result of preordered aggregation of raw data. In fact, one cannot believe that the ethical passe-partout of AI is enough to prevent technological determinism from producing forms of power and awe. Ethics does not neutralize the idea of affordance, understood as a

---

[26] Turing (1950, 433).

[27] Ebers (2020, 92).

[28] Hildebrandt and O'Hara (2020, 1–15). Pariotti interestingly reflects upon the difference between soft regulation and soft law (2017, 8–27).

[29] Watcher and Mittelstadt (2019, 494–620).

limit or opportunity for social action within the technological medium.[30] Both the AI and the production of training data are extractive and non-relational methods[31] that absorb from the materiality of the consumable environmental resources and from human interactions and relationships, which certainly has an ethical impact in terms of costs and benefits.[32] On the other hand, the building of individual autonomy contributes to create a personal idea of justice,[33] so that ethics cannot have a univocal meaning and cannot be a valid imperative toward everybody (*erga omnes*) like a legal obligation. As rightly observed by Floridi, information and communication technologies (ICTs) "have re-ontologized the systems":[34] programmatically armouring AI through fundamental rights safeguards both as the basis of legality of AI and as the basis of the ethics of AI does not solve the complexity of underlying issues.[35] On these premises, the analysis of the ethical tests conducted by some scholars of the Oxford Internet Institute is interesting.[36] According to these authors, the rules of the ethical test applicable to AI are defined by the same rules and habits that inform the cognitive environment where the artifacts of AI are built. The study starts from three cases that show how the use of algorithms can determine the possibility of error in the interpretation of reality. Such are: the transformation of data into evidence; the justification of an action that is not ethically neutral; and the imputation of responsibility. These three cases can in turn give rise to ethical questions: unfounded proof can give rise to unjustified actions; an inaccessible proof can cause opacity; a misleading proof (it is not true that algorithms are free of bias, because they reflect the values of the developers, pre-existing social values, technical constraints, and contextual data) can give rise to bias; a non-transparent result can cause discriminatory effects; some transformative effects on individuals can affect individual autonomy; in the end

---

[30] Ibid.

[31] Zuboff (2019, 128).

[32] Stuermer et al. (2017, 247–262).

[33] Stevens (2020, 156, 168).

[34] Floridi (2010, 4).

[35] Graber (2020, 194–213).

[36] Mittelstadt et al. (2016, 4).

traceability is the relevant factor for ensuring moral responsibility.[37] This research strand, which is part of the so-called Information Ethics, deeply analyzes the ethical implications of technology of information, from the creation of the information to its use. If we consider the works on information ethics by Floridi, there is a profound divergence between the philosophical studies on ethics and ethics guidelines. These studies start from the assumption that information has an intrinsic ethical value that it can be universally acceptable to the extent that it is not subjected to coercion[38] and that it arises from the contextual sharing of the information space (defined as "infosphere") between human agents and artificial agents. Both have in fact a *relational self*[39] that does not allow a separation between reality and virtual space. In the context of this analysis, this perspective appears much more interesting, at least from a speculative point of view, compared to a model of duplication of rights under which the ethical guidelines have been conceived, because it does not contemplate a duplication between real and artificial space and claims for the autonomy of information ethics as an autonomous branch of information philosophy.

5 Conclusions: Lessons from Ethics for the Law of AI?

Some believe that excessive emphasis is placed on the impact of AI on the law, whereas instead there would be different other factors to be considered—including politics, financial possibilities, the institutional setup, and ultimately ethics—which help to determine how the foundational legal values of a legal system are integrated within it.[40] However, it is inevitable to reflect on the role of the law with respect to ethical norms that are modeled on legal prescriptions. Besides an awkward attempt at an ethics that replicates the legal precepts, it seems increasingly

---

[37] Ibidem, 4–10.
[38] Floridi (2013, 322).
[39] Floridi (2015, 11).
[40] Surden (2020, 721).

compelling to frame legal models that measure up specialized knowledge and can transform the challenges presented by AI into forms of inclusive and integrated knowledge. Probably, the fragmented and sectoral nature of the provisions in the field of artificial intelligence has created a basic misunderstanding: that the role of law could be limited to the legal design of the algorithms as tailored on the applicable legislation, and for this reason the European legislator has been probably disappointed by the cognitive gap of being able to do all that can be done with technology. In this way, an ethical approach would address the hope of creating the best of all possible worlds, especially if it complies with fundamental rights. In practice, as explained, this has produced two phenomena that should not be underestimated: on the one hand, the express demand for compliance of ethics to the law; on the other hand, the leveling of ethical principles and rights, which weakens the purpose of the conformity to legal rules, betraying its precise delimitation of the assumptions; on the other hand, it obscures the scope and implications of the ethical precepts. So, ethics or the law, after all, for artificial intelligence? If legal experience conveys mechanisms of reflexive elaboration of knowledge in the broader meaning, ethics seems to be a somewhat unusual and not very productive example. If instead one believes that the law of the fourth industrial revolution has its own new lexicon, then it is necessary to be aware that linguistic metaphors can change, as well as the awareness of what legal issues and legal knowledge imply besides the basic effect of producing sanctions. This concern is amplified if we look at the preferred option of EU law, namely in the AI Act, to ensure the proper functioning of trustworthy AI systems in the single market. This policy option is represented in fact by an EU horizontal instrument following a proportionate risk-assessment approach that leaves all providers of non-high-risk AI systems to follow a code of conduct to voluntarily apply the mandatory requirements provided for high-risk AI systems.[41] In substance, the ethical approach, strongly encouraged by the European Parliament, relates to the legal conceptualization of the threshold of acceptability of

---

[41] Artificial Intelligence Act, https://eur-lex.europa.eu/legal-content/EN/TXT/PDF/?uri=CELEX: 52021PC0206&from=EN. https://eur-lex.europa.eu/legal-content/EN/TXT/PDF/?uri=CELEX: 52021PC0206&from=EN, 9.

AI systems "whose use is considered unacceptable as contravening Union values, for instance by violating fundamental rights".[42]

In conclusion, if ethics is just another word for "waiting for Godot" and Godot is the law to be adopted, in the case of AI, law and ethics are then put in a position to be compatible although in a quite simplistic way, that is finally determined by the requirements provided by the law. And it could not be otherwise.

References

Bignami, F. (2018). *Comparative Law and Regulation. Understanding the Global Regulatory Process*. Elgar.

Böckenforde, W. (1967). *La formazione dello Stato come processo di secolarizzazione* (a cura di M. Nicoletti). Morcelliana.

Bradford, A. (2015). Exporting Standards: The externalization of the EU's Regulatory Power Via Markets. *International Law Review of Law and Economics*, 42, 158–173.

Bradford, A. (2019). *The Brussels Effect. How the European Union Rules the World*. Oxford University Press.

Catanzariti, M. (2020a). Enhancing Policing Through Algorithmic Mass-Surveillance. In L. Marin, S. Montaldo (eds.), *The Fight Against Impunity* (pp. 239–255). Hart.

Catanzariti, M. (2020b). La razionalit. algoritmica dei processi decisionali. In S. Gozzo, C. Pennisi, V. Asero, R. Sampugnaro (eds.), *Big Data e processi decisionali* (pp. 149–165). Egea.

Cath, C., Floridi, L., Mittelstadt, B., Taddeo, M., Watcher, S. (2018). Artificial Intelligence and the 'Good Society': The US, EU, and UK approach. *Science and Engineering Ethics*, 24, 505–528.

Chiti, E., Marchetti, B. (2020). Divergenti? Le strategie di Unione Europea e Stati Uniti in materia di intelligenza artificiale. *Rivista della Regolazione dei Mercati*, 1, 28–50.

---

[42] Ibidem, 12.

Cremona, M., Scott, J. (2019). Introduction. In M. Cremona, J. Scott (eds.), *EU Law Beyond EU Borders: The Extraterritorial Reach of EU Law* (pp. 1–20). Oxford University Press.

Ebers, M. (2020), Regulating AI and Robotics: Ethical and Legal Challenges. In M. Ebers, S. Navas Navarro (eds.), *Algorithms and Law* (pp. 37–99). Cambridge University Press.

Ebers, M., Cantero Gamito, M. (2021). Algorithmic Governance and Governance of Algorithms: An Introduction. In M. Ebers, M. Cantero Gamito (eds.), *Algorithmic Governance and Governance of Algorithms: Legal and Ethical Challenges* (pp. 1–22). Springer.

Eisler, R. (1987). Human Rights: Towards an Integrated Theory for Action. *Human Rights Quarterly*, 9, 287.

Floridi, L. (2010). Ethics After the Information Revolution. In *The Cambridge Handbook of Information and Computer Ethics* (pp. 3–19). Cambridge University Press.

Floridi, L. (2013). *The Ethics of Information*. Oxford University Press.

Floridi, L. (2015). *The Online Manifesto. Being Human in Hyperconnected Era*. Springer.

Graber, C.B. (2020). Artificial Intelligence, Affordances and Fundamental Rights. In M. Hildebrandt, K. O'Hara (eds.), *Life and the Law in the Era of Data-Driven Agency* (pp. 194–213). Elgar.

Hildebrandt, M., O'Hara, K., (2020). Introduction: Life and the Law in the Era of Data-Driven Agency. In M. Hildebrandt, K. O'Hara (eds.), *Life and the Law in the Era of Data-Driven Agency* (pp. 1–15). Elgar.

Mantelero, A. (2018). AI and Big Data. A Blueprint for a Human Rigths, Social and Ethical Impact Assessment. *Computer Law & Security Review*, 34(4), 754–772.

McCrudden, C. (2013). In Pursuit of Human Dignity: An Introduction to Current Debates. In C. McCrudden (ed.), *Understanding Human Dignity* (pp. 1–58). Oxford University Press.

Mittelstadt, B.D., Allo, P., Taddeo, M., Wachter, S., Floridi, L. (2016). The Ethics of Algorithms: Mapping the Debate. *Big Data & Society*, 3(1), 1–21.

Orgad, L., Reijers, W. (2020). How to Make the Perfect Citizen? Lessons from China's Model of Social Credit System. EUI Working Paper RSCAS 28. https://cadmus.eui.eu/bitstream/handle/1814/66910/RSCAS%20202028.pdf

Pariotti, E. (2013). *Diritti umani: concetto, teoria, evoluzione*. Cedam.

Pariotti, E. (2017). Self-regulation, concetto di diritto, normatività giuridica. *Ars Interpretandi*, 2, 9–28.

Punzi, A. (2003). L'ordine giuridico delle macchine. La Mettrie Helvetius d'Holbach. L'uomo macchina verso l'intelligenza collettiva. Giappichelli.

Rawls, J. (1999). *A Theory of Justice*. Harvard University Press.

Renda, A. (2021). Moral Machines. The Emerging EU Policy on "Trustworthy AI". In W. Barfield (ed.), *The Cambridge Handbook of Algorithms* (pp. 667–690). Cambridge University Press.

Sheppele, K.L. (2018, July). *Rule of Law Retail and Rule of Law Wholesail*. ver fassunsblog.de.

Síthigh, D.M., Siems, M. (2019). The Chinese Social Credit System: A Model for Other Countries? EUI Working Paper LAW 1. https://cadmus.eui.eu/bit stream/handle/1814/60424/LAW201901.pdf.

Stevens, D. (2020). In Defense of 'Toma': Algorithmic Enhancement of a Sense of Justice. In M. Hildebrandt, K. O'Hara (eds.), *Life and the Law in the Era of Data-Driven Agency* (pp. 156–174). Elgar.

Stuermer, M., Abu-Tayeh, G., Myrach, T. (2017). Digital Sustainability: Basic Conditions for Sustainable Digital Artifacts and Their Ecosystems. *Sustainability Science*, 2, 247–262.

Surden, H. (2020). The Ethics of AI in Law: Basic Questions. In M.D. Dubber, F. Pasquale, S. Das (eds.), *Oxford Handbook of Ethics of AI* (pp. 720–736). Oxford University Press.

Turing, A.M. (1950). Computing Machinery and Intelligence. *Mind*, 49, 433–460.

Wachter, S., Mittelstadt, B. (2019). A Right to Reasonable Inferences: Re-thinking Data Protection Law in the Age of Big Data and AI. *Columbia Business Law Review*, 2, 494–620.

Waldman, A.E. (2020). Algorithmic Legitimacy. In W. Barfield (ed.), *The Cambridge Handbook of Algorithms* (pp. 107–120). Cambridge University Press.

Yeung, K., Lodge, M. (2019). *Algorithmic Regulation*. Oxford University Press.

Yeung, K., Howes, A., Pogrebna, G. (2020). AI Governance by Human Rights—Centered Design, Deliberation, and Oversight: An End to Ethics Washing In M.D. Dubber, F. Pasquale, S. Das (eds.), *The Oxford Handbook of Ethics of AI* (pp. 78–106). Oxford University Press.

Zuboff, S. (2019). *The Age of Surveillance Capitalism. The Fight for a Human Future and the New Frontier of Power*. Public Affairs.

7

Introduction to Computational Ethics

Ljupčo Todorovski

1 Introduction

In a recent article, Segun (2020) argues for establishing the field of computational ethics. In contrast with the prevailing discourse of the traditional robot ethics, on one hand, and the more recent machine ethics, on the other, the computational ethics focuses on the practical issue of making the ethical decisions computable, i.e., transforming them into algorithms. Computational ethics aims at providing computer scientists and engineers with a technical framework for building intelligent

---

L. Todorovski (✉)
Faculty of Mathematics and Physics, University of Ljubljana, Ljubljana, Slovenia
e-mail: ljupco.todorovski@fmf.uni-lj.si

Department of Knowledge Technologies, Jožef Stefan Institute, Ljubljana, Slovenia

© The Author(s), under exclusive license to Springer Nature
Switzerland AG 2023
A. Završnik and K. Simončič (eds.), *Artificial Intelligence, Social Harms and Human Rights*, Critical Criminological Perspectives,
https://doi.org/10.1007/978-3-031-19149-7_7

systems capable of making ethical decisions that also includes minimal standards for an artificial agent to be considered ethical. Computational ethics is therefore more pragmatic and has a narrower, more technical focus than the related fields of robot ethics and machine ethics. The first covers the wider area of how the development of robots will affect ethical and social interaction with humans and therefore addresses the issue of designing ethical robots only implicitly (Kuipers 2018). The second related area of machine ethics is concerned with the profound impact that intelligent agents might have on our legal, ethical, social, and economic landscape (Anderson and Leigh Anderson 2011).

The notion of computational ethics is closely related to the infocentrism or infocentric view (also referred to as technocentric bias) on ethics of artificial agents (Torrance 2012). This view assumes that autonomous, artificial agents can take ethical decisions on their own, despite their inability to put ethics in the wider context of emotion, consciousness, or empathy, all being very relevant for the moral thinking and experience. The consequence of this assumption is that ethical phenomena can be cast in computational terms and therefore modeled and reasoned about by artificial agents. Albeit naïve, we are going to follow this assumption throughout this chapter to be able to focus on representing efforts toward computational modeling of ethical decisions. The reader interested in an in-depth criticism of the infocentrism and computational ethics conducted through contrasting them with orthogonal, more complex stances should read (Torrance 2012).

While many previous surveys, overviews, and volumes have been published on the topics of robot and machine ethics, see, e.g., (Anderson and Leigh Anderson 2011), the introductions to and overviews of approaches to the specific area of computational ethics are rare (Segun 2020). There is a very recent notable exception of (Tolmeijer et al. 2021) that provides such an exhaustive, systematic survey for computer scientists. The goal of this chapter is different, we aim here at introducing the basics of computational ethics field through an overview of the current literature and taxonomical systemization of computational approaches to the task of incorporating ethics-related decisions in intelligent systems.

We start our introduction with clustering the approaches to computational ethics in two classes of bottom-up and top-down approaches.

Section 2 introduces these two classes by defining their scope and discussing their advantages and disadvantages. In Sect. 3, we introduce and provide examples of top-down approaches, which rely on manual transformation of ethical theories to algorithms and decision models. We match the approaches with the corresponding ethical theories they encode. Section 4 introduce bottom-up approaches, which automatically learn decision models from examples of ethical decisions made by humans and overviews recent work on them. Section 5 discusses the issue of computational complexity of ethical decision-making and the consequences of the complexity on further development of the field of computational ethics. Finally, Sect. 6 concludes the chapter with a summary and an overview of open venues for further research in computational ethics.

2 Bottom-Up vs Top-Down Approaches

Allen et al. (2005) introduce a distinction between two main types of approaches to computational ethics: bottom-up and top-down, a very relevant distinction being followed by many other studies (Kim et al. 2021; Tolmeijer et al. 2021). Bottom-up approaches are based on efforts to train artificial agents based on exemplary human behavior, so they acquire skills that are necessary to take, or more precisely, emulate ethical decisions made by humans. These approaches rely on the use of machine learning (Langley 1995) to acquire knowledge and skills from training examples: they are bottom-up, since they induce top-level rules or models for ethical reasoning from low-level, observation data. On the other hand, top-down approaches aim at manual encoding of theories of ethical and moral behavior into algorithms. They rely on human effort toward selecting an ethical principle and/or theory, formally defining it, often using symbolic logic, and implementing its formal definition into an ethical decision support system.

Following the great success of machine learning algorithms (especially neural networks) to acquire various human skills in the wide range of domains, from recognizing visual patterns (hand-written digits and letters or faces) through text translation and game playing, to medical diagnosis, bottom-up approaches gain traction in computational ethics as well. However, learning ethical models from examples involves but a few issues that we are going to address here: the (in)ability of models to capture complex ethical norms and principles, quality of training data, and understandability of the learned models.

The first issue of (in)ability is related to a well-known *naturalistic fallacy* or error of deriving an "ought" from an "is" (Kim et al. 2021). The problem with bottom-up induction of ethical models from observations is that they assume that what "is" being frequently observed (since many of the machine learning methods deploy statistical methods, frequency of observations plays an important role) relates to an "ought"-to-be-followed norm. The latter can, in principle and in many documented cases, in practice, violate valid ethical principles and norms (Miller et al. 2017). Also, many recent studies show that models obtained with machine learning algorithms tend to replicate human bias and prejudices (Brennan et al. 2009).

The latter is closely related to the sensitivity of the concepts induced with machine learning on the quality of training data (Wolf et al. 2017). One would conjecture that this issue can be adequately addressed by carefully selecting exemplary human behavior for training artificial agents. However, recent studies of behavioral ethics show that human decision-makers often fail to consider ethical aspects, due to a phenomenon referred to as "ethical fading" (Bazerman and Tenbrunsel 2011). For example, business managers often follow formal cost–benefit analysis to take rational business decisions. Cost–benefit analysis takes the moral dimension of the "purely business and rational" decisions out of the equation and therefore neglects it in the decision-making process. The phenomenon of "ethical fading" can be observed in many other domains: Egler and Ross (2020) show that expert judgments are often vulnerable to biases and irrelevant factors, making the problem of selecting appropriate training data in bottom-up approaches far from simple or trivial.

Consequently, machine learning often relies on biased data, leading to biased and discriminatory decision models. When the latter are being used for taking autonomous decisions, they might lead to substantial replication and boosting of human prejudices and/or unethical decisions.

The problem is alleviated on a higher level due to the wide-spread use of opaque models in machine learning, i.e., models that cannot provide understanding or explanation of their decisions (Brennan et al. 2009; Pasquale 2015). The issue of black-box models in machine learning has been addressed in the field of explainable and trustworthy artificial intelligence (OECD 2020), where black-box models are being replaced by transparent ones (Rudin 2019) or algorithms for explaining the decisions of opaque models are being developed (Ribeiro et al. 2016).

Transparent decisions and decision-making models are crucial for the future of the bottom-up approaches to computational ethics: only transparent ethical decisions can be checked for their validity and applicability in real applications. For example, autonomous vehicles widely use transparent rule-based systems to implement computational ethics, *"… many companies have shifted to rule-based AI, an older technique that lets engineers hard-code specific behaviors or logic into an otherwise self-directed system."* (Brandom 2018). The rule-based systems are typical representatives of top-down approaches that are based on a long research tradition of using symbolic logic for ethical reasoning and represent a relevant alternative to machine learning approaches described above. Bringsjord et al. (2006) in one of the seminal articles introducing top-down approaches state *"one approach is to insist that robots only perform actions that can be proved ethically permissible in a human-selected deontic logic—that is, a logic that formalizes an ethical code."*

Following the top-down approaches, ethical decisions are modeled and implemented as systematic, rule-based systems encoded in the formalism of symbolic logic (Thomason 2008). Logic-based approaches are widely used in autonomous vehicles for implementing the driving mechanisms and traffic-related decisions making, even though in the same application domain, pattern recognition mechanisms and machine learning are primarily based on machine learning. One of the reasons for the popularity of logic-based, top-down approaches might lie in the fact that formal, symbolic logic is a rare formalism being common in computer science as well as ethical philosophy (Kim et al. 2021). Reasoning and decision-making follow clear and human understandable rules of deductive logic and logical proofs. Therefore, these systems take decisions that are transparent, and the reasoning can be explained to and shared with humans, an important advantage over the bottom-up approaches.

In the related literature, the dichotomy of top-down and bottom-up systems is often discussed in parallel with distinguishing between system 1 and system 2 human cognitive reasoning (Kim et al. 2021). Humans use system 1 thinking most of the time and is like the one of the bottom-up, machine learning approaches: the system 1 reasoning is very fast, based on intuition, and not transparent in terms of inability to explain the reasoning process or the decisions taken. In contrast, system 2 thinking is slow, based on analysis and logical deduction, and transparent. It is reasonable to conjecture that system 2 thinking is more appropriate for ethical decision-making: the transparent decision can be effectively checked by humans and is more likely to detect unethical behavior (Bazerman and Sezer 2016).

3 Top-Down Approaches

Top-down approaches to computational ethics are based on translating human knowledge, i.e., ethical theories into algorithms and implementations. These are often based on logical, symbolic reasoning on an if–then rules, which allows for applying the general encoded theories to a given specific situation. The caveat of the top-down systems is that the process of translation of theories to algorithms is prone to errors and misinterpretations. However, the long tradition of using logical, symbolic reasoning in AI also provides ample, elaborated methods for establishing, checking the correctness, and debugging large collections of if–then rules.

Table 1 summarizes the four major ethical theories being encoded by top-down approaches (Kuipers 2018; Tolmeijer et al. 2021). *Consequentialism* relates the moral stance of a decision with its consequences (Sinnott-Armstrong 2019). There are two instances of consequentialist principles that are often considered in computational ethics. Do-no-harm principle holds all actions with harmful consequences to be ethically impermissible, rendering lack of action permissible. A more strict version of the do-not-harm principle, proposed by Asimov in his first law

7 Introduction to Computational Ethics 167

Table 1 Overview of the four major ethical theories considered by top-down approaches to computational ethics, adopted from (Tolmeijer et al. 2021)

Ethical theory	Decision criteria	Mechanism
Consequentialism Utilitarianism	Utility and overall well-being	Selecting an action that maximizes utility
Deontological ethics	Rules and duties	Suitability of an action to the rule(s)
Virtue ethics	Virtues	Instantiation of virtues to specific cases

of robotics, forbids robots to let harmful consequences happen when the latter can be avoided by performing actions.

Utilitarianism is a variety of consequentialism that follows the slogan "the greatest happiness for the greatest number": it states that an action is ethical, if it maximizes a given quantitative measure of utility, which usually relates to the overall welfare of individuals in society (Sinnott-Armstrong 2019; Kuipers 2018). The computational approaches to ethics often rely on utilitarianism since it allows for the deployment of standard optimization algorithms to the task of selecting ethical decisions. Numerous approaches from game and decision theory are applicable to this task. However, the efficient computation of optimal decisions is directly related to the parsimony of the decision model in terms of the number of decision factors that it considers. This makes the process of encoding appropriate decision models tedious and time consuming (Kuipers 2018). In addition, the result of the encoding might be an overly complex decision model leading to high computational complexity of the decision-making process, which might render computational approaches inapplicable to practical problems. Later in the chapter, we are going to revisit this issue by considering the computational complexity of ethical decision-making and its consequences.

In *deontology*, that studies duty (*deon* in Greek), the moral stance of an action is in accordance with established moral duties, rules, constraints, and/or norms (Alexander and Moore 2020). The latter can be very conveniently transformed into logical rules used in turn for computational reasoning about the ethical actions and decisions. AI has a plethora of tools and algorithms for reasoning from rules and constraints. Another advantage of using deontological rules is their comprehensibility that

168   **L. Todorovski**

makes decisions transparent and easy to explain or understand. Note however, that the deontological rules often lead to unexpected consequences that are to be meticulously encoded as rule exceptions. Also, one can question the validity and justification of a chosen set of deontological rules (Kuipers 2018).

Finally, *virtue ethics* (Hursthouse and Pettigrove 2016) differ from the theories introduced above in its focus: instead of focusing on ethical merit of agent's actions, it focuses on the moral character of the agent. An ethical action is therefore in line with the moral disposition of a virtuous human. Its transformation to algorithms is based on the conjecture that individual acquires virtues through experience, computationally modeled through positive and negative cases, i.e., examples of virtuous and unscrupulous behavior. This makes it suitable for case-based reasoning, where the decisions in a specific situation are taken in analogy with the actions taken in similar cases, retrieved from a regularly updated repository of previously encountered cases.

Bringsjord et al. (2006) in their pioneering, seminal work on implementing deontological norms using formal logic and reasoning methods to support ethical decision-making of artificial agents emphasize three strong arguments for the deployment of deontic logic in computational ethics. First, ethical philosophers use deontic logic to formalize ethical norms and dilemmas to be able to reason about them. Second, AI and computer science in general is based on logic. Third, formal methods for checking and proving the correctness of logical claims, strengthen the trust in the decisions made by artificial agents. The correctness of the decisions can be checked both deductively, by deriving formal proofs of software correctness, and inductively, by checking the software on carefully selected test cases. The possibility of deductive check is especially important since it avoids the caveats of unreliable inductive reasoning. Finally, (Bringsjord et al. 2006) illustrate the utility of the approach on a simple example of health-care robots taking decisions related to the survival and well-being of patients, showing the advantages of demonic rules over utilitarianism.

Many researchers in computational ethics have followed these initial ideas. A recent example is a study by Pereira and Saptawijaya (2007). They show that ethical decisions can be implemented as abductive logic

7 Introduction to Computational Ethics 169

programs capable of modeling moral dilemmas, including the double-effect principle of explaining the permissibility of a harmful action; the latter being permissible in cases when it represents a means for bringing up good. The abductive logic programs combine a-priori deontic rules with agent posteriori preferences on consequences, thus allowing the combination of deontological ethics with consequentialism. More specifically, preferences on consequences can be enforced following the utility theory or following a set of deontic rules. Following this approach, authors show that the computational approach encoding the principle of double effect as the moral rule, can deliver preferred moral decisions in the context of classic trolley problem (Thompson 1976).

Further prominent example of encoding the utilitarian ethics into algorithms is the HERA software library for modeling hybrid ethical reasoning agents developed by Lindner et al. (2017). Authors have shown that HERA allows for the implementation of various ethical principles like utilitarianism and the aforementioned principle of double effect. The approach of HERA is hybrid in a sense that, instead of committing to a single ethical theory, e.g., optimizing utility or logical reasoning about the moral permissibility of actions and action plan, it allows for combining multiple theories. If several different ethical theories and/or principles decide that an action plan is permissible, it is more likely that the plan will be ethically acceptable to more individuals. On the other hand, if different principles disagree upon the permissibility of an action plan, artificial agents can share the uncertainty with humans and seek assistance on selecting the optimal plan. Finally, different ethical stances taken by artificial robots can be taken by combining different sets of ethical norms.

To illustrate the utility of the HERA library, Lindner and Bentzen (2017) implement the artificial intelligence IMMANUEL. Furthermore, Lindner and Bentzen (2019) show that HERA can implement the second formulation of Kant's categorical imperative, which requires that an agent never treat someone as a means only, but always also as an end for reaching a certain goal. The implementation of HERA is conducted through logical reasoning about the effects of actions on individuals involved in a certain situation. The illustrative example presented in (Lindner and Bentzen 2019) shows that HERA allows for reasoning that

170　L. Todorovski

goes beyond the ethical principles of utilitarianism and the principle of double effect: plan that would be accessed as permissible following these two principles is found to conflict with the Kant's categorical imperative. Along the same line of research, Lindner et al. (2020) address the issue of computability and computational complexity of algorithms for taking ethical decisions, a topic, we are going to revisit in Sect. 5.

4　Bottom-Up Approaches

The bottom-up approaches to implementing ethics is based on a conjecture that artificial agent can be trained to act morally from a data set consisting of correctly labeled (permissible and impermissible) actions. In Sect. 2, we highlighted few problems with the approaches in this class, mostly related to the quality of the training examples. Here we are going to continue that discussion and provide several examples of specific bottom-up approaches.

Guarini (2006) proposes training an artificial neural network with examples consisting of cases labeled as ethically permissible or impermissible. The trained network should be general enough to classify not only the training cases, but also new one, unseen in the training phase, with respect to their permissibility. The neural network was trained on modest set of 22 training cases, and its classification accuracy was assessed on 62 new, test cases labeled by 60 students of ethics course. The results show the ability of the neural network to generalize well from the training to the test cases: for example, the network correctly classified suicide cases, even though no suicidal cases were present in the training data.

Note however that the presented approach has two important limitations. The first is the obvious inability of neural networks (as opaque, black-box models) to generate arguments for the classification as output. Thus, the decisions taken by the network remain opaque. Also, the neural network is limited on classification from the cases descriptions: a trained network cannot consider moral arguments about the permissibility of a given case nor able to revise its classification in the presence of such arguments. Note that this is a general limitation of neural networks, we discussed in Sect. 2.

The second limitation is the high sensitivity to the distribution of the cases in the training data. For example, if a certain agent (Jill) was more frequently present in the training cases than another one (Jack), different classifications would be obtained for the same case involving Jack or Jill. In other words, the neural network would find a certain case permissible for Jack, but impermissible for Jill, or vice versa, which is an obvious reasoning fallacy. Again, note that this fallacy is an instance of the *naturalistic fallacy* or error of deriving an "ought" from an "is" introduced in Sect. 2. Since, the training algorithm observes what Jack and Jill "are" doing, the resulting neural networks learns what they "ought" to do: differentiating the training cases with the acting agents leads to different sets of "ought" (classification) rules for Jill and Jack.

This kind of sensibility to training data combined with the model's limited abilities to explain its decisions renders the approach inapplicable in practice, since it is very difficult to establish trust in such a system. To allow the learning agent unbiased training cases, Abel et al. (2016) propose a reinforcement learning approach to training the artificial agent. In reinforcement learning (Sutton and Barto 2018), the agent takes a pro-active role in collecting training examples through interaction with the environment. However, those examples are not labeled as positive or negative (i.e., agents do not have information on the permissibility of the actions taken): instead, the agent receives a positive or negative reward for its actions. The algorithms for reinforcement learning then search for an agent decision model that maximizes the received reward. If the reward is related to the permissibility of the actions taken, the agent is expected to learn how to behave ethically in the given environment. The experiments presented in the paper show the ability of the approach to learning the opaque decision model for probabilistic reasoning about the permissibility of relatively simple ethical decisions.

The problematic issue with approaches based on reinforcement learning is the formulation of an appropriate reward function that will guide the agent toward a good decision model. Wu and Lin (2017) propose the approach of "ethics shaping" to address this issue by using inverse reinforcement learning. The latter allows for extracting a reward function from observed actions of an expert (in this case, virtuous human) in a given environment. The proposed method then relies on minimizing the discrepancy between the acts of the agent's decision model (in the terminology of reinforcement learning, we refer to the model as policy of the artificial agent) and the human decision model aggregated from observational data. Note however, that this approach assumes that the human ethical choices are always impeccable, and is therefore sensitive to bias training data, that might include unethical behavior as discussed previously in Sect. 2. Furthermore, the obtained decision model is still black-box and incapable of explaining the agent's decisions.

5 Computational Complexity and Computability

In the final section of this chapter, we are going to discuss the computational complexity of the presented approaches to computational ethics. This is an important aspect of the applicability of the proposed approaches for taking decisions, timely and efficiently. The focus will be on the logic-based approaches, where the results of the HERA system have been systematically presented (Lindner et al. 2020).

Before presenting the results, let us introduce the basics of computational complexity and computability. The field of computer science that addresses these two issues is computational complexity theory that studies the taxonomical classification of problems with respect to their complexity in terms of resources required to algorithmically solve them. Different kinds of resources are being considered, computational time and memory space being the two most prominent ones. Here, we are interested in those two. The computational time relates to the time needed to solve a class of ethical decision problems, which directly relates to the ability of the decision models to deliver decisions efficiently and in real time. The computational space relates to the amount of memory needed to compute the decision.

On the highest level of the taxonomical classification of problems is the computability dichotomy: one class includes problems that can be solved algorithmically and the other include incomputable problems. In the latter class of computable problems, several important subclasses

7 Introduction to Computational Ethics   173

have been defined that include problems with related computational complexity. The spaces of particular interest to our discussion are:

- P is the class of problems solvable in time that is proportional to the polynomial of the decision problem size.[1] To put it in simple, albeit imprecise words, the problems in this class are considered efficiently solvable by computers.
- $PSPACE$ includes problems solvable using polynomial space, i.e., the amount of memory that is proportional to the polynomial of the problem size. It is not clear whether these problems are efficiently solvable in polynomial time: One of the open questions in computer science is whether the classes P and PSPACE are equivalent or not.
- $PSPACE\text{-}complete$ is the subclass of the most difficult problems in PSPACE. In principle, this means that they are more complex for algorithmic solving than the problems in PSPACE. For these decision problems, it is impossible to compute the optimal decision exactly and efficiently: all we can hope for are algorithms for computing sub-optimal approximations of the optimal decision.
- $co\text{-}NP\text{-}complete$ is the space of decision problems that are complements of problems in the $NP\text{-}complete$ space. The complement of a decision problem is a problem, where the decisions "yes" and "no," e.g., whether an action or action plan is permissible or not, are switched around. For co-NP-complete problems, one can verify whether a given decision is *impermissible* in polynomial time. However, computing the optimal decisions cannot be computed efficiently, much like in the case of the PSPACE-complete problems.

Now, having these classes in mind, let us return to our computational ethics approaches. The proof of the Proposition 2 in (Lindner et al. 2020) shows that efficient (polynomial time) algorithms can be implemented for deciding whether a plan is ethically permissible with respect to the deontic principle. This is an important result that reconfirms the high relevance of the numerous approaches to computational

---

[1] The size of the decision problem is measured in the number of logical (typically if–then) decision rules in the decision model.

ethics based on deontic logic that has been developed upon the seminal work of Bringsjord et al. (2006), elaborated in Sect. 3.

Note however, further results presented by Lindner et al. (2020) classify other problems of ethical decision-making into the classes of *PSPACE-complete* and *co-NP-complete*, which renders them very difficult for exact algorithmic solving. First, deciding whether a plan is morally permissible according to the principles of utilitarianism or Asimovian principle, that is a special, restrictive case of the general do-not-harm norm, are both in the class of *PSPACE-complete* decision problems (check Theorems 1 and 3 in (Lindner et al. 2020)). These results show that algorithms for the exact computation of action plans that follow the utilitarianism ethical theory (see Sect. 3) are out of reach. Note that the restrictive Asimov's formulation of the do-not-harm principle are specific instances of the general consequentialism ethical theory, where ethical actions are selected by maximizing the utility (check Table 1 and the corresponding paragraphs of Sect. 3). Thus, we can conclude that maximization of the utility is the problem that is PSPACE-complete and any approach that seeks for optimizing the utility of actions' consequences cannot be implemented with an efficient algorithm.

Finally, deciding the ethical permissibility of the general do-not-harm principle (not necessarily its specific, stricter Asimov's variant discussed above) and double-effect principle are both in the co-NP-complete class of most complex computational problems introduced above (see Theorems 4 and 6 in (Lindner et al. 2020)). It is not surprising that the more general do-not-harm principle is more complex to decide upon than the stricter variant. For explaining the complexity of the decision models based on the double-effect principle, we should recall from Sect. 3 that this principle follows both consequential and deontological ethical theories. On one hand, the principle is deontological since it establishes the moral stance of an agent's action to an ethical norm. On the other hand, the principle combines reasoning about action consequences and agent goals: only positive consequences should be intended by goals or are means to the goals, and the positive consequences should overweight the negative ones. Note that the dichotomy of positive and negative consequences also follows the deontic norms. And the condition that positive sequences should prevail introduces an ultraistic principle. This explains why do-not-harm principle is hard to implement and why the Trolley problem, the solution of which always require consideration of side-effect harmful consequences, is so relevant in important in the studies of computational ethics.

In sum, computational complexity of decision problems related to ethical decision-making is often prohibitive to implementation of efficient algorithms. This is a serious limitation of the top-down approaches following the consequentialists ethical theories, including utilitarianism. The latter can be more efficiently addressed by opaque, black-box models obtained with machine learning. Thus, we can conjecture that decision models, trained using machine learning, bottom-up approaches, represent computationally efficient surrogates for making decisions that approximate the optimal decisions that cannot be computed efficiently.

6   Conclusion

The chapter overview approaches to computational ethics, a field of AI that studies algorithms for making ethically permissible decisions. The overview includes typical, exemplary approaches taken in the field and discusses them in terms of their capability to properly address various ethical principles and theories. At a first glance, it seems that top-down approaches based on symbolic logic are superior to the ones based on machine learning. However, the analysis of the computational complexity of the problems encountered in ethical decision-making, shows the ratio and necessity for considering bottom-up approaches as serious candidates for further developments in the field of computational ethics.

To this end, the most promising direction for further research is the hybrid methods that combine top-down and bottom-up approaches (Kim et al. 2021). The combination holds promise to deliver efficient decision-making models that can tackle computationally demanding problems that include moral principles related to the consequentialism and utilitarianism. There are two possible venues to be followed on the way toward hybrid methods. The first relies upon the deployment of algorithms for learning in logic: machine learning algorithms for inductive logic programming and probabilistic logic learning (De Raedt and Kersting 2003). These algorithms learn logical theories from observational data, i.e., the learned models are transparent and expressed in logic. For the purpose of computational ethics, one should validate their ability to learn transparent decision models for ethical decisions making. Another direction for building hybrids is to start with existing methods for learning opaque, black-box decision models from exemplary behavior. To obtain explanations of such decision models, one can deploy methods for explaining decisions of black-box models, recently developed in the field of explainable artificial intelligence (Ribeiro et al. 2016). Note however, that such hybrid approaches would confront the problems of dealing with biased training data or, alternatively, obtaining unbiased training data consisting of examples related to impeccable ethical decisions taken by humans, both issues being actively researched in machine learning.

Acknowledgements The research leading to this chapter has received funding from the Slovenian Research Agency, under the research project "Human Rights and Regulation of Trustworthy Artificial Intelligence" (No. V5-1930).

References

Abel, D., MacGlashan, J., and Littman, M. L. (2016). Reinforcement learning as a framework for ethical decision making. In *Proceedings of the AAAI Workshop: AI, Ethics, and Society, Technical Report WS-16–02.*
Alexander, L. and Moore, M. (2020). Deontological ethics. *The Stanford Encyclopedia of Philosophy.* https://plato.stanford.edu/
Allen, C., Smit, I., and Wallach, W. (2005). Artificial morality: Top-down, bottom-up, and hybrid approaches. *Ethics and Information Technology, 7(3):* 149–155.
Anderson, M. and Leigh Anderson, S., (Eds.). (2011). *Machine Ethics.* Cambridge University Press.

Bazerman, M. H. and Sezer, O. (2016). Bounded awareness: Implications for ethical decision making. *Organizational Behavior and Human Decision Processes, 136*: 95–105. https://doi.org/10.1016/J.OBHDP.2015.11.004

Bazerman, M. H. and Tenbrunsel, A. E. (2011, April). Ethical breakdowns. *Harvard Business Review,* 58–65.

Brandom, R. (2018). Self-driving cars are headed toward an AI roadblock. *The Verge, July 2018 issue on Real-World AI*.

Brennan, T., Dieterich, W., and Ehret, B. (2009). Evaluating the predictive validity of the COMPAS risk and needs assessment system. *Criminal Justice and Behavior, 36(1)*: 21–40. DOI:https://doi.org/10.1177/009385480832 6545

Bringsjord, S., Arkoudas, K., and Bello, P. (2006). Toward a general logicist methodology for engineering ethically correct robots. *IEEE Intelligent Systems, 21(4)*: 38–44. https://doi.org/10.1109/MIS.2006.82

De Raedt, L. and Kersting, K. (2003). Probabilistic logic learning. *ACM SIGKDD Explorations Newsletter, 5(1)*: 31–48. https://doi.org/10.1145/959 242.959247

Egler, M. and Ross, L. D. (2020). Philosophical expertise under the microscope. *Synthese, 197(3)*: 1077–1098.

Etzioni, A. and Etzioni, O. (2017). Incorporating ethics into artificial intelligence. *The Journal of Ethics, 21(4): 403–418,* http://www.jstor.org/stable/45204573

Guarini, M. (2006). Particularism and the classification and reclassification of moral cases. *IEEE Intelligent Systems, 4*: 22–28. https://doi.org/10.1109/MIS.2006.76

Hursthouse, R. and Pettigrove, G. (2016). Virtue ethics. *The Stanford Encyclopedia of Philosophy*. https://plato.stanford.edu/

Kim T. W., Hooker, J., and Donaldson, T. (2021). Taking principles seriously: A hybrid approach to value alignment in artificial intelligence. *Journal of Artificial Intelligence Research, 70*: 871–890. https://doi.org/10.1613/jair.1.12481

Kuipers, B. (2018). How can we trust a robot? *Communications of the ACM, 61(3)*: 86–95. https://doi.org/10.1145/3173987

Langley, P. (1995). *Elements of Machine Learning*. Morgan Kaufmann.

Lindner, F. and Bentzen, M. M. (2017). The hybrid ethical reasoning agent IMMANUEL. In *Proceedings of the Companion of the 2017 ACM/IEEE International Conference on Human-Robot Interaction* (pp. 187–188). https://doi.org/10.1145/3029798.3038404

178   **L. Todorovski**

Lindner, F. and Bentzen, M. M. (2019). A formalization of Kant's second formulation of the categorical imperative. https://arxiv.org/abs/1801.03160.

Lindner, F., Bentzen, M. M., and Nebel, B. (2017). The HERA approach to morally competent robots. In *Proceedings of the 2017 IEEE/RSJ International Conference on Intelligent Robots and Systems, IROS 2017* (pp. 6991–6997).

Lindner, F. Mattmüller, R. and Nebel, B. (2020). Evaluation of the moral permissibility of action plans. *Artificial Intelligence, 287*: 103350. https://doi.org/10.1016/j.artint.2020.103350

Miller, K. W., Wolf, M. J., and Grodzinsky, F. (2017). This "ethical trap" is for roboticists, not robots: on the issue of artificial agent ethical decision-making. *Science and Engineering Ethics, 23*: 389–401. https://doi.org/10.1007/s11948-016-9785-y

OECD. (2020). *Recommendation of the Council on Artificial Intelligence.* OECD/LEGAL/0449.

Pasquale, F. (2015). *The Black Box Society: The Secret Algorithms that Control Money and Information.* Harvard University Press.

Pereira, L. M., & Saptawijaya, A. (2007). Modelling morality with prospective logic. In *Proceedings of the Thirteenth Portuguese Conference on Progress in Artificial Intelligence, EPIA-07* (pp. 99–111). Springer-Verlag, Berlin, Heidelberg.

Ribeiro, M. T., Singh, S., and Guestrin, C. (2016). "Why should I trust you?": Explaining the predictions of any classifier. In *Proceedings of the twenty-second ACM SIGKDD International Conference on Knowledge Discovery and Data Mining, ICDM-2016* (pp. 1135–1144). https://doi.org/10.1145/2939672.2939778

Rudin, C. (2019). Stop explaining black box machine learning models for high stakes decisions and use interpretable models instead. *Nature Machine Intelligence 1*: 206–215. https://doi.org/10.1038/s42256-019-0048-x

Segun, S. T. (2020). From machine ethics to computational ethics. *AI & Society, 36*: 263–276. https://doi.org/10.1007/s00146-020-01010-1

Sinnott-Armstrong, W. (2019). Consequentialism. *The Stanford Encyclopedia of Philosophy.* https://plato.stanford.edu/

Sutton, R. S. and Barto, A. G. (2018). *Reinforcement Learning: An Introduction* (2nd Ed.). MIT Press.

Tolmeijer, S., Kneer, M., Sarasua, C., Christen, M., and Bernstein, A. (2021). Implementations in machine ethics: A survey. *ACM Computing Surveys, 53(6)*: Article 132. https://doi.org/10.1145/3419633

Thomason, R. (2008). Logic and artificial intelligence. *The Stanford Encyclopedia of Philosophy.* https://plato.stanford.edu/

Thomson, J. J. (1976). Killing, letting die, and the trolley problem. *Monist: An International Quarterly Journal of General Philosophical Inquiry, 59*: 204–217.

Torrance, S. (2012). Artificial agents and the expanding ethical circle. *AI & Society, 28*: 399–414. https://doi.org/10.1007/s00146-012-0422-2

Wolf, M. J., Miller, K. W., and Grodzinsky, F. S. (2017). Why we should have seen that coming: Comments on Microsoft's Tay "experiment", and wider implications. *The ORBIT Journal, 1(2)*: 1–12. https://doi.org/10.29297/orbit.v1i2.49

Wu, Y.-H. and Lin, S.-D (2017). A low-cost ethics shaping approach for designing reinforcement learning agents. In *Proceedings of the Thirty-Second AAAI Conference on Artificial Intelligence, AAAI-18* (pp. 1687–1694).

Part IV
Policy, Regulation, Governance: AI and Harm Prevention

8

Artificial Intelligence and Human Rights: Corporate Responsibility Under International Human Rights Law

Lottie Lane ⓘ

1 Introduction

Private businesses are key developers of artificial intelligence (AI). In their capacity as creators of AI systems, businesses play a crucial role in ensuring that the systems are human-centric, and in particular that they respect human rights. By now, several AI guidelines and principles explicitly address the role of businesses developing AI (e.g. Access Now and Amnesty International 2018; BSR 2018), but a lack of clarity concerning the position of AI businesses under international human rights law remains. When the United Nations human rights system was developed shortly after the second world war, the focus was placed on protecting individuals from States rather than from private businesses

---

L. Lane (✉)
Department of Transboundary Legal Studies, Faculty of Law,
University of Groningen, Groningen, The Netherlands
e-mail: c.l.lane@rug.nl

© The Author(s), under exclusive license to Springer Nature
Switzerland AG 2023
A. Završnik and K. Simončič (eds.), *Artificial Intelligence, Social Harms and Human Rights*, Critical Criminological Perspectives,
https://doi.org/10.1007/978-3-031-19149-7_8

183

184   L. Lane

and the framework's drafters did not envisage the incredible developments in technological developments that would occur in the decades that followed. Progress towards legal certainty for businesses generally has undoubtedly been made with the adoption of (non-legally binding) international standards to protect human rights from private businesses, however, significant questions regarding the responsibilities of businesses developing AI remain: What are these responsibilities under international human rights law and what challenges exist to achieving compliance with these standards?

This chapter takes a normative approach to answering these questions, aiming to provide readers with backgrounds in computer science and AI ethics with an overview of the role of AI businesses in building human-centric AI from a human rights perspective. The chapter first briefly explains the negative impacts that AI developed by private businesses can have on human rights (Part 2). Part 3 lays down the general legal framework regarding businesses' responsibilities under international human rights law, including under the United Nations Guiding Principles on Business and Human Rights (UN Human Rights Council 2011). This section also addresses key developments in business and human rights such as the draft binding treaty on business and human rights and the proposal for European Union legislation on mandatory human rights due diligence (HRDD) for businesses. To identify more specific standards of behaviour expected from businesses in this context as well as some key challenges to ensuring human rights protection, the framework is applied to the development of AI in Part 4. Insight is gained from human rights and AI governance initiatives (e.g. Access Now and Amnesty International 2018) which specifically address AI businesses' conduct. Conclusions are drawn in Part 5.

2   Negative Impact of AI on Human Rights

Despite the potential for AI to positively contribute to the realisation of human rights, we have already seen countless situations in which human rights have been put at risk, if not actually violated by the use of AI in many contexts. As awareness of the risks that AI poses to human rights increases, more and more situations of potential harm are being exposed, leading to increased recognition of the need for a human rights-based approach to AI (e.g. McGregor et al. 2019).

The typical example is privacy and data protection, whether regarding the collection, storage and use of personal data used in AI or the use of facial recognition for police surveillance (e.g. United Kingdom Court of Appeal 2020). However, AI poses risks to a much broader range of human rights. Over the last few years we have witnessed numerous instances of discrimination caused by reliance on automated decision-making (e.g. Dastin 2018), interference with access to social security through the digital welfare state (e.g. Casey 2019; Human Rights Law Centre 2019; cited in UN General Assembly 2019), and potentially drastic implications in the criminal justice sector and the right to a fair trial (e.g. Ulenaers 2020), to name a few.

Beyond these risks to specific rights, AI also poses significant challenges to accountability for human rights abuse caused by reliance on the technology.[1] This partly comes down to the lack of the related concept of transparency that pervades AI (Felzmann et al. 2020; Edwards and Veale 2017). Many algorithms (and machine learning algorithms in particular)[2] are very complex, which can result in infamous "black box" AI systems, where not even the engineer who created the system is able to say how exactly it came to a certain conclusion (Informatics Europe and EUACM 2018, 9; Kroll et al. 2017; Council of Europe 2017, 38). Such opacity can have a significant consequence on victims' right of access to an effective remedy under international human rights law (UN General Assembly 1966) due to the inability to adequately challenge the system's results. Put simply: if we do not know how a result/decision has been

---

[1] In business and human rights literature, "accountability" is typically seen as comprising the two elements of: (1) answerability; and (2) enforcement. Answerability requires relevant actors to justify and explain their conduct, whereas enforcement deals primarily with the sanctioning of those actors for non-compliance with applicable standards and access to effective remedy for any victims harmed by non-compliance (see Bernaz 2021).

[2] Machine learning algorithms are defined as algorithms "'trained' by exposing them to a large number of examples and rewarding them for drawing appropriate distinctions and making correct decisions" (Informatics Europe and EUACM 2018).

186   L. Lane

reached and even whether a result or decision was reached using AI, it is extremely difficult to effectively challenge such a result (Lane 2022a).[3]

3 General Legal Framework on Business and Human Rights

Businesses have a central role in the development of AI, even when it is ultimately used in the public sector. However, despite the indisputable links between AI, businesses and human rights, the international legal framework lags somewhat behind. Not only in relation to AI itself, which is not explicitly addressed by any international human rights law treaty or other primary sources of international law, but also, and more generally, in relation to businesses that have a negative impact on human rights. In light of the exponential growth and use of AI, it is important to fully understand who is responsible for what in relation to human rights. Progress is being made in delineating States' human rights obligations vis-a-vis AI (e.g. UN Committee on Economic, Social and Cultural Rights (CteeESCR) 2021; UN Committee on the Rights of the Child 2021; Lane 2022b), but the rather underdeveloped nature of "business and human rights" under international law leaves several uncertainties as to the responsibilities of businesses. Clarity is not only important for businesses themselves, but for all AI actors, including individuals and groups negatively affected by AI—the present uncertainties have a considerable impact on ensuring accountability and access to remedies; if we do not know for what businesses are responsible, how can we hold them accountable and ensure that victims get the redress they deserve? To shed light on this, the following paragraphs briefly consider the position of businesses under international human rights law (Sect. 3.1) before zooming in on corporate responsibility under international human rights law (Sect. 3.2).

---

[3] This issue was raised in the "SyRI" case (District Court of The Hague 2020), although in the context of the right to privacy.

3.1 Position of Businesses Under International Human Rights Law

As private entities, businesses do not have any direct obligations under international human rights law. Only States have direct obligations, which are considered to be "vertical" (owed by the State to individuals) rather than "horizontal" (owed by private actors to individuals) (Lane 2018, 15). Consequently, it is not currently possible to bring a case directly against businesses on the basis of human rights at the international level.

Nonetheless, businesses are not entitled to a "free pass" vis-a-vis human rights. One of the States' human rights obligations is to protect individuals' human rights from the harmful activities of third parties, including businesses (Lane 2018, 29–34). This requires States to adopt national laws, policies and other measures to prevent companies from interfering with the enjoyment of human rights. The obligation to protect human rights has been applied by international and regional human rights adjudicatory bodies to result in the "indirect horizontal effect" of human rights (Lane 2018), whereby States are required to take certain measures to protect individuals' rights from non-State actors. This has particularly been given content through States' duty of due diligence as well as obligations to regulate businesses (UN CteeESCR 2017). While this goes some way towards protecting individuals from businesses, the way in which these obligations are applied does not provide clarity of what human rights standards, if any, are directly applicable to businesses—understandably given the State-centric legal framework, human rights adjudicatory bodies tend to shy away from clarifying what concrete standards businesses themselves should follow vis-à-vis human rights and focus only the conduct of States (Lane 2018). Much more light is shed on the standards applicable to businesses by non-binding instruments addressing corporate human rights responsibility.[4]

---

[4] The term "responsibilties" rather than "obligations" is used in relation to businesses throughout this chapter. This is to distinguish the binding nature of the standards applicable to States under primary sources of international law from the non-binding nature of standards applicable to businesses under "soft-law" instruments.

3.2 Corporate Human Rights Responsibility

Due to the limitations of the international legal framework and the significant negative impact that businesses can have on the enjoyment of human rights, soft-law and non-binding initiatives have been developed by many different actors to try to hold businesses responsible for the harm they cause to human rights, and to try to sculpt out their responsibilities under international law.

Initially, voluntary business and human rights initiatives that considered issues such as sustainability and corporate social responsibility more broadly gained more support than initiatives that aimed to subject businesses to direct responsibilities or obligations.[5] As a case in point was the UN Draft Norms on the Responsibilities of Transnational Corporations and other Business Enterprises with regard to Human Rights (UN SubCommission on the Promotion and Protection of Human Rights 2003), which were heavily opposed for trying to place "State-like obligations" on businesses (Jägers 2011). However, in 2011, the United Nations Guiding Principles on Business and Human Rights (UNGPs— UN Human Rights Council 2011) were adopted. The UNGPs were drafted by former UN Special Representative of the Secretary-General on human rights and transnational corporations and other business enterprises, the late John Ruggie, after consultation with a wide range of stakeholders (UN Human Rights Council 2011, para. 12). Despite various valid criticisms of the UNGPs (e.g. López 2013; Hamm 2021), by now they are typically considered to be the most well-known and widely supported standards on business and human rights at the international level. Since being unanimously endorsed by the UN Human

---

[5] E.g. the UN Global Compact initiative launched in 2000, which is a sustainability initiative comprising labour, environment and anti-corruption as well as human rights principles (UN Global Compact 2021). Another example is the International Organization for Standardization's "ISO 26000" (2010), which provides guidance on corporate social responsibility, including aspects of human rights. The Organisation for Economic Cooperation and Development (OECD) Guidelines for Multinational Enterprises. First adopted in 1976 to address responsible business conduct more broadly, a chapter on human rights was included in the Guidelines in 2011 (OECD 2011) and guidance on HRDD for businesses was adopted in 2018 (OECD 2017). The Guidelines are unique in that they are the only international initiative concerning business and human rights that has an enforcement mechanism (Lane et al. 2021).

Rights Council in 2011, the non-binding UNGPs have been followed by a large number of businesses and States, have provided inspiration for national legislation on HRDD (Business and Human Rights Resource Centre 2021a) and draft EU legislation on HRDD (European Parliament 2021) and have paved the way for the drafting of a binding international treaty on business and human rights (Open-Ended Intergovernmental Working Group on Transnational Corporations and other Business Enterprises with respect to Human Rights 2020).[6] They have also been the subject of a huge amount of scholarly debate (Rasche and Waddock 2021) and have been used as applicable standards in corporate human rights benchmarking schemes (World Benchmarking Alliance 2021; Ranking Digital Rights 2020). Arguably, the UNGPs lay down the core definition of corporate human rights responsibility, and will therefore form the focus of the next section of this chapter.

3.2.1 Corporate Responsibility to Respect Human Rights

Turning to the content of the UNGPs, the Principles comprise three inter-related pillars, each containing various guidelines addressed to businesses or States. Pillar 1 concerns the State's duty to protect human rights, which "lies at the very core of the International human rights regime" (as suggested in Sect. 3.1). The UNGPs reiterate that the duty to protect human rights requires the adoption of policies, the regulation of businesses and adjudication of cases concerning business and human rights (Principles 1–10). Pillar 2 lays down the corporate responsibility to respect human rights, which requires businesses to "avoid infringing on the rights of others and to address adverse impacts with which they are involved" (Principles 11–24). This will be explained in more detail below. Pillar 3 contains principles regarding access to an effective remedy

---

[6] The third revised draft of the treaty, which was published in August 2021 by the Open-Ended Intergovernmental Working Group on Transnational Corporations and other Business Enterprises with respect to Human Rights (2020) established for the purpose in 2014, stays within the current legal framework of binding obligations for States. The draft is ultimately aimed at protecting individuals' human rights from businesses and would go some way towards this if adopted, businesses are not given enforceable human rights obligations at the international level through the treaty.

for victims of corporate human rights abuse. Principles 25–31 require the existence of grievance mechanisms for individuals to complain about human rights abuse and to be provided with a remedy where appropriate. This includes non-judicial grievance mechanisms, such as businesses' own mechanisms for responding to adverse human rights impacts they cause or to which they contribute (Principle 29).

Overall, the UNGPs follow a "know and show" approach, requiring businesses to know internally and show externally how they are addressing risks to people (Commentary to Principle 15). The responsibility applies throughout a business' own operations and its business relationships throughout its value chain and must be embedded throughout all business functions. In other words, respect for human rights has to become "part of the DNA of doing business" (Office of the United Nations High Commissioner for Human Rights and Carr Centre for Human Rights Policy 2020). Additionally, even if a business were to "do good" elsewhere, for example through philanthropy or corporate social responsibility or sustainability schemes, it cannot use this to offset its negative impacts on human rights (Commentary to Principle 11).

The UNGPs apply to *all* business enterprises, with the consequence that the responsibilities are general enough to apply to all sectors. Therefore, what precisely the UNGPs mean for different business contexts, e.g. AI, has to be further delineated (see Sect. 4). However, the UNGPs do provide important guidance to businesses as to what these more general responsibilities are, dividing corporate respect for human rights into three core components (Principle 15): (1) adoption of a policy commitment to respect human rights (Principle 16); (2) adoption of HRDD processes to identify, prevent, mitigate and account for how the business addresses its human rights impacts (Principles 17–21); and (3) adoption of processes to enable the remediation of any adverse impacts the business cases or to which it contributes (Principle 22).

First, a policy commitment is typically quite a general statement confirming the business' commitment to human rights but must be approved at the most senior level of the business, informed by relevant expertise, be publicly available and sufficiently communicated, and, crucially, be "reflected in operational policies and procedures necessary to embed it throughout the business enterprise" (Principle 16). In this vein, as well as communicating the commitment to employees, the business should, for example, provide training for relevant employees (Commentary to Principle 16). In other words, the commitment must be genuine and implemented in practice, rather than a lip-service exercise.

Second, while all three components of the responsibility to respect human rights should be fulfilled by businesses, due diligence really lies at its heart. HRDD is the component that features most often in national legislation on business and human rights, it is the focus of the future EU legislation on business and human rights, and it has also been included in the current draft of the international treaty on business and human rights (Open-Ended Intergovernmental Working Group on Transnational Corporations and other Business Enterprises with respect to Human Rights 2021, Articles 6(2), (3) and (4)). The United Nations Office of the High Commissioner for Human Rights' interpretive guide to the UNGPs (2012, 6) defines HRDD as an "ongoing management process that a reasonable and prudent enterprise needs to undertake, in the light of its circumstances (including sector, operating context, size and similar factors) to meet its responsibility to respect human rights". Due diligence is a rather open-ended concept and its precise requirements and complexity depend on "the size of the business enterprise, the risk of severe human rights impacts, and the nature and context of its operations" (United Nations Office of the High Commissioner for Human Rights 2012; UNGPs, Principle 17). Accordingly, there is no one-size-fits-all solution, so guidance on how to implement it needs to be provided to businesses in different contexts and sectors. Having said that, the UNGPs do provide a general outline applicable to all businesses, including those developing AI. This outline shows businesses how to proactively manage potential and actual adverse human rights impacts with which they are involved. There are four key steps to be conducted on an ongoing basis: (1) Identifying and assessing actual or potential adverse human rights impacts with which they may be involved either through their own activities or as a result of their business relationships (Principle 18); (2) Integrating the findings from impact assessments across relevant internal functions and processes and take appropriate action according to their involvement in the adverse impact and the extent of their leverage in addressing the adverse impact (Principle 19);

(3) Tracking the effectiveness of their response, with the aim of driving continuous improvement (Principle 20); and (4) Communicating how they address their human rights impacts, particularly when concerns are raised by or on behalf of affected stakeholders (Principle 21).

Finally, processes to enable the remediation of adverse impacts may relate, for example, to operational grievance mechanisms allowing businesses to resolve complaints by people who consider themselves to have suffered due to their operations. This may be done by a business on its own or in cooperation with others. When a business has been alleged to have committed a crime, for example, the business will likely need to cooperate with judicial grievance mechanisms (Commentary to Principle 22).

4   AI, Business and Human Rights

The question now arises: What does this mean for AI businesses? Several aspects of HRDD require further elaboration for businesses developing AI, particularly bearing in mind the idiosyncrasies of AI and the challenges that come with them. International human rights law does not yet give us the answer. Certain initiatives dealing with the governance of AI, however, do contribute to giving content to AI businesses' responsibility to respect human rights.

In the following paragraphs, two international initiatives that explicitly address this question are discussed with a view to identifying how AI businesses can respect human rights. The first is a declaration adopted by Access Now and Amnesty International (2018), containing principles for both States and businesses with regard to machine learning systems, equality and discrimination. The second initiative is a report by the non-profit organisation Business for Social Responsibility (BSR 2018), which applies to AI more generally. Neither initiative is legally binding. However, they do provide guidance that is helpful to States (as users of AI but also as regulators of AI businesses) and other law and policymakers, as well as businesses developing AI. Specific guidance on how AI businesses should implement HRDD, as the heart of corporate respect

8 Artificial Intelligence and Human Rights: Corporate ... 193

for human rights, forms the basis of Sect. 4.1, while several key challenges to achieving corporate respect for human rights in relation to AI are introduced in Sect. 4.2.

4.1 AI and Human Rights Due Diligence

There is no one way of conducting HRDD for AI systems—there are many options open to AI businesses regarding the scope and logistics of the processes involved. For instance, businesses may conduct these processes themselves, but they may also be conducted by third parties. The scope of HRDD (and within that, human rights impact assessments—HRIA) that businesses undertake can also vary widely, with some pertaining to particular products, services or activities, whereas others are more general, company-wide processes (Yeung 2019). Additionally, businesses may have considerable freedom to decide to conduct a HRIA and choose the parameters of the assessment themselves, but are sometimes legally required to have HRIAs conducted, either by themselves or an independent third party (Mantelero 2018, 754; Yeung 2019, 71).

Whichever option applies to an AI business, the initiative by Access Now and Amnesty International (2018) provides (non-exhaustive) standards that can be followed during HRDD processes. The initiative is entitled the "Toronto Declaration: Protecting the right to equality and non-discrimination in machine learning systems". Although it is limited to non-discrimination and equality, there are some more general points included—particularly concerning HRDD—that are applicable to a broader range of human rights and AI systems that do not involve machine learning. After a number of general paragraphs on using the framework of international human rights law to tackle the harmful effects of AI, the Declaration is structured similarly to the three pillars of the UNGPs. It first details the human rights obligations of States using machine learning systems before addressing corporate responsibility and, finally, the right to an effective remedy.

The Declaration's paragraphs on corporate responsibility focus squarely on HRDD. For the most part, these paragraphs reiterate and apply to machine learning the four elements of HRDD under the UNGPs. Accordingly, the Declaration flags several ways to help *identify risks*, which should include those "commonly associated with machine learning systems", relating to the range of data used to train such systems and the inherent bias that may be present in such data, etc. (Access Now and Amnesty International 2018, paragraph 45). Suggested methods are regular HRIA throughout a system's life cycle, as well as "live, regular tests and audits", independent reviews and measures to mitigate identified risks, among others (paragraph 31). Such measures could involve the meaningful inclusion of potentially affected groups in the design, testing and review phases of a system (paragraph 31(b)).

The Declaration further elaborates how businesses developing machine learning systems can *prevent risks* to human rights (paragraph 47). This involves having diverse machine learning development teams to try to better "identif[y] bias by design" (paragraph 47(b) and having high-risk systems audited by independent third parties (paragraph 47(c)). Crucially, the Declaration clearly states that machine learning systems with risks that are "too high or impossible to mitigate" should not be deployed (paragraph 48).

In terms of *tracking the effectiveness of their responses*, the Declaration emphasises the need for quality and assurance checks and auditing to be conducted through the whole life cycle of a machine learning system on an ongoing basis (paragraph 49). The importance of this for reducing the risks of feedback loops that can be caused by AI is also noted here (paragraph 49).[7]

Finally, the Declaration details businesses' responsibility to be transparent, *communicating* their efforts to respect human rights and linking this to accountability for individuals or groups affected by a machine learning businesses' operations (paragraph 50). This involves transparency of the HRDD processes adopted to identify risks, the measures taken to address those risks and informing affected individuals as to how they can complain about interference with their human rights caused by a machine learning system (paragraph 51). The Declaration also calls

---

[7] In this context, "feedback loops" refers to the reinforcement or even exacerbation of existing discrimination reflected in data used in machine learning systems in particular. For discussion see Liu (2020).

8 Artificial Intelligence and Human Rights: Corporate ... 195

for transparency of "technical specifications and details of the machine learning and its functions, including samples of training data and details of the source of data" (paragraph 51(b)). Notably absent from the Declaration, however, is any mention of safeguards that should be in place in relation to the sharing of this information (for example, to prevent violations of privacy, Lane 2022b).[8] Throughout the Declaration, attention is drawn to the need to have independent review and assessment of AI systems in some situations, although exactly when this is necessary is not always made clear (Lane 2022a, see e.g. paragraph 31(b)). The crux of the Declaration, that businesses should not deploy machine learning systems that pose risks to human rights that are "too high or impossible to mitigate" (paragraph 48), is clear. If this is identified during a business' HRDD processes, it should either make adjustments to mitigate the risks, or put an end to the project (Lane 2022a).

The BSR report takes a slightly different approach—although it follows the foundational principles set out in the UNGPs, it suggests five elements to HRDD that build on the Principles and directly addresses the idiosyncrasies of AI as a developing technology, pinpointing key concerns for AI businesses (BSR 2018, 5): (1) Future testing HRDD; (2) Addressing impacts across the product and service value chain; (3) Rights-based approaches to AI opportunities; (4) Human rights by design and (5) Business leadership in collective action and public policy.

For reasons of space, a full discussion of the five elements is not possible here, but several noteworthy points that also highlight some of the challenges to achieving HRDD in relation to AI can be addressed. The first relates to the need to "future-proof" HRDD. Here, the report notes that because of the rapid and unpredictable development of AI technologies, it is necessary to develop "due diligence methods capable of informing human rights identification and mitigation strategies that are resilient to a range of different plausible scenarios and that consider potential cascading impacts" (BSR 2018, 7). BSR argues that although

---

[8] For a discussion of risks to privacy posed by making certain algorithmic information transparent, see Felzmann et al. (2020).

196   L. Lane

the criteria typically used to identify which human rights issues to prioritise in HRDD[9] (as allowed by the UNGPs, Commentary to Principle 17; Principle 24) provide information on what negative impacts are possible in theory, they do not "provide enough insight into the certain and multiple different versions of the future that might unfold". BSR proposes a "future-testing methodology based on a structured approach to test human rights mitigation strategies against a range of high-level future scenarios", with the aims of: (1) determining how an impact's diversity may change over time and (2) testing whether the mitigation strategy proposed can stand up against the potential different futures (BSR 2018, 7–8). Addressing these two core points could help businesses to develop effective HRDD tools and measures to prevent human rights harm.

The second point of note is the need to learn from HRDD in other sectors. BSR suggests that AI businesses look to how businesses in other sectors conduct human rights impact assessments (BSR 2018, 9) and consider steps that businesses in other sectors have taken to "demystify the complexity of their supply chains" (BSR 2018, 10). This is crucial in the relatively young AI sector, where understanding of supply chains and potential human rights issues (and of the sector itself) is particularly low (BSR 2018, 10). Not only could this provide important information to the general public, but it can help to highlight to regulators, law- and policy-makers, investors, etc., what issues to focus on in order to best encourage human rights-friendly AI (BSR 2018, 10).

The report also suggests learning from other tools within the AI sector, namely "privacy by design", which many businesses have already adopted. BSR claims that this could be used to "mainstream human rights in the development of AI" and embed the much broader "human rights by design" (BSR 2018, 13). While this is still in its infancy, some examples of AI businesses working towards such an approach already exist,[10] and academic literature suggesting ways to design for human

---

[9] These include the scope, remediability and likelihood (i.e. the severity) of a negative impact as well as the attribution of the impact to the business and the business' leverage over entities in its business relationships to stop them from causing harm (BSR 2018, 7–8).

[10] Research on this is being undertaken by IBM and others, for example (see Gebru et al. 2020; BSR 2018, 14).

rights in AI and to conduct human HRIAs for AI is increasing (e.g. Aizenberg and van den Hoven 2020; Mantelero and Esposito 2021).

Ultimately, the BSR report makes it very clear that HRDD should involve a wide range of employees within an AI business (including, e.g. those in legal, sales and marketing departments as well as machine learning engineers) who need to be adequately informed and trained, the entire supply chain (and to use leverage in this respect),[11] and all stages of AI systems' life cycle. Businesses are also urged to collaborate with other (business and policy) actors to help fill governance gaps and inform new policies (BSR 2018, 16).

Taken together, the guidance in the initiatives provides a much more solid basis for AI businesses to begin developing HRDD processes. However, as the BSR report acknowledges, there is still much to be learned concerning how exactly HRDD can be conducted in this context. AI businesses also face specific challenges in conducting HRDD and respecting human rights more generally.

4.2 Challenges to Achieving Corporate Respect for Human Rights with Respect to AI

The shortcomings of the legal framework addressed in Sect. 3 present challenges for businesses wishing to develop human rights-compliant AI. In addition to these (and the challenges regarding transparency mentioned above), there are several key challenges related to the nature and idiosyncrasies of AI and its uses that pose obstacles to AI businesses achieving respect for human rights in practice. This section does not contain an exhaustive discussion of such obstacles, however it introduces several salient issues concerning human rights due diligence.[12]

One such challenge has been partially addressed above—the unpredictability of many AI systems. Despite the guidance provided by BSR,

---

[11] One way of achieving this could be through contractual clauses with suppliers/customers/business partners.

[12] Additional challenges pertain, for example, to the difficulties in ensuring accountability and the right to an effective remedy in light of the sheer number of rights-holders that may be affected by an AI system and the potentially "billions of decisions" with regard to which claims of human rights harm may be lodged (BSR 2018, 5).

198   **L. Lane**

even with careful planning and consideration it may not actually be possible to predict whether a certain AI system would have a negative impact on human rights and if so, what precisely that impact would be. This makes it crucial that a system be subject to extensive testing before it is passed on to the entity planning to deploy it, with continuous impact assessments throughout all stages of the process. An added element of complexity here is the role of humans external to the AI's development that may affect the impact of a system. In semi-automated decision-making, for instance (e.g. the use of AI systems in judicial decision-making and by employers filtering applications for job vacancies) the added variable of a "human-in-the-loop", the attitude, behaviour and potential bias of whom are not predictable by the algorithm, makes it even harder for the business developing the system to envisage the actual impact of their creation.[13]

Some of the guidance provided by the UNGPs and BSR can be helpful in this respect, particularly concerning the use of leverage. However, it would also help to clearly delineate the responsibility of the developers of the system vs. the deployers of the system—where one ends and the other begins needs to be clearly agreed upon. Yeung (2019, 55–62) suggests several ways in which responsibility could be delineated, drawing on existing approaches to legal responsibility from various legal regimes, including "risk/negligence-based models" and "strict responsibility". However, this presents challenges in its own right, particularly when human–AI interactions in the use of AI and the complex value chains (and the "many hands") are added to the equation (Yeung 2019, 62–67). Part of this issue is distinguishing *contributing to* human rights harm caused by AI from being *directly linked to* it. The two are explicitly distinguished in the UNGPs (Principle 17(a)) and although the distinction can be unclear under any circumstances, it is especially complicated in the face of AI's unpredictability (Microsoft 2020). Whether a result of the fast pace of developments or the opaqueness or complexity of algorithms, AI's unpredictability poses challenges to identifying from where the harm stems. As Microsoft (2020) points out, this could be from the

---

[13] There are additional concerns of humans-in-the-loop becoming "complacent, over-reliant or unduly diffident" when dealing with systems that are supposedly accurate and objective, which may not always be the case (Zerilli et al. 2019).

algorithm itself, the data used to train it, or the way in which the AI is used. This has a consequence for human rights accountability—if it is not possible to pinpoint what caused the harm, it makes it more complex to determine who was responsible for the harm, and to what degree.

5 Conclusion

This chapter has provided an overview of corporate responsibility for human rights in the context of AI. The potential for AI to negatively impact human rights is evident, but the international human rights law framework does not (yet) set down clear standards for businesses developing AI, and it remains to be seen exactly what impact ongoing legally binding initiatives at the international and EU level will have on these businesses. The clearest standards available under international law are found in the non-binding UNGPs, which elaborate the corporate responsibility to respect human rights. The UNGPs are extremely helpful in their delineation of three core elements of the responsibility (a policy commitment, HRDD and processes for the remediation of human rights harm), but more specific guidance is sorely needed for AI businesses aiming to create human rights-compliant systems.

Such guidance is, to an extent, provided in initiatives by non-governmental and non-profit organisations that explicitly take a human rights-based approach. The Toronto Declaration follows the UNGPs and includes several guidelines for businesses to follow when conducting HRDD. A large focus of the Declaration is the transparency of both AI systems and HRDD processes, which was identified in Sect. 2 as playing a major role in the risks that AI poses to human rights. A more extensive discussion of HRDD and AI is provided in the report published by BSR. BSR identifies five key elements to HRDD building on those in the UNGPs and addressing in a more direct manner suggestions for and the challenges faced by businesses trying to respect human rights in practice. This includes the need to future-proof AI HRDD processes in light of the unpredictability of AI, learning from other sectors in providing transparency of supply chains, the use of leverage and the need to adopt a "human-rights-by-design" approach to AI. Other obstacles are closely linked to human rights accountability and the right to an effective remedy, which are themselves challenged by the huge number of rights-holders that can be affected by AI systems.

The guidance provided in the initiatives is undoubtedly helpful for businesses, but now that the principles underpinning HRDD have been identified, further action needs to be taken to determine how exactly businesses can successfully embed HRDD into their operations. There is no one-size-fits-all answer to this, as much will depend on the size of an AI business, the complexity of its supply chain and of course the type of AI systems it develops. Collaboration between practitioners, law- and policy-makers and academics is crucial here to clarify AI businesses' responsibilities and to translate corporate respect for human rights vis-a-vis AI into workable processes in practice. With more and more countries adopting mandatory HRDD legislation and in light of legal developments at the international and EU level, this should be done sooner rather than later.

References

Access Now and Amnesty International. 2018. "The Toronto Declaration: Protecting the right to equality and non-discrimination in machine learning systems". https://www.accessnow.org/cms/assets/uploads/2018/08/The-Toronto-Declaration_ENG_08-2018.pdf.

Aizenberg, Evgeni and Jeroen van den Hoven. 2020. "Designing for human rights in AI". *Big Data & Society*, 7(2). https://doi.org/10.1177/205395172 0949566

Bernaz, Nadia. 2021. "Conceptualizing corporate accountability in international law: Models for a business and human rights treaty". *Human Rights Review* 22: 45–64. https://doi.org/10.1007/s12142-020-00606-w.

Business and Human Rights Resource Centre. 2021a. "National & regional movements for mandatory human rights & environmental due diligence in Europe". Last updated June 25, 2021. https://www.business-humanrights.org/en/latest-news/national-regional-movements-for-mandatory-human-rig hts-environmental-due-diligence-in-europe/.

Business and Human Rights Resource Centre. 2021b. "European Parliament adopts key report with recommendations to EU Commission on mandatory due diligence & corporate accountability". Accessed August 5, 2021. https://www.business-humanrights.org/en/latest-news/european-parliament-committee-on-legal-affairs-publishes-report-with-recommendations-to-eu-commission-on-mandatory-due-diligence/.

Business for Social Responsibility. 2018. "Artificial intelligence: A rights-based blueprint for business. Paper 3: Implementing human rights due diligence". https://www.bsr.org/reports/BSR-Artificial-Intelligence-A-Rights-Based-Blueprint-for-Business-Paper-03.pdf.

Casey, Simone. 2019. "The targeted compliance framework: Implications for job seekers". *National Social Security Rights Network*, July 25, 2019.

Council of Europe. 2017. Study on the human rights dimensions of aureate data processing techniques (in particular algorithms) and possible regulatory implications. MSI-NET(2016)06 rev3.

Dastin, Jeffrey. 2018. "Amazon scraps secret AI recruiting tool that showed bias against women". *Reuters*, October 11, 2018. https://www.reuters.com/article/us-amazon-com-jobs-automation-insight-idUSKCN1MK08G.

District Court of The Hague, The Netherlands. 2020. ECLI:NL:RBDHA:2020:1878.

Edwards, Lilian, and Michael Veale. 2017. "Slave to the algorithm? Why a 'right to an explanation' is probably not the remedy you are looking for". *Duke Technology and Law Review* 16: 18–84.

European Parliament. 2021. "Resolution of 10 March 2021 with recommendations to the Commission on corporate due diligence and corporate accountability". 2020/2129(INL)).

Felzmann, Heike, Eduard Fosch-Villaronga, Christoph Lutz, and Aurelia Tamò-Larrieux. 2020. "Towards transparency by design for artificial intelligence". *Science and Engineering Ethics* 26: 3333–3361 https://doi.org/10.1007/s11948-020-00276-4.

Gebru, Timnit, Jamie Morgenstern, Briana Vecchione, Jennifer Wortman Vaughan, Hanna Wallach, Hal Daumé III, and Kate Crawford. 2020. "Datasheets for datasets". University of Cornell Working Paper. Accessed August 5, 2021. https://arxiv.org/abs/1803.09010.

Hamm, Brigitte. 2021. "The struggle for legitimacy in business and human rights regulation—A consideration of the processes leading to the un guiding principles and an international treaty". *Human Rights Review*. https://doi.org/10.1007/s12142-020-00612-y.

Human Rights Law Centre. 2019. "Preventing technology from entrenching inequality: Submission to the United Nations Special Rapporteur on extreme poverty and human rights". May 20, 2019. https://www.ohchr.org/Documents/Issues/Poverty/DigitalTechnology/HumanRightsLawCentre.pdf.

Informatics Europe and EUACM. 2018. "When computers decide: European recommendations on machine-learned automated decision making". https://www.acm.org/binaries/content/assets/public-policy/ie-euacm-adm-report-2018.pdf.

International Organization for Standardization. 2010. "ISO 26000 social responsibility". Accessed July 28, 2021. https://www.iso.org/iso-26000-social-responsibility.html.

Jägers, Nicola. 2011. "UN Guiding Principles on Business and Human Rights: Making headway towards real corporate accountability?" *Netherlands Quarterly of Human Rights* 29 (2): 159–163. https://doi.org/10.1177/016934411102900201.

Kroll, Joshua A., Joanna Huey, Solon Barocas, Edward W. Felten, Joel R. Reidenberg, David G. Robinson, and Harlan Yu. 2017. "Accountable algorithms". *University of Pennsylvania Law Review* 165: 633–705. https://www.jstor.org/stable/26600576.

Lane, Lottie. 2018. "The horizontal effect of international human rights law in practice: A comparative analysis of the general comments and jurisprudence of selected United Nations human rights treaty monitoring bodies". *European Journal of Comparative Law and Governance* 5: 5–88. https://doi.org/10.1163/22134514-00501001.

Lane, Lottie. 2022a. "Clarifying human rights standards through artificial intelligence initiatives". *International and Comparative Law Quarterly 71(4): 915-944.* https://doi.org/10.1017/S0020589322000380

Lane, Lottie. 2022b forthcoming. "Artificial intelligence and human rights: Corporate responsibility in AI governance initiatives". Nordic Journal of Human Rights.

Lane, Lottie, Stephanie Triefus, and Chiara Macchi. 2021. "Vulnerability and business and human rights". *Human Rights Here*, October 1, 2021. https://www.humanrightshere.com/post/vulnerability-and-business-and-human-rights.

Liu, T. Lydia. 2020. "When bias begets bias: A source of negative feedback loops in AI systems". *Microsoft Research Blog*, January 21, 2020. https://www.microsoft.com/en-us/research/blog/when-bias-begets-bias-a-source-of-negative-feedback-loops-in-ai-systems/.

López, Carlos. 2013. "The 'Ruggie process': From legal obligations to corporate social responsibility?" In *Human Rights Obligations of Business: Beyond the Corporate Responsibility to Respect?* edited by Surya Deva and David Bilchitz, 58–77. Cambridge University Press: Cambridge

Mantelero, Alessandro. 2018. "AI and Big Data: A blueprint for a human rights, social and ethical impact assessment". *Computer Law & Security Review* 34: 754–772. https://doi.org/10.1016/j.clsr.2018.05.017.

Mantelero, Alessandro and Maria Samantha Esposito. 2021. "An evidence-based methodology for human rights impact assessment (HRIA) in the development of AI data-intensive systems". *Computer Law & Security Review* 41: 1–35. https://doi.org/10.1016/j.clsr.2021.105561.

McGregor, Lorna, Daragh Murray and Vivian Ng. 2019. "International human rights law as a framework for algorithmic accountability". *International and Comparative Law Quarterly* 68: 309–343. https://doi.org/10.1017/S00205 89319000046.

Microsoft. 2020. "Human rights report: Fiscal year 2020". Accessed August 5, 2021. https://www.microsoft.com/en-us/corporate-responsibility/human-rights.

Office of the United Nations High Commissioner for Human Rights and Carr Centre for Human Rights Policy. 2020. "Addressing human rights risks in technology company business models". February 24, 2020. https://www.ohchr.org/Documents/Issues/Business/B-Tech/ConceptNote_and_Age nda.pdf.

Open-Ended Intergovernmental Working Group on Transnational Corporations and other Business Enterprises with respect to Human Rights. 2020. "Third Revised Draft of a Legally Binding Instrument to Regulate, in International Human Rights Law, the Activities of Transnational Corporations and other Business Enterprises". August 17, 2021. https://www.ohchr.org/en/hrbodies/hrc/wgtranscorp/pages/igwgontnc.aspx.

Organisation for Economic Cooperation and Development Guidelines for Multinational Enterprises. 2011. "OECD guidelines for multinational enterprises: 2011 edition". https://www.oecd.org/daf/inv/mne/48004323. pdf.

Organisation for Economic Cooperation and Development Guidelines for Multinational Enterprises. 2017. "OECD due diligence guidance for responsible business conduct". http://mneguidelines.oecd.org/due-diligence-guidance-for-responsible-business-conduct.htm.

Ranking Digital Rights. 2020. "2020 indicators". Accessed July 29, 2021. https://rankingdigitalrights.org/2020-indicators/#G.

Rasche, Andreas and Sandra Waddock. 2021. "The UN Guiding Principles on Business and Human Rights: Implications for corporate social responsibility research". *Business and Human Rights Journal*: 1–14. https://doi.org/10.1017/bhj.2021.2.

Ulenaers, Jasper. 2020. "The impact of artificial intelligence on the right to a fair trial: Towards a robot judge?" *Asian Journal of Law and Economics* 11 (2): 1–38.

United Kingdom Court of Appeal, R (on the application of Edward Bridges) v The Chief Constable of South Wales Police EWCA Civ 1058.

United Nations Committee on Economic, Social and Cultural Rights. 2017. "General comment no. 24 on state obligations under the International Covenant on Economic, Social and Cultural Rights in the context of business activities". E/C.12/GC/24.

United Nations Committee on Economic, Social and Cultural Rights. 2021. "General comment no. 25 on science and economic, social and cultural rights (article 15 (1) (b), (2), (3) and (4) of the International Covenant on Economic, Social and Cultural Rights)". E/C.12/GC/25.

United Nations Committee on the Rights of the Child. 2021. "General Comment No. 25 on Children's Rights in Relation to the Digital Environment". CRC/C/GC/25.

United Nations General Assembly. 1966. "International Covenant on Civil and Political Rights". United Nations, Treaty Series, vol. 999, 171

United Nations General Assembly. 2019. "Report of the Special Rapporteur on extreme poverty and human rights". October 11, 2019. A/74/493.

United Nations Global Compact. 2021. "Who we are". Accessed July 28, 2021. https://www.unglobalcompact.org/what-is-gc.

United Nations Sub-Commission on the Promotion and Protection of Human Rights. 2003. "Norms on the Responsibilities of Transnational Corporations and Other Business Enterprises with regard to Human Rights". https://und ocs.org/en/E/CN.4/Sub.2/2003/12/Rev.2.

United Nations Human Rights Council. 2011. "Report of the Special Representative of the Secretary-General on the issue of human rights and transnational corporations and other business enterprises, John Ruggie: Guiding Principles on Business and Human Rights: Implementing the United Nations 'Protect, Respect and Remedy' Framework". A/HRC/17/31.

United Nations Office of the High Commissioner for Human Rights. 2012. "The corporate responsibility to respect human rights: An interpretive guide". Accessed July 29, 2021. https://www.ohchr.org/documents/publicati ons/hr.pub.12.2_en.pdf.

World Benchmarking Alliance. 2021. "Corporate human rights benchmark". Accessed July 29, 2021. https://www.worldbenchmarkingalliance.org/public ation/chrb.

Yeung, Karen. 2019. "Responsibility and AI: A study of the implications of advanced digital technologies (including AI systems) for the concept of responsibility within a human rights framework". Council of Europe Study DGI(2019)05.

Zerilli, John, Alistair Knott, James Maclaurin, and Colin Gavaghan. 2019. "Algorithmic decision-making and the control problem". *Minds and Machines* 29: 555–578.

9

As Above so Below: The Use of International Space Law as an Inspiration for Terrestrial AI Regulation to Maximize Harm Prevention

Iva Ramuš Cvetkovič and Marko Drobnjak

1   Introduction

Artificial intelligence (AI) is deemed to be capable of addressing several scientific and commercial goals, aimed at preventing harm on Earth and in outer space, but due to its unpredictable, changeable, and undefined nature its use opens various ethical, political, and legal issues (Soroka and Kurkova 2019, p. 132). It has been linked to concerns and skepticism, as it often is the case in transition periods, such as the past transition toward information and communication technologies (ICT),

---

I. Ramuš Cvetkovič (✉) · M. Drobnjak
Institute of Criminology at the Faculty of Law, Ljubljana, Slovenia
e-mail: iva.ramus@pf.uni-lj.si

M. Drobnjak
e-mail: marko.drobnjak@pf.uni-lj.si

© The Author(s), under exclusive license to Springer Nature
Switzerland AG 2023
A. Završnik and K. Simončič (eds.), *Artificial Intelligence, Social Harms and Human Rights*, Critical Criminological Perspectives,
https://doi.org/10.1007/978-3-031-19149-7_9

207

which is in numerous perspectives today considered not only beneficial, but invaluable to humanity (Criado and Gil-Garcia 2019). The following subchapters will examine in which areas AI is nowadays being used for the prevention of harm and how these areas are regulated. This will be done by presenting the use of AI in preventing harm on Earth and in outer space, as well as by comparing the regulation of such use in both areas, in order to comparatively evaluate the effectiveness and appropriateness of such use and its regulation and to propose some ways forward, translating certain aspects from space law into general regulatory framework for AI ("as above so below" approach).

The authors are following the established distinction between *narrow* and *strong* AI[1] technology, where *narrow* AI technology marks current AI systems, specifically designed for a certain task or series of tasks, which are not directly translatable to other unrelated activities, and not completely autonomous (in other words: systems, that act *as if* they were intelligent), whereas *strong* AI is marking currently inexistent technology which is, however, planned to be developed in a way allowing it to be completely autonomous and capable of developing into fully independent cognitive system, meeting or even surpassing human-level cognition (*actually* intelligent systems) (Russel and Norvig 2016, p. 1020; Surden 2019). Such distinction is relevant particularly for the assessment of AI regulation, as *narrow* and *strong* AI systems will have to be regulated differently, especially in the field of responsibility and liability for the harm caused by such technologies, as they require and allow different levels of human involvement and scrutiny.

This chapter focuses only on the use of AI for the prevention of harm, in particular, the prevention of materialized harm done to persons, property, or environment. The scope of analysis is therefore limited to the

---

[1] AI usually stands for machine learning approaches from computer sciences. It has become a popular term in social sciences as it is a perfect fit for various tech solutions that can be found under its umbrella. Thierer et al. (2017: 9) hypothetically prescribed two dimensions of AI, where weak or narrow AI stands for typical methodological approaches from computer science while strong stands for sophisticated solutions that are not developed yet: "*Weak AI systems are not genuinely 'intelligent' in the human sense of the word. In contrast, a 'stronger' AI system might perform competently in several different fields*". With critical consideration of those two perspectives, we will address AI as a potential for reaching broader social benefits and preventing harm.

harm deriving from the adverse changes of the environment and environmental degradation, including, but not limited to climate change, environmental pollution, extreme weather conditions, and natural disasters—environmental harm, reaching the threshold of "significant harm". Such an understanding of the term harm corresponds with the use of harm in international law, especially in the well-established customary no-harm principle (ILC 2001). Environmental protection is one of the main conditions for effective protection of fundamental human rights, as environmental harm often results in impairment of health, loss of lives, greater social inequality and social injustice, forced migration, and disadvantage to future generations (Warner et al., 2010; Tyagi et al. 2014; Rieu-Clarke 2020). Therefore, environmental harm encompasses criminological implications and is strongly linked to the concept of social harm (White 2013), as it directly or indirectly impacts the quality of human lives (Manisalidis et al. 2020). Limiting the scope of harm to materialized environmental harm, means that this chapter examines a small section of an otherwise broader field of harm prevention, leaving out violations of human rights, especially the right to privacy, certain democratic principles, and other intangible values and goods.

When speaking about AI regulation from the perspective of harm prevention, we mean regulation allowing AI technologies to be used in order to tackle environmental challenges, but at the same time ensuring that AI is not misused, exploited, monopolized, discriminatory as in beneficial to only certain chosen subjects or used in a way which does not maximize harm prevention.

In the following text, the current and potential uses of AI in harm prevention on Earth (Sect. 2) and in outer space (Sect. 3) are going to be presented. Then, the evolving framework for AI is outlined by defining the key principles for the use of AI in harm prevention on Earth (Sect. 4), followed by a specific regulatory framework applicable in outer space, where the legal principles of space law that could be relevant for the AI and harm prevention are analyzed (Sect. 5). Based on a comparison of two regulatory regimes some ways forward will be proposed, showing potential of translating some of the legal principles of space law into developing legal regulation of AI on Earth (Sect. 6).

Finally, in the conclusion (Sect. 7) the evaluation of the appropriateness of the "as above so below" approach is made.

2 AI Preventing Harm on Earth

This subchapter demonstrates the use of AI-based solutions on Earth, in areas such as *managing natural disasters* (3.1), *agriculture* (3.2), and *transportation* (3.3), where AI is capable of predicting and preventing harm.

2.1 Natural Disasters

In developing machine models for natural disaster prediction and management, approaches based on various AI technologies have proven to be extremely useful. Such approaches can be used, for example, to predict the occurrence, direction and consequences of landslides, fires, ground subsidence, and floods, which may serve as guidance for evacuation of humans and for taking appropriate disaster managing actions (choosing appropriate strategy, tools, personnel, etc.), especially in the areas with higher risks of natural disasters (Yousefi et al. 2020; Ghorbanzadeh et al. 2019; Mohan et al. 2021). Currently, even earthquakes can be predicted to some extent, by using various approaches based on neural networks, which seems promising for tackling this geological phenomenon with AI in the future (Asim et al. 2017; Mousavi et al. 2020). The main advantage of AI technology in natural disaster management is the improvement of the response time of rescue teams, which is crucial for saving human lives and preventing environmental harm.

2.2 Agriculture

In agriculture, AI is being used to optimize agricultural procedures or to comply with sustainability policies. As part of the so-called "smart agriculture", AI stands for data analysis and the introduction of solutions based on robotics, such as automatism, decision support, remote and direct detection of events, and satellite imaging (Walter et al. 2017). This approach, moreover, is characterized by "edge computing", with the help of which it is claimed to be possible to ensure the reliability of the food supply for the entire world population (O'Grady et al. 2019). Using drones in swarms to support agricultural activity can also be understood as smart agriculture. In this way, it is possible to better monitor the areas which are difficult to access, resulting in higher productivity over a more extended period (Spanaki et al. 2021). Furthermore, there are considerations to weave all kinds of data from agriculture, industry, supply chains, distribution, as well as from social networks with sensory data in the form of temperature and the like to optimize the agrifood industry (Misra et al. 2020). The adoption of smart agriculture is also crucial from a competitiveness perspective, as it allows regions that depend heavily upon the success of the agricultural sector to better adapt to the market, which allows rural regions to develop and therefore increases social benefit. AI and the corresponding transformation of traditional agriculture into modern agriculture enable the development of business models in agriculture that, thanks to machine learning, can be an example for agriculture in general (Panpatte et al. 2021). The use of AI in agriculture enables better use of resources and more innovative agriculture that can meet the demand for food on a global scale. It can therefore be concluded that the use of AI in agriculture can, if regulated and used properly, contribute to sustainability and consequently further in preventing harm (famine, environmental degradation, excessive pollution, increase in natural disasters, etc.…) arising from unsustainable agricultural practices.

2.3 Traffic

The use of AI can lead to the optimization of traffic solutions in cities (Rogov et al. 2020), as it is possible to use traffic data to predict congestion and plan the fastest and shortest routes, as well as to manage, for example, traffic signal infrastructure, thus reducing the risk of congestion (Soomro et al. 2018). Efficient traffic management and selection of the best routes for public transport can be achieved precisely through the use of AI and computer models that take into account the actual traffic situation and thus enable the prediction of the best traffic routes (Okrepilov et al. 2022). Moreover, with the help of AI, it is possible to address the full range of other transport segments that deal with transport challenges leading to better predictability of traffic, easier accessibility of transport modes, and less dependence on the availability of transport (Miles et al. 2006). The same applies to non-road transport, i.e., air transport (Wangermann et al. 1998; Degas et al. 2022), rail transport (Bešinović et al., 2021), or shipping (Rawson et al., 2021) in different weather conditions. AI in transportation guides (through apps such as Google Maps or Apple Maps) the best routes from origin to destination regardless of the mode of transportation, predicts the safest use of routes, and selects the most economical routes. Especially the latter is relevant for mitigating the harmful impact of traffic on the environment and human health (Rodrigue, n. d.; WHO 2000; Foster et al. 2021). By efficiently and safely monitoring traffic, AI is furthermore capable of predicting and preventing accidents (which often, especially in the case of air transport, water transport, or railway transport, can cause substantive environmental harm) from occurring, and in this way minimizes harm and maximizes social benefit.

These examples show the possibility to use data and machine learning to develop solutions enabling better quality of life for people on Earth while preventing environmental and social harm. In order to do so, there must exist an efficient regulatory framework, establishing principles guiding AI toward harm prevention (Wilkinson et al. 2016), which are going to be discussed below.

3 AI Preventing Harm in Outer Space

In this subchapter we are going to present how narrow AI is currently used in outer space activities, and in the end briefly touch upon how strong AI is planned to be used in the future.

Although AI is increasingly used and is planned to be used in different spheres of human space activities, including but not limited to the *traditional* space activities—launch, remote sensing, telecommunication, and navigation services, as well as *next-generation space programmes*—on-orbit servicing, collision avoiding mechanisms, remediation of space debris, deep space exploration, and space mining (Martin, Freeland, 2020, pp.279, 280), we will here focus on three types of space activities using AI aimed at preventing or mitigating environmental social harm, namely, *space debris remediation* (3.1), *collision avoiding mechanisms* (3.2), and *collecting data for monitoring environmental harm* (3.3).

3.1 Space Debris Remediation

Space debris, artificial objects in outer space that are no longer functional, but are still traveling at a very high speed, are becoming one of the main threats of harm in outer space, as there are approximately 15,000 pieces of space debris larger than 10 cm, about 200,000 pieces between 1 and 10 cm and millions of pieces smaller than 1 cm (Gregersen 2022). Most of the pieces are too small to be tracked by currently available technology (NASA 2021). The amount of space debris is growing rapidly. One reason is that there are more and more space objects launched every year, as the number of space-faring states and private actors in the space sector is steadily increasing. Another reason is that the amount of space debris increases through collisions between such pieces, resulting in fragmentation of existing pieces into even smaller fragments, which on their own again engage in further collisions (Kessler and Cour-Palais 1978)— this phenomenon is known as the Kessler syndrome (Lyall and Larsen 2009).

Space debris presents a threat to (1) the functioning space objects in outer space, (2) to the International Space Station (ISS) with astronauts on board; and (3) to people and the environment on Earth. There are several examples of space objects being damaged or destroyed by pieces of debris, from minor accidents, such as the one in 2016, when European Space Agency (ESA) discovered that its Copernicus Sentinnel-1A satellite was hit by just a millimeter-sized particle which resulted in a small power reduction (ESA 2016), to a major Cosmos-Iridium satellite collision in 2009, where an inactive satellite Cosmos 2251 collided with an active Iridium 33 satellite, resulting in almost 2000 new pieces of debris, larger than 10 cm, and several thousand smaller pieces (NASA 2009; Weeden 2010). Space debris further poses a serious threat to the ISS and the astronauts on board. Soon after the 2021 performance of an anti-satellite test (ASAT), a piece of the destroyed satellite hit ISS Canadian-built robotic arm and created a 5 mm hole (Rigby and Carter 2021). The risk of collision with the newly created cloud of orbital debris resulting from the ASAT forced the astronauts aboard the ISS to adjust the ISS' course and even take shelter (Ahmed 2021; Heilweil 2021; McFall-Johnsen 2021; Strickland 2021). Space debris may cause harm to people or environment on Earth by contributing to climate change by harming the ozone layer, causing environmental pollution through toxic substances or materials falling to Earth and posing risk to the essential satellite services, which help protect human lives and environment (Pietkiewicz 2019).

The calls have been made that space debris problem might be tackled with the assistance of AI. ESA announced that it plans to launch the first space mission aimed at removing space debris (ClearSpace-1) in 2026, which is going to be equipped with AI camera for locating debris (ESA 2020; Macaulay 2020). If successful, AI will contribute to minimizing and mitigating potential harm arising from the threat of space debris. However, during the process of space debris removal several legal issues may arise, which are going to be addressed below.

3.2 Collision Avoiding Mechanisms

Another risk for the occurrence of harm in outer space is collisions between man-made space objects. This risk is heightened as the number of space objects increases. This can be contributed to several factors: (1) the cost of commercial launches has decreased in recent years, enabling more and more actors to launch satellites; (2) hardware development has evolved as to cover a great variety of activities which can now be performed by space objects; (3) the constructions of several mega-constellations, consisting of thousands of individual satellites have been carried out. However, the "rules of the road" to govern traffic in outer space and contribute to collision prevention, have not yet been adopted (Frandsen 2022).

Even though international and national registers of space objects launched into outer space exist (Schmidt-Tedd and Soucek 2020; UNOOSA 2022), statistics show that the registration system is inefficient and incomplete, as the registrations do not occur in timely fashion or sometimes do not occur at all, and therefore it is challenging to keep track of every object in outer space (Hertzfeld 2021). This is especially the case with small satellites, which are particularly difficult to track, guide, and control (von der Dunk 2016).

AI systems are being used to prevent space object collisions, which result in harmful consequences—either the creation of more space debris, pollution of outer space or impairment of a satellite used for harm prevention on Earth (e.g., satellites used in natural disaster management). The role of AI in satellite collision prevention is both direct and indirect. *Indirectly*, AI prevents collisions by effectively monitoring operations of large satellite constellations, including positioning of the individual satellites, communication, and their end-of-life management (Bratu et al. 2021, p. 427). Furthermore, AI is involved in preventing harm through avoidance of collisions by being an important part of the manufacturing process (Schmelzer 2020), thus minimizing the chance of human error in the production phase and ensuring a better functioning of the satellite once it is launched into outer space. *Directly*, AI is involved in satellite collision prevention through directly monitoring "the health" of satellites, namely, keeping a constant watch on satellite's sensors and other equipment, alerting in case of malfunction or a threat of collision, and in some cases, even by carrying out corrective action (Schmelzer 2020; Bratu et al. 2021). In order words, AI plays an important role in controlling and navigating space objects (Schmelzer 2020). It does so by being able to look at the patterns of other functioning space objects, pieces of space debris as well as celestial bodies and other objects present in outer space (Schmelzer 2020). SpaceX has already installed such AI collision-preventing system on some of its satellites (Chatterjee 2022), however reports indicate that in some instances their satellites barely avoided the crash with other satellites (Arti 2022; Chatterjee 2022), which puts in question the efficiency of their AI system. SpaceX is not the only one using AI for the purpose of avoiding collisions in outer space. ESA is currently developing a collision-preventing system, which will automatically assess the risk and probability of collisions in outer space and will upon such an assessment decide or partake in the decision-making process in order to establish the appropriate corrective action (a step toward *strong* AI). Such action may be either to conduct a responsive maneuver to avoid the forthcoming threat, or to send out orders and signals to other satellites involved in the potential collision to carry out such a maneuver on their own (ESA 2019; Bandivadekar Berquand 2021; Bratu et al. 2021). Despite the usefulness of already existing collision-preventing mechanisms as well as the expected efficiency of those under development, concerns regarding potential vulnerability of such systems arise. Consequently, in case of failures or errors of such AI systems, the issue of liability appears (Schmelzer 2020), which is going to be tackled below in further detail.

3.3 Monitoring Environmental Harm Through Data Collecting

There is substantially more data for monitoring environmental harm available nowadays, due to the increased number of satellites in outer space (Abashidze et al. 2022). Besides the development and the increased use of AI for the analysis of the so-called "space Big Data"—enormous amount of data gathered from satellites and other space missions, which can be useful in mitigating harm on Earth, several AI tools are deployed in outer space in order to contribute to sustainability and to prevent harm, such as remote sensing of the Earth with the aim of tackling environmental pollution, climate change, and monitoring natural disasters (Bratu 2021; Martin and Freeland 2021).

An example of such technology is Copernicus, a program for providing information services that (in part) draw information from satellite Earth observation (Copernicus, n. d.; European Commission 2016). There already exist initiatives (CALLISTO, n. d.) to integrate AI technology into such systems (Dumitru et al. 2019) in order to make them more efficient, faster, and finally better at preventing harm.

4 Development of Regulatory Framework on Earth

The development of AI and its regulation was fast and uncoordinated. We are currently in a phase where international binding regulation of AI has not yet been constructed. Instead, the development of AI regulation is fragmented, as it is taking place on different levels (international, regional, and national level), by different subjects (governments, organizations, private actors), prioritizing different interests (national security, human rights, commercial interests, etc.), and regulating different fields (industry, criminal justice, environment, etc.) (Soendergaard 2021). The hype of regulating AI, stimulated by "race-rhetoric" and seeking the "first mover advantage", has resulted in a process of adopting numerous AI-related documents (mostly of a non-binding nature), marked as a "race to AI regulation" (Smuha 2021).

This subchapter will not analyze these documents in detail, but will instead present the identified policies and principles that are the most often found in such documents. These principles can therefore be marked as "general" in a sense that they do not pertain to a specific field and that they are generally accepted on an international (or at least regional) level, as well as enshrined in several national documents from different states, but are not in any way constructed as a coherent unit. Upon close examination of the existing national, regional, and international documents relating to the AI regulation, the following principles have been identified as the leading guiding principles on the use of AI (from the most common principle to the least common): transparency, justice and fairness, non-maleficence, responsibility, privacy, beneficence, freedom and autonomy, trust, sustainability, dignity, and solidarity (Jobin et al. 2019).

A wide consensus over these principles indicates that they are most likely to be the basis of binding legal AI regulations. This is confirmed by the fact that some of them are already included in the EU proposal of an AI Act (see European Commission 2021), which is going to, once adopted, create a general legal framework for the use of AI in the EU (Glauner 2022).

We are going to present in further detail the principles that are most relevant for the prevention of harm, namely, *transparency, non-maleficence, responsibility and accountability, beneficence, sustainability,* and *solidarity. Transparency* principle covers efforts to increase the explicability and interpretability of AI, as well as to encourage all acts of communication and disclosure, and in this way minimizes harm (Jobin et al. 2019). *Non-maleficence* principle refers to safety and security, including risk management aimed at preventing AI from causing foreseeable or even unintentional harm, even though harm is in this sense mostly understood as social harm (Jobin et al. 2019). *Responsibility and accountability* principles are widely represented in the AI regulations, however they are rarely defined and often understood in a very unharmonized way, as different liability schemes and different responsible subjects are being named (Jobin et al. 2019). *Beneficence* principle is aimed at the promotion of human well-being, the creation of socio-economic opportunities and economic prosperity. The undefined issue remains who are the actual subjects that are recipients of such benefits. As observed by Jobin et al. (2019), the private sector usually understands this principle as to be sufficed by AI benefiting the customers of their products, however, many other sources claim that this principle requires AI to be shared and to benefit everyone, using terms such as "humanity", "society", "as many people as possible", "the planet", or "the environment". We conclude that in the latter there is a more general and appropriate understanding of the scope of the beneficence principle and that it significantly contributes to the AI being used for minimizing harm and maximizing social benefit. The principle of *sustainability* states that the use of AI must be aimed toward environment protection, the improvement of ecosystems and biodiversity, and contributing to fairer and more equal societies (Jobin et al. 2019). Lastly, the principle of *solidarity* refers to the implications of AI in the labor market—redistribution of benefits must not disrupt social cohesion, must protect potentially vulnerable persons or groups and must prevent sacrificing social solidarity in the name of "radical individualism" (Jobin et al. 2019).

5 Specific Regulatory Framework Applicable in Outer Space

Despite the fact that AI may be used in outer space activities to increase their benefit to the society and to prevent harm, such use nevertheless raises concerns with regard to responsibility and liability for damages, transparency, level of autonomy and human control (Filling Space 2021). This is why we must now look at the applicable regulatory framework in order to establish whether such framework truly allows and demands AI to prevent harm to the greatest extent possible.

The basis for AI regulation in outer space can be deduced from the principles enshrined in the Treaty on Principles Governing the Activities of States in the Exploration and Use of Outer Space, including the Moon and Other Celestial Bodies—Outer Space Treaty (OST),[2] which has already in major part crystalized into customary international law and is therefore applicable to all states (Jakhu and Freeland 2016). While Martin and Freeland (2020, pp. 298–301) already extracted the relevant principles from OST, namely, the use and exploration of outer space carried out for the benefit of all countries (Article I), in accordance with international law (Article III) and for peaceful purposes (Article IV), state authorization and supervision of space activities (Article VI), liability for damages caused by space objects (Article VII), jurisdiction and control of the registering state (Article VIII), acting due regard to the interest of other states (Article IX), and information sharing (Article XI); and show their potential effects on the AI regulation, we are going to tackle here in more detail only those principles that we deem are *particularly relevant* for the implementation of AI to prevent harm.

Firstly, the exploration and use of outer space (which is considered the province of all mankind) must be carried out for the *benefit and in the interests of all countries,* irrespective of their degree of economic or scientific development, and must further be free, *without discrimination* of any kind, on a basis of equality and in accordance with international

---

[2] *Treaty on Principles Governing the Activities of States in the Exploration and Use of Outer Space, Including the Moon and Other Celestial Bodies,* 27 January 1967, 610 UNTS 205, 18 UST 2410, TIAS No 6347, 6 ILM 386 (entered into force on 10 October 1967).

law, as enshrined in Article I of the OST (emphasis added). This means that the use or exploration of outer space, including use and exploration conducted with the inclusion of AI technologies, must not be discriminatory and must therefore not bring benefits to certain countries at the expense of others. Even more, according to this principle, the use and exploration must be done for the benefit and in the interest of all countries, it could be argued that this means not only a negative obligation not to cause social harm to other states, but a positive obligation to grant every state some kind of benefit or interest arising from the use and exploration of outer space. According to the commentary on the Article I, however, the exact meaning of this principle and its effects are dubious, but what can be agreed on is that it strives to ensure participation of non-space-faring countries in the benefits arising from exploration and use of outer space, without clearly defining what such benefits are (Hobe, 2009). In the broadest interpretation, this principle demands that AI in outer space is beneficial to all states, and in the narrowest interpretation prohibits AI in outer space to be harmful. The principle in Article I is therefore, in any case, directing the use of AI in outer space toward preventing harm.

Secondly, Article VI of the OST declares that states bear international responsibility for national activities in outer space, carried out by both governmental and non-governmental entities, and must *authorize* and *supervise* such activities (emphasis added). The process of authorization is usually carried out under the state's national legislation setting out specific conditions for authorization, but due to the open language of the OST, states are allowed a certain degree of discretion and may exercise authorization by other means (Gerhard 2009). In both cases, however, the conditions must be formulated to be capable of ensuring safety and compliance with other principles of the OST (*ibidem*). It follows from this provision, that also AI technology, used or incorporated in space activities, will have to first be subject to authorization and then to continuous supervision of the respective state. This furthermore means that states will have to play their part in maintaining the security of an AI-enhanced space activity as well as guarantee that its automation, navigation, and communication systems remain safe (Martin and Freeland 2020, p. 299). This is important especially taken together with the fact that independent self-regulation carried out by private actors in the absence of state supervision leads to the accumulation of authority and regulatory power in the hands of private actors and consequently to fragmentation of approaches and disharmonized regulation (Soroka and Kurkova 2019, p. 137). Furthermore, the lack of state supervision may result in an unbalance between private and public interests, especially to the benefit of the former. Hence, this principle establishes a procedural safeguard regarding AI in space activities, as well as to some extent material requirements of safety and compliance with OST, therefore increasing the standard of harm prevention.

Article VII of the OST establishes *liability* for damages caused by a space object. Subsequently to the OST, the Convention on International Liability for Damage Caused by Space Objects—Liability Convention (LIAB)[3] was adopted, which further details liability arising from space activities. It regulates liability in two ways, depending on where the damage has occurred. If the damage occurred on Earth or to an aircraft in flight, the launching state[4] of the space object that caused damage is absolutely liable to pay compensation—*absolute liability* (Article II of the LIAB), whereas if the damage occurred elsewhere, the liability arises only in cases of a fault on the side of the launching state or the fault of persons for whom it is responsible—*fault liability* (Article III of the LIAB). The principle of liability is primarily aimed at recovering harm (Preamble of the LIAB). Its effect, however, is even wider—the establishment of state liability increases prevention of harm, as it encourages and stimulates states to pay additional diligence to prevent damage and consequently avoid liability. Even though liability in space treaties concerns states, this does not mean that private companies, agencies, or organizations are not obliged to prevent harm. Usually, states have legislation in place which allows them to seek redress from the subject[5]

---

[3] Convention on International Liability for Damage Caused by Space Objects, 29 March 1972, 961 UNTS 187, 24 UST 2389, 10 ILM 965 (1971) (entered into force 1 September 1972).

[4] The term *launching state* is in Article I(c) of the LIAB defined as a "state which launches or procures the launching of a space object; or a state from whose territory or facility a space object is launched".

[5] Typically, that subject is the private entity that created and launched space object and is controlling its actions in outer space, however the specific issues arise in case of on-orbit

actually responsible for the damage for which they were liable under the LIAB and the OST. It has been argued, however, that the current liability regime is insufficient, as it falls short of directly addressing the liability of private space-faring companies (Reinert 2020, pp. 339, 351). With the incorporation of AI into space objects, the liability regime faces even more challenges. Firstly, the distinction between *narrow* and *strong* AI will probably make the assessment of fault in case of fault liability more difficult, as *strong* AI will, it is anticipated, reach a high level of autonomy, which will make it difficult if not impossible to ascribe fault to the launching state. Another difficulty arising during the process of establishing fault is the issue of predictability of damages, which is crucially linked to the required standard of care (Soroka et al. 2022, p. 128). Martin and Freeland (2020, pp. 302–303) suggest that in certain cases the launching state could be *exonerated* from liability pursuant to Article VI of the LIAB (emphasis added). This Article establishes that if the damage resulted from gross negligence or from an act or omission done with intent to cause damage on the part of a state claiming compensation or of natural or juridical persons it represents, fault could be ascribed to the programmers or supervisors of AI technology (instead of fault being ascribed to the launching state), if they act negligently or deceitfully, or, damage in outer space arising from decision created by AI should be instead of fault liability governed by absolute liability. Chatzipanagiotis (2020) rejects the idea of such extension of absolute liability, but instead proposes that the issue of defining fault in case of AI decisions could be solved by establishing detailed international rules of conduct which would serve to guide the assessment whether the required standard of care was respected. Despite the issues regarding the establishment of fault in cases of space objects with AI components, especially in cases of *strong* AI, liability regime in outer space ensures that victims of harm receive adequate compensation and, in this way, minimize harmful effects caused by space objects. To a certain degree liability contributes to the prevention of harm, as the awareness of liability in case of fault encourages states (and other subjects) to act with due care

---

transfer of ownership or in case of difficulties establishing causal link between space object and damages.

9 As Above so Below: The Use of International Space ... 223

when conducting space activities. We conclude that overall liability is an important factor in preventing harm, even in cases of space objects with AI components.

According to Article VIII of the OST, a state that registered space object *retains jurisdiction and control* over such object while it is in outer space or on a celestial body (emphasis added). Jurisdiction and control are not impacted by the fact that space object concludes its mission and becomes non-functional (Schmidt-Tedd and Mick 2009), which implies a very broad understanding of the extent of this principle. The result of this provision in the case of AI is therefore that human intervention is expected after the initial programming of AI (Martin and Freeland 2020, pp. 299–300). Such an obligation can be seen as a materialization of jurisdiction and especially control, which entails also the right to adopt technical rules in order to achieve the mission or the goal of the space object and, if necessary, to direct, stop, modify, and correct the elements of the space object or its mission (Schmidt-Tedd and Mick 2009), especially if read together with the obligation of state to authorize and supervise space activities from Article VI of the OST, described above. Even though it might seem that human intervention is needed only in cases of *narrow* AI, which is not fully autonomous and needs human supervision for its functioning, even in cases of *strong* AI the risk of unforeseeable harm remains. Precisely because of the unpredictable behavior of AI, the possibility of human intervening with an AI system to change its decision or deactivate it, is crucial (Martin and Freeland 2020, p. 300).

Article IX of the OST obliges states using and exploring outer space to act with *due regard to the corresponding interests of all other states* (emphasis added). In particular, this means that a state must prove that it has done everything in its power to prevent harm from occurring (Marchisio 2009). Article IX further obliges states to *avoid harmful contamination of outer space* and *adverse changes in the environment of the Earth* resulting from the introduction of extraterrestrial matter and, where necessary, to adopt appropriate measures for this purpose (emphasis added). In case of potentially harmful interference with the activities of other states, consultations should take place. Even though it is not clearly defined, what exactly is harmful contamination in the sense of Article IX, it has been established that it covers any contamination which would result in harm to a state's space experiments or programs (Cypser 1993, pp. 324–325), and in that sense covers, *inter alia*, space debris (Marchisio 2009). Following this interpretation, harmful contamination includes contamination caused by space activities or space objects with AI components. Article IX is therefore aimed toward preventing harm arising out of the use and exploration of outer space, including the involvement of AI.

Article XI of the OST stipulates that the states conducting activities in outer space should *inform* the Secretary-General of the United Nations as well as the public and the international scientific community, to the *greatest extent feasible and practicable*, of the *nature, conduct, locations, and results of such activities* (emphasis added). This provision defines the means for achieving certain goals set out in Article I of the OST, namely, the obligation to carry out exploration and use of outer space for the benefit and in the interests of all countries, irrespective of their degree of economic or scientific development, as it materializes fair and equitable access to information gathered and knowledge acquired through the carrying out of space activities for all nations (Mayence and Reuter 2009). Nature, conduct, locations, and results of space activities, which shall be disclosed, include in particular all kinds of information regarding the mission objectives, technical information regarding the construction of a certain space object and its respective launching facilities, launching schedules, flight paths or orbit positions, results of scientific experiments carried out in outer space, scientific knowledge gained concerning the setup of the solar system, or earth observation data obtained by satellites (Mayence and Reuter 2009). The information regarding AI technology incorporated into space objects, therefore, falls within the scope of the information that needs to be disclosed according to the aforementioned principle. On the other hand, the threshold of disclosure set out in Article XI, namely, *to the greatest extent feasible and practicable*, leaves the door open for a wide discretion, taking into account, for example, intellectual property rights or strategic military objectives (Mayence and Reuter 2009). When defining the threshold, the emphasis must, however, be put on the word *greatest* (Mayence and Reuter, 2009). In this regard, this Article at least creates participation rights and an entitlement for non-space-faring states to access

Earth observation data regarding general environmental conditions and the prevention and handling of natural disasters and other dangers, or data concerning the general exploration of the solar system (Mayence and Reuter 2009). In general, it can be stated that, as limiting and vague as it is, Article XI ensures a certain level of public supervision over space activities of states, including those containing AI components. Public supervision increases the awareness and transparency of space activities, which can result in more effective prevention of harm which could be caused by such activities.

This framework, however, is not all-encompassing. There are several potential problems arising from the use of AI in outer space, which will be difficult to resolve using only the existing legal framework. The first potential problem is linked to the removal of space debris, and concerns the absence of the state of registry's consent to the removal of a piece belonging to an object it registered, according to Article VIII of the OST, the state of registry retains jurisdiction and control over its registered space object and parts thereof. If AI system would autonomously decide to remove a piece of debris, should it then first identify the state of registry and seek its consent, or should there be an exception to the principle from Article VIII? In other words, in the clash of obligations of preventing harm and respecting Article VIII—which obligation prevails and must be prioritized? Another potential problem concerns the use of data gathered by satellites. Do space law provisions apply only to the process of AI collecting such data in outer space or also to the process of AI processing and interpreting such data (which can be done in outer space or on Earth)? What happens if the data is falsely or insufficiently interpreted and ends up causing damage or failing to prevent harm? May such damage be defined as "damages caused by a space object", invoking liability?

Despite offering a good starting point for extracting basic principles governing the use of AI in outer space, a more detailed regulation and compliance standards for AI in outer space on an international, regional, and national level will need to be developed, in order to ensure that AI develops in a way that is beneficial and not harmful (Martin and Freeland 2020, pp. 281, 294).

6 Comparison and Ways Forward

In this subchapter, we are going to draw parallels between aforementioned ethical and soft-law principles regarding the use of AI on Earth and certain space law principles, which are relevant for the use of AI in outer space. We are going to identify differences and similarities toward regulating harm prevention and on this basis show, how some of the legal principles of space law may provide guidance for ways forward in translating the existing non-binding principles into a binding international law.

Firstly, the principle of beneficence to a certain extent corresponds to the principle of benefit for all from Article I of the OST, decreeing free use and exploration of outer space (including activities with AI) without discrimination of any kind and in the interest and benefit of all countries. However, whereas interpretations of the subject recipient under the beneficence principle vary, Article I clarifies that the subject recipients are all states. However, Article I is not only clearer, but also wider, as it establishes that outer space is the province of all mankind. The inclusion of the word mankind, despite not being entirely clear, strongly signifies that the harm prevention effects of space regulation are directed at a wider circle of beneficiaries as, for example, offering benefits merely to the consumers, i.e., those that have purchased AI services. From the perspective of harm prevention, it is clear that the interpretation covering the benefits and interests of more subjects is going to produce more positive effects on harm prevention than merely offering benefits to the selected subjects. This is especially the case when AI is used for tackling global challenges, which can only be efficiently addressed on a global level, such as climate change, environmental pollution, or mass-scale natural disasters. The way forward should therefore follow the example of space law, and any future AI regulation should enshrine a wide interpretation of the beneficence principle, offering benefits stemming from AI use to all countries irrespective of their degree of economic development, in order to minimize harm and maximize social benefit globally.

Secondly, the transparency principle and the information sharing principle enshrined in Article XI of the OST draw strong parallels. Although both principles lack precise definition, space law decrees that information regarding space missions (including certain information about the AI components of such missions or space objects) must be shared to the *greatest* extent feasible and practicable, meaning it does not suffice to establish a mere minimal standard of transparency, but that information should be shared in as much such sharing of information does not infringe upon safety, security, intellectual property rights, or other rights that may be impaired through absolute transparency. If transparency is to serve the goal of preventing harm, then information sharing must not be merely a formality, but has to actually be aimed at assuring the materialization of harm prevention. This is only possible through the exchange of certain substantive information. Space law therefore illustrates the way forward as seeking the upper limits of transparency and information sharing, which can still protect AI from cyber-attacks, terrorism, infringement of rights, misuse, or misfunction, but at the same time allows for high public scrutiny over its functioning and consequently more awareness, responsibility and oversight, and thus a higher harm prevention effect.

Third principle, the principle of non-maleficence, regarding the ensuring of security and risk management of AI, may be observed in several space law provisions. In particular, Article VIII, establishing that the state of registry retains jurisdiction and control over its space object (including objects with AI components), and Article VI, demanding a state to not only authorize space activities, but also continuously supervise them. Both provisions lay ground for human oversight over AI used in outer space, which is going to be particularly important once *strong* AI, possessing full autonomy and decision-making capability, is designed and deployed. Before that occurs, more detailed rules governing risk management and thus preventing harm will have to be adopted. In the area of human supervision ensuring security and minimizing risks, both, non-maleficence principle as well as Articles VI and VIII of the OST need a more detailed regulation on how precisely such supervision shall be carried out in order to achieve the highest possible harm prevention.

Fourthly, both examined regulatory frameworks contain principles regarding responsibility and accountability. However, whereas soft-law and ethical guidelines are not unified in answering the questions of who and to what extent is responsible, liable, or accountable for damages arising out of activity with AI components, space law provides for a clear liability framework. It differentiates between strict or absolute liability for damage occurring on earth or to aircraft in flight (with the option of exoneration in cases of gross negligence or intentional damage on side of the victim), meaning compensation must be paid irrespective of existence of fault, and fault-based liability in outer space, where the launching state is held liable only in cases where its fault or the fault of persons under its control is proven. This is how space law in a way differentiates between damage done to actors who have willingly entered into risk of damage occurring by participating in space activity and those that did not: this sentiment is a potentially elegant way of proceeding in AI regulation, as strict liability with the possibility of exoneration could be ideal for cases where damage was to occur on a larger scale, for example in densely populated areas where the victims of AI damage have no control over its use, while fault-based approach could be used in areas where all actors involved had or are using AI, and are therefore aware of the risks and are reaping benefits. The former is especially appropriate given the still high risk of AI use. However, it should be mentioned that both existing frameworks seem to neglect the ever-increasing role of private actors in the international fora. This will require attention in future as holding private actors only indirectly liable through holding states liable may not prove satisfactory for a range of reasons, from forum shopping to poor practices of states.

Fifth comparison can be made between the principle of sustainability and corresponding provisions of space law. Even though we did not find a provision in space law that would directly translate into the principle of sustainability, there are several provisions found in the OST that contribute to this end. One of them, already elaborated upon above, is the benefit and interest of all countries and be the province of all mankind (Article I), implying that a space activity (including its AI components) must not benefit just one state or a region, but must be beneficial globally. Similar effects may be observed from the obligation to ensure that activities are carried out with due regard to the interests of other states (Article IX). It has been suggested that the term "mankind" refers not only to the present, but also to the future generations (Gorove

1972), which would be another indicator of the need for sustainability. Being mindful of the fact that sustainability means taking into account the interests of not only one, but all parts of the world, as well as not merely the present, but also future generations, should be a way forward to further regulate principle of sustainable AI.

Lastly, we turn toward the principle of solidarity. Even though this principle is mainly understood as solidarity on the labor market, we argue that it is parallel to certain provisions in space law, for example Article I of the OST. To illustrate, solidarity may be *mutatis mutandis* applied from relations between workers and employers to relations between states, as the effects of the provision that the use and exploration of outer space must benefit all countries, including developing countries or non-space-faring countries are: minimizing the differences between them and space-faring countries, enabling all to gain benefits from outer space, and thus preventing discrimination and the rise of radical individualism. Inclusion of all states, the prevention of discrimination, and ensuring that benefits and interests of all are respected, are principles important not just in outer space, but on Earth as well. Threats to the environment such as climate change, natural disasters, extreme weather changes, the issues of agriculture and transport are issues which can only be fully addressed through global sustainability and solidarity.

7 Conclusion

This chapter demonstrates how certain principles of space law might serve as a useful guidance in the process of developing an international legal framework for the use of AI on Earth, at least looking from the perspective of harm prevention, and by doing so, argues for the so-called "as above so below" approach. It can be concluded that this may be done only in cases where principles on AI regulation are defined in several different ways, and is especially useful in cases where definitions are affected by the interests of private actors, and thus trying to limit the scope of AI regulatory framework in order to gain more freedom regarding the profits, distribution of benefits, or the way the activities are conducted. An example of such a definition affected by private interests is one of the definitions of beneficence principle. Showing that whereas sharing benefits merely with consumers suffices for respecting such definition of the beneficence principle from ethical AI guidelines, space law, in contrast, establishes that the recipients of (at least a certain amount of) benefits are all states and consequently, their inhabitants.

There must, on the other hand, exist a limit to the translation of space law into the AI regulation. The main arguments for such limitation are that space law developed in a particular political as well as factual context. It emerged during the cold war, in the context of an arms race and uncertainties regarding which of the two main space powers would reach outer space first, which resulted in several safeguards and compromises. Furthermore, space law regulates activities in outer space, which is an extremely hazardous environment, where damage may occur despite the use of numerous precautions and the deployment of the most advanced technology. That is why a stricter liability scheme in outer space, for example, is justified.

However, partially these arguments are applicable to AI as well. AI technologies are not yet developed to their full potential, and it is not clear which state or private actor is going to be the first one to develop fully autonomous, *strong* AI. It is further unclear how such AI will be used. Just as for outer space, we are not aware and cannot picture the extent of possibilities in the use and exploration of the emerging field. Additionally, using AI in certain high-risk activities may be marked as extremely hazardous as well. This is why the establishment of safeguards in order to ensure that AI is aimed at preventing harm and maximizing social benefit for all is needed.

Another argument against full translation of space principles into the AI regulatory framework is that even in space law, there are several unanswered questions and issues arising from the potential use of AI. It is therefore not yet a comprehensive framework capable of dealing with every legal dilemma regarding AI. This is true, and regulation of AI will therefore probably continue in two parallel ways, the general regulation on Earth as well as a more specialized regulation in space law. However, if we want the two regulatory frameworks to be as efficient, harmonized, and harm-prevention-oriented as possible, they might draw from each other and take into account the good practices or principles aimed at minimizing harm.

Acknowledgements The research leading to this article has received funding from the Slovenian Research Agency, research project "Human Rights and Regulation of Trustworthy Artificial Intelligence" (no. V5-1930).

The authors would like to sincerely thank Katja Grünfeld and Pika Šarf for reading the first manuscript and for their feedback, which enriched our work.

Literatures

Abashidze, A., Ilyashevich, M., Latypova, A.. (2022). Artificial Intelligence and Space Law. *Journal of Legal, Ethical and Regulatory, 25*(3), 1–13.

Ahmed, Issam. (2021). Space Debris 'Event' Forces ISS Crew to Take Evasive Action (Update). *PhysOrg*. Retrieved from: https://phys.org/news/2021-11-space-junk-station-astronauts-docked.html. Accessed on 27 July 2022.

Arti. (2022). Fact Check: SpaceX and Its Capabilities Outperforming NASA? *Analytics Insight*. Retrieved from: https://www.analyticsinsight.net/fact-check-spacex-and-its-ai-capabilities-outperforming-nasa/#:~:text=Like%20the%20Dragon%2C%20SpaceX's%20shuttle,satellite%20crashes%20has%20ignited%20discussion. Accessed on 28 July 2022.

Asim, K. M., Martínez-Álvarez, F., Basit, A., & Iqbal, T. (2017). Earthquake Magnitude Prediction in Hindukush Region Using Machine Learning Techniques. *Natural Hazards, 85*(1), 471–486.

Bandivadekar, Deep, & Berquand, Audrey. (2021). Five Ways Artificial Intelligence Can Help Space Exploration. *The Conversation*. Retrieved from: https://theconversation.com/five-ways-artificial-intelligence-can-help-space-exploration-153664. Accessed on 28 July 2022.

Bešinović, N., De Donato, L., Flammini, F., Goverde, R. M., Lin, Z., Liu, R., ... & Vittorini, V. (2021). Artificial Intelligence in Railway Transport: Taxonomy, Regulations and Applications. *IEEE Transactions on Intelligent Transportation Systems*.

Bratu, Ioana. (2021). *Artificial Intelligence for Future Lunar Societies: A Critical Analysis of the Liability Problem.* 5th Global Moon Village Workshop & Symposium, December 6–8, Nicosia, Cyprus.

Bratu, Ioana, Lodder, Arno R., & van der Linden, Tina. (2021). Autonomous Space Objects and International Space Law: Navigating the Liability Gap. *Indonesian Journal of International Law ,18*(3), 423–446.

CALLISTO. Retrieved from: https://callisto-h2020.eu/project/. Accessed on: 28 July 2022.

Chatterjee, Poulomi. (2022). How SpaceX Is Using AI to Advance Its Ambitions. *Analytics India Magazine*. Retrieved from: https://analyticsindiamag.com/how-spacex-is-using-ai-to-advance-its-ambitions/. Accessed on: 27 July 2022.

Chatzipanagiotis, Michael. (2020). Whose Fault Is It? Artificial Intelligence and Liability in International Space Law. *71th International Astronautical Congress (IAC)—The Cyberspace Edition*, 12–14 October.

Copernicus. *About Copernicus*. Retrieved from: https://www.copernicus.eu/en/about-copernicus. Accessed on: 28 July 2022.

Criado, Ignacio J., Gil-Garcia, & Ramon J. (2019). Creating Public Value Through Smart Technologies and Strategies: From Digital Services to Artificial Intelligence and Beyond. *International Journal of Public Sector Management, 32*(5), 438–450.

Cypser, Darlene A.. (1993). International Law and Policy of Extraterrestrial Planetary Protection. *Jurimetrics—Journal of Law. Science & Technology, 33*(2), 315–339.

Degas, A., Islam, M. R., Hurter, C., Barua, S., Rahman, H., Poudel, M., ... & Aricó, P. (2022). A Survey on Artificial Intelligence (ai) and Explainable AI in Air Traffic Management: Current Trends and Development with Future Research Trajectory. *Applied Sciences, 12*(3), 1295.

Dumitru, Corneliu, Schwarz, Gottfried, Castel, Fabien, Lorenzo, Jose, & Datcu, Mihai. (2019). Artificial Intelligence Data Science Methodology for Earth Observation. Retrieved from: https://www.researchgate.net/publication/335916984_Artificial_Intelligence_Data_Science_Methodology_for_Earth_Observation. Accessed on: 28 July 2022.

ESA. (2016). *Copernicus Sentinel-1A Satellite Hit by Space Particle*. Retrieved from: https://www.esa.int/Applications/Observing_the_Earth/Copernicus/Sentinel-1/Copernicus_Sentinel-1A_satellite_hit_by_space_particle#:~:text=ESA%20engineers%20have%20discovered%20that,to%20identify%20the%20affected%20area. Accessed on: 27 July 2022.

ESA. (2019). *Automating Collision Avoidance*. Retrieved from: https://www.esa.int/Space_Safety/Space_Debris/Automating_collision_avoidance. Accessed on: 27 July 2022.

ESA. (2020). *Earth's First Space Debris Removal Mission.* Retrieved from: https://www.esa.int/ESA_Multimedia/Videos/2020/11/Earth_s_first_s pace_debris_removal_mission. Accessed on: 27 July 2022.

European Commission. (2016). *Study to examine the socioeconomic impact of Copernicus in the EU: Report on the Copernicus downstream sector and user benefits.* Retrieved from: https://op.europa.eu/en/publication-detail/-/public ation/97a5cf70-aa5f-11e6-aab7-01aa75ed71a1. Accessed on: 27 July 2022.

European Commission. (2021). *Proposal for a Regulation of the European Parliament and the Council: Laying Down Harmonised Rules on Artificial Intelligence (Artificial Intelligence Act) and Amending Certain Union Legislative Acts.* Retrieved from: https://eur-lex.europa.eu/legal-content/EN/ALL/? uri=CELEX:52021PC0206. Accessed on: 29. 7. 2022.

Filling Space. (2021). *How Can Space Law Address Artificial Intelligence in Space?* . Retrieved from: https://filling-space.com/2021/05/07/how-can-space-law-address-artificial-intelligence-in-space/. Accessed on: 25 July 2022.

Foster, Vivien, Zhang, Fan, Li, Shanjun, Xing, Jianwei. (2021). Can Policy Measures Reduce the Environmental Impact of Urban Passenger Transport? *World Bank Blogs.* Retrieved from: https://blogs.worldbank.org/transp ort/can-policy-measures-reduce-environmental-impact-urban-passenger-tra nsport. Accessed on: 31 July 2022.

Frandsen, Hjalte Osborn. (2022). Looking for the Rules-of-the-Road of Outer Space: A Search for Basic Traffic Rules in Treaties, Guidelines and Standards. *Journal of Space Safety Engineering, 9,* 231–238.

Gerhard, M., et al. (2009). *Article VI.* In S. Hobe (Ed.), *Cologne Commentary on Space Law* (Vol. 1, pp. 103–123). Carl Heymanns Verlag.

Ghorbanzadeh, O., Blaschke, T., Gholamnia, K., & Aryal, J. (2019). Forest fire Susceptibility and Risk Mapping Using Social/Infrastructural Vulnerability and Environmental Variables. *Fire, 2*(3), 50.

Glauner, Patrick. (2022). *An Assessment of the AI Regulation Proposed by the European Commission.* In Sepehr Ehsani et al. (Eds.), *The Future Circle of Healthcare: AI, 3D Printing, Longevity, Ethics, and Uncertainty Mitigation.* Heidelberg: Springer.

Gorove, Stephen. (1972). *The Concept of "Common Heritage of Mankind": A Political, Moral or Legal Innovation?.* San Diego Law Review, 9, 390–403.

Gregersen, Erik. (2022). space debris. *Britannica.* Retrieved from: https://www. britannica.com/technology/space-debris. Accessed on: 27 July 2022.

Heilweil, Rebecca. (2021). The Space Debris Problem Is Getting Dangerous. *Vox*. Retrieved from: https://www.vox.com/recode/2021/11/16/22785425/international-space-station-russia-missle-test-debris. Accessed on: 27 July 2022.

Hertzfeld, Henry R. (2021). Unsolved Issues of Compliance with the Registration Convention. *Journal of Space Safety Engineering, 8*(3), 238–244.

Hobe, S., et al. (2009). *Article I*. In S. Hobe (Ed.), *Cologne Commentary on Space Law* (Vol. 1, pp. 25–44). Carl Heymanns Verlag.

ILC. (2001). *Draft Articles on Prevention of Transboundary Harm from Hazardous Activities, with Commentaries*. UN Doc. A/RES/56/82, 56 UN GAOR Supp (No. 49), Geneva, p. 154.

Jakhu, Ram, & Freeland, Steven. (2016). *The Relationship Between the Outer Space Treaty and Customary International Law*. 67th International Astronautical Congress (IAC).

Jobin, Anna; Ienca, Marcello; Vayena, Effy. (2019). The Global Landscape of AI Ethics Guidelines. *Nature Machine Intelligence, 1*, 389–399.

Kerrest, Armel, Smith, Lesley Jane. (2009). Article VII. In Stephan Hobe et al. (Eds.), *Cologne Commentary on Space Law*, (Vol. 1, pp. 126–145). Cologne: Carl Heymanns Verlag.

Kessler, Donald J., & Cour-Palais, Burton G. (1978). Collision Frequency of Artificial Satellites: The Creation of a Debris Belt. *JGR Space Physics, 38*(A6), 2637–2646.

Lafferranderie, Gabriel. (2005). Jurisdiction and Control of Space Objects and the Case of an International Intergovernmental Organisation (ESA). *Zeitschrift für Luft- und Weltraumrecht, 54*(2), 228–242.

Lyall, Francis; Larsen, Paul B. (2009). *Space Law: A Treatise*. Surrey: Ashgate.

Macaulay, Thomas. (2020). AI to Help World's First Removal of Space Debris. *TheNextWeb*. Retrieved from: https://thenextweb.com/news/ai-to-help-worlds-first-removal-of-space-debris. Accessed on: 27. 7. 2022.

Manisalidis, Ioanis; Stavropoulou, Elisavet; Stavropoulos, Agathangelos; Bezirtzoglou, Eugenia. (2020). *Environmental and Health Impacts of Air Pollution: A Review* , 8 Frontiers in Public Health 14, Retrieved from: https://doi.org/10.3389/fpubh.2020.00014/full. Accessed on: 27 July 2022.

Marchisio, Sergio. (2009). Article IX. In Stephan Hobe et al. (Eds.), *Cologne Commentary on Space Law* (Vol. 1, pp. 169–188). Cologne: Carl Heymanns Verlag.

Martin, Anne-Sophie, Freeland, Steven. (2020) Artificial Intelligence—A Challenging Realm for Regulation Space Activities. *Annals of Air and Space Law, XLV*, 275–306.

Martin, Anne-Sophie, & Freeland, Steven. (2021). The Advent of Artificial Intelligence in Space Activities: New Legal Challenges. *Space Policy, 55*. online.

Mayence, Jean-François, & Reuter, Thomas. (2009). Article XI. In Stephan Hobe et al. (Eds.), *Cologne Commentary on Space Law* (Vol. 1 , pp. 189–206). Cologne: Carl Heymanns Verlag.

McFall-Johnsen, Morgan. (2021). *Russia Pushes the International Space Station Away from '90s US Rocket Debris—the 2nd Space-Junk Scare This Week. Insider.* Retrieved from: https://www.businessinsider.com/international-space-station-swerves-to-avoid-rocket-debris-2021-12. Accessed on: 27 July 2022.

Miles, J. C., & Walker, A. J. (2006, September). The Potential Application of Artificial Intelligence in Transport. In *IEE Proceedings-Intelligent Transport Systems* (Vol. 153, No. 3, pp. 183–198). IET Digital Library.

Misra, N. N., Dixit, Y., Al-Mallahi, A., Bhullar, M. S., Upadhyay, R., & Martynenko, A. (2020). IoT, Big Data and Artificial Intelligence in Agriculture and Food Industry. *IEEE Internet of Things Journal*.

Mohan, K. V. M., Satish, A. R., Rao, K. M., Yarava, R. K., & Babu, G. C. (2021, October). Leveraging Machine Learning to Predict Wild Fires. In *2021 2nd International Conference on Smart Electronics and Communication (ICOSEC)* (pp. 1393–1400). IEEE.

Mousavi, S. M., & Beroza, G. C. (2020). A Machine-Learning Approach for Earthquake Magnitude Estimation. *Geophysical Research Letters, 47*(1), e2019GL085976.

NASA. (2021). *Space Debris and Human Spacecraft*. Retrieved from: https://www.nasa.gov/mission_pages/station/news/orbital_debris.html. Accessed on: 27 July 2022.

NASA. (2009). *The Collision of Iridium 33 and Cosmos 2251: The Shape of Things to Come*. Retrieved from: https://ntrs.nasa.gov/citations/20100002023. Accessed on: 27 July 2022.

O'Grady, M. J., Langton, D., & O'Hare, G. M. P. (2019). Edge Computing: A Tractable Model for Smart Agriculture? *Artificial Intelligence in Agriculture, 3*, 42–51.

Okrepilov, V. V., Kovalenko, B. B., Getmanova, G. V., & Turovskaj, M. S. (2022). Modern Trends in Artificial Intelligence in the Transport System. *Transportation Research Procedia, 61*, 229–233.

Panpatte, S., & Ganeshkumar, C. (2021). Artificial Intelligence in Agriculture Sector: Case Study of Blue River Technology. In *Proceedings of the*

236 I. Ramuš Cvetkovič and M. Drobnjak

Second International Conference on Information Management and Machine Intelligence (pp. 147–153). Singapore: Springer.

Pietkiewicz, Michał. (2019). *Protection of the Space Environment Against Space Debris Pollution. Studia Prawnoustrojowe, 45,* 215–227.

Rawson, A., Brito, M., Sabeur, Z., & Tran-Thanh, L. (2021). A Machine Learning Approach for Monitoring Ship Safety in Extreme Weather Events. *Safety Science, 141,* 105336.

Reinert, Alexander P. (2020). *Updating the Liability Regime in Outer Space: Why Spacefaring Companies Should Be Internationally Liable for Their Space Objects. William. & Mary Law Review, 62* 1, 325–356.

Rieu-Clarke, Alistair. (2020). *The Duty to Take Appropriate Measures to Prevent Significant Transboundary Harm and Private Companies: Insights from Transboundary Hydropower Projects. International Environmental Agreements: Politics, Law and Economics, 20,* 667–682.

Rigby, Mark, Carter, Brad. (2021). A Chunk of Chinese Satellite Almost hit the International Space Station. They Dodged It—But the Space Junk Problem Is Getting Worse. *The Conversation.* Retrieved from: https://the conversation.com/a-chunk-of-chinese-satellite-almost-hit-the-international-space-station-they-dodged-it-but-the-space-junk-problem-is-getting-worse-171735. Accessed on: 27 July 2022.

Rodrigue, Jean-Paul. *Transportation and the Environment.* Retrieved from: https://transportgeography.org/contents/chapter4/transportation-and-enviro nment/. Accessed on: 27 July 2022.

Rogov, A. A., Statsenko, A. A., Obukhov, I. V., & Smirnova, A. A. (2020, January). Development of Artificial Intelligence Systems for Megacities Transport Infrastructure Management. In *2020 IEEE Conference of Russian Young Researchers in Electrical and Electronic Engineering (EIConRus)* (pp. 1663–1666). IEEE.

Russell, Stuart, Norvig, Peter. (2016). *Artificial Intelligence: A Modern Approach* (3rd Edition). Essex: Pearson.

Schmelzer, Ron. (2020). "How Is AI Helping to Commercialize Space?" *Forbes.* Retrieved from: https://www.forbes.com/sites/cognitiveworld/2020/03/21/ how-is-ai-helping-to-commercialize-space/?sh=3118f09b7c9f. Accessed on: 28. 7. 2022.

Schmidt-Tedd, Bernhard, Mick, Stephan. (2009). Article IX. In Stephan Hobe et al. (Eds.), *Cologne Commentary on Space Law* (Vol. 1, pp. 146–168). Cologne: Carl Heymanns Verlag.

Schmidt-Tedd, Bernhard, & Soucek, Alexander. (2020). Registration of Space Objects. *Oxford Research Encyclopedia of Planetary Science.* Retrieved from: https://doi.org/10.1093/acrefore/9780190647926.001.0001/acrefore-9780190647926-e-95. Accessed on: 28 August 2022.

Smuha, N. A. (2021) From a 'Race to AI' to a 'Race to AI regulation': Regulatory Competition for Artificial Intelligence. *Law Innovation and Technology, 13*(1), 57–84.

Soendergaard, Peter. (2021). Multinational AI Governance—The Threat of "Fragmentation of AI". *2021.AI*. Retrieved from: https://2021.ai/multinational-ai-governance-fragmentation-ai/. Accessed on: 2 August 2022.

Soomro, S., Miraz, M. H., Prasanth, A., & Abdullah, M. (2018). *Artificial Intelligence Enabled IoT: Traffic Congestion Reduction in Smart Cities.*

Soroka, Larysa, Danylenko, Anna, & Sokiran Maksym (2022). *Legal Issues and Risks of Artificial Intelligence Use in Space Activity. Philosophy and Cosmology, 28*, 118–135.

Soroka, Larysa, & Kurkova, Kseniia (2019). *Artificial Intelligence and Space Technologies: Legal, Ethical and Technological Issues. Advanced Space Law, 3*,131–139.

Spanaki, K., Karafili, E., Sivarajah, U., Despoudi, S., & Irani, Z. (2021). Artificial Intelligence and Food Security: Swarm Intelligence of AgriTech Drones for Smart AgriFood Operations. *Production Planning & Control*, 1–19.

Strickland, Ashley. (2021). Space Junk Hit the International Space Station, Damaging a Robotic Arm. *CNN*. Retrieved from: https://edition.cnn.com/2021/06/01/world/iss-orbital-debris-robotic-arm-scn/index.html. Accessed on: 27 July 2022.

Surden, Harry. (2019). *Artificial Intelligence and Law: An Overview. Georgia State University Law Review, 35*(4), 1305–1337.

Thierer, A. D., Castillo O'Sullivan, A., & Russell, R. (2017). *Artificial Intelligence and Public Policy*. Mercatus Research Paper.

Tyagi, Swati, Garg, Neelam, & Paudel, Rajan. (2014). Environmental Degradation: Causes and Consequences. *European Researcher, 81*(8-2), 1491–1498.

UNOOSA. (2022). *United Nations Register of Objects Launched into Outer Space*. Retrieved from: https://www.unoosa.org/oosa/en/spaceobjectregister/index.html. Accessed on: 28 July 2022.

Von der Dunk, Frans. (2016.) Liability for Damage Caused by Small Satellites—A Non-Issue? In *Irmgard Marboe, Small Satellites: Regulatory Challenges and Chances* (pp. pp. 154–173). Leiden: Brill.

Walter, Achim, Finger, Robert, Huber, Robert, & Buchmann, Nina. (2017). Smart Farming Is Key to Developing Sustainable Agriculture. *PNAS*. Retrieved from: https://doi.org/10.1073/pnas.1707462114. Accessed on 31 July 2022.

Wangermann, J. P., & Stengel, R. F. (1998). Principled Negotiation Between Intelligent Agents: A Model for Air Traffic Management. *Artificial Intelligence in Engineering, 12*(3), 177–187.

Warner, K., Hamza, M., Oliver-Smith, A. et al. (2010). Climate Change, Environmental Degradation and Migration. *Nat Hazards, 55*, 689–715.

Weeden, Brian. (2009). Iridium-Cosmos Collision. *Secure World Foundation.* Retrieved from https://swfound.org/media/6575/swf_iridium_cosmos_collision_fact_sheet_updated_2012.pdf. Accessed on 27 July 2022.

White, R. (2013). *Environmental Harm—An Eco-Justice Perspective.* Policy Press.

WHO. (2000). *Transport, Environment and Health.* Report. WHO Regional Publications, European Series, No. 89. Retrieved from: https://www.euro.who.int/__data/assets/pdf_file/0003/87573/E72015.pdf. Accessed on 31 July 2022.

Wilkinson, M. D., Dumontier, M., Aalbersberg, I. J., Appleton, G., Axton, M., Baak, A., & Mons, B. (2016). The FAIR Guiding Principles for Scientific Data Management and Stewardship. *Scientific Data, 3*(1), 1–9.

Yousefi, S., Pourghasemi, H. R., Emami, S. N., Pouyan, S., Eskandari, S., & Tiefenbacher, J. P. (2020). A Machine Learning Framework for Multihazards Modeling and Mapping in a Mountainous Area. *Scientific Reports, 10*(1), 1–14.

10

Democratizing the Governance of AI: From Big Tech Monopolies to Cooperatives

Katja Simončič and Tonja Jerele

1 Introduction

Today, artificial intelligence (AI) solutions are so ubiquitous in many parts of the world, that many individuals are blissfully unaware of how much they rely on them in their everyday life (European Commission 2017). AI is, for example, used in the public domain in education and taxation processes, in the context of smart cities, judicial systems, election campaigns as well as in insurance, banking, and other business sectors. Furthermore, AI is thought to be one of the main components in the

---

K. Simončič (✉)
Ministry of Labour, Social Affairs and Equal Opportunities of the Republic of Slovenia, Ljubljana, Slovenia
e-mail: Katja.simoncic@yahoo.com

T. Jerele
Faculty of Social Sciences, University of Ljubljana, Ljubljana, Slovenia
e-mail: tonja.jerele@fdv.uni-lj.si

© The Author(s), under exclusive license to Springer Nature Switzerland AG 2023
A. Završnik and K. Simončič (eds.), *Artificial Intelligence, Social Harms and Human Rights*, Critical Criminological Perspectives,
https://doi.org/10.1007/978-3-031-19149-7_10

239

upcoming "revolution" in the production of goods, named Industry 4.0, "a concept that propagates the combination of the Internet of Things, big data, social media, cloud computing, sensors, artificial intelligence, robotics, and the application of the combination of these technologies to the production, distribution and use of physical goods" (Fuchs 2019, 77). It is therefore important in what way, by whom, and on which data, the AI systems are getting built and what implications this has for the individual users.

Currently, the development of the majority of AI applications takes place in only nine mega-corporations—Google, Apple, Amazon, Facebook, IBM, Microsoft in the United States, Tencent, Baidu, and Alibaba in China (hereinafter Big Tech) whose commitment to increase profit for its shareholders does not always align with what's best for the well-being, individual liberties, and democratic values of the large part of the global population (Webb 2019). Shen (2017) notes that while around 7,9 billion people live on this planet, only 10,000 people in seven countries are writing code for all of the AI that is being developed. If humans are on the route to creating Artificial General Intelligence (AGI) that represents the human condition that will influence all of humanity, then AI and AGI being developed need to account for the whole range of human condition (Montes and Goertzel 2019) and not just the small circle of individuals that have been able to gain access to elite education or procure a highly coveted position in one of the "big nine."

There is a growing concern among policymakers, researchers, and the wider public, that these companies hold a monopoly over the research and development of not only AI but the whole ecosystem around it as well. In a recent report, the US House Judiciary Subcommittee on antitrust (Subcommittee 2020) stated that Google, Apple, Amazon, and Facebook do enjoy monopoly power and advised a legal reform to be undertaken that would force the companies to split parts of their business (Feiner 2020).

To prevent the concentration of political and economic power in the hands of a small circle of individuals and with it the social harm that occurs as a consequence and to, rather, start developing AI for social good, we find that decisive actions to regulate the ownership of data are crucial and timely. Time to act is running out, seeing that once we start to rely on algorithms to make decisions for us it will be much more difficult to stop sharing our personal data and lose all the perks that come with it (Harari 2018b). We commend the efforts certain groups and people are making in this direction, such as the push to institute a global governance regime of AI by some of the tech insiders (Webb 2019), various initiatives calling for greater democratization, transparency, and inclusion in the research and development of AI or advocating for systemic changes to the current situation, as well as efforts from the EU and others to create legal regimes for the regulation of AI (Walch 2020). However, it seems that many of the solutions proposed will most likely merely widen the circle of those few on the top, without shifting any real power to those on the bottom.

Aside from nationalizing Big Tech, which, considering the current state of things might lead to more problems than solutions, this chapter attempts to look at other, less advocated ways of protecting our democratic values in relation to AI development, focusing particularly on the example offered by cooperatives. In order to address current democratic shortages and their social consequences, reorganizing Big Tech companies according to the principles of cooperatives is one of the possible solutions we should consider. In the very least, the principles followed by cooperatives serve as a reminder of all that must change in Big Tech in order for AI to serve the many, not the few.

In this chapter we will firstly consider different aspects of AI monopolization and look into the socially harmful effects that have consequently arisen. In the second half of the chapter, we will investigate what AI for social good could look like and examine the principles that could be useful when designing a more democratic AI.

2 Tech Companies as Monopolies

A monopoly is a company that has monopoly power in the market for a particular good or service (FTC, nd), making it practically impossible for competing companies to enter the market. It's often a company that operates under large economies of scale, requires a lot of capital, offers a product that has no substitute, may possess technological superiority, controls resources, and "prompts government mandate ensuring its sole existence." It also creates substantial entry barriers—perhaps ones created by the firm's conduct itself—that permit the firm to exercise substantial market power for an appreciable period (U.S. Dep't of Justice 2008). Various aspects of monopolies are extremely problematic, such as price-fixing (i.e. the ability to set a price they choose), a decrease in quality of the products or services due to the monopolistic position as well as a lack of incentive for innovation, and the issue of cost-push inflation (i.e. the company can set any price they want, consequently raising costs for consumers to increase profit) (Amadeo 2021).

In 2020, after a 16-month investigation into competitive practices at Apple, Amazon, Facebook, and Google, the US House Judiciary Subcommittee on antitrust has released a report (Subcommittee 2020) stating that the four companies enjoy monopoly power and suggested that congress should reform antitrust laws which would lead to a potential split/segregation of parts of their business (Feiner 2020). According to the report, Facebook, a company that generates its revenue predominantly from selling advertisement placements, has monopoly power in online advertising as well as in the social networking markets (Subcommittee 2020, 170). Amazon, on the other hand, has monopoly power over most of its third-party sellers (publicly described as "partners" and behind closed doors as "internal competitors"), as well as over many of its suppliers. According to official numbers, the company's market share of US e-commerce is around 40%, yet based on the information Subcommittee staff gathered during its investigation the number is closer to 50% or higher. The company reportedly controls about 65 to 70% of all US online marketplace sales. Apple holds monopoly power over software distribution on iOS devices, allowing the company to generate extraordinary profits from the App Store and its Service Business. These profits are derived by extracting rents from developers who either pass on price increases to consumers or reduce investments in new services. According to the Subcommittee staff: "Apple's ban on rival app stores and alternative payment processing locks out the competition, boosting Apple's profits from a captured ecosystem of developers and consumers." (Subcommittee 2020, 345) Lastly, according to the report, Google, which serves as a sort of infrastructure for essential services online, has a monopoly of

10 Democratizing the Governance of AI: From Big Tech ...

the online general search and search advertising market. The company, for example, owns Chrome, the world's most popular browser; YouTube; Google Maps with which it captures over 80% of the market for navigation mapping service and Google Cloud with which the company hopes to dominate the Internet of things (Feiner 2020).

Until recently, Big Tech has been tirelessly ensuring the public and the legislators that they are not monopolies. Harm to consumer welfare is hard to prove if, as in the case of Facebook, the services it offers are for free and since other digital platforms like LinkedIn, Pinterest, Reddit, Youtube, TikTok could be perceived as potential substitutes. Furthermore, Facebook's spending on research and development is among the highest in the world, indicating that the company most clearly does not lag in innovation as is usually the case when a company holds due to its presumed monopolistic position (Menaldo 2021).

Current Big Tech companies not only have a monopoly over their user base in their respective fields—which allows them to collect vast amounts of personal digital data (also known as Big Data)—and ad revenue, they are actively working on achieving a hegemonic position as providers of cloud computing as well. In the last five or so years, cloud computing has become an ever more important service and the fastest-growing segment in the IT and technology platforms sector. Due to the increasing demand for more computational power to run machine learning (ML) algorithms and store vast amounts of data, companies are increasingly turning to the cloud. Mosco (2015, 517) defines cloud computing as a "model for enabling on-demand network access to a shared pool of ubiquitous, configurable computing resources (e.g., networks, servers, storage, applications, and services) that can be rapidly provisioned and released with minimal management effort or service provider interaction.... it enables distant storage, processing, and distribution of data, applications, and services for individuals and organizations."

Leading companies in cloud computing right now are Amazon Web Services (AWS), a subsidiary of Amazon, which currently holds 32% of the market share, Microsoft Azure follows with 20%, and Google Compute Engine (9%) with Chinese giants Alibaba (6%), and Tencent (2%) following closely behind, particularly in Asian markets (Richter 2021). AWS has been known to use its dominant position in "online sales to undercut the competition in pricing cloud services. It has been so successful in this practice of predatory pricing … that smaller companies have either been driven out of the marketplace or forced to concentrate on narrow niche positions" (Mosco 2015). Many experts in the field warn that in the coming years, due to the nature of ML—the more data the system gets, the better the decisions it will make—customers are more likely to get locked into an initial vendor. This means that the current leaders in cloud computing and in ML will probably lead the next era of tech and are poised to become the most powerful companies in history (Burrows 2018).

Increasingly, governmental organizations (like the CIA and NSA in the United States), political campaigns (like the Obama re-election campaign of 2012), and other institutions are using commercial cloud computing and big data services as well, bringing together "leaders in digital capitalism and the surveillance state to create a marriage that would certainly benefit both parties" (Mosco 2015). This only strengthens the political and social power these companies hold and signifies another step in their agenda to position themselves as essential services.

Another issue that comes up when discussing monopolization and new digital technologies is Intellectual Property (IP) Rights. Birch et al. (2020) postulate that IP rights transforming into a financial instrument, investment asset, and a tradable commodity in recent years has resulted in "the creation and fortification of IP monopolies, particularly in the context of emerging technologies – including the aggregation and analysis of personal data," which has an increasing role in the research process as well as contributes to the growth of academic entrepreneurship. Some companies are refusing to move their operations to the cloud out of fear that the providers of services will be able to access and use insights generated from their data (Rao 2020).

Due to having a de facto monopoly of data collection and storage, computing power, and IP rights, Big Tech also has an increasing connection with elite universities—the companies provide the resources and the universities provide the experts in the field (Ahmed and Wahed 2020), which gives Big Tech a great deal of say about what is and isn't being developed, and for what purpose. A growing body of research

(Birhane et al. 2021; Birch et al. 2020, Montes and Goertzel 2019; Ahmed and Wahed 2020; boyd and Crawford 2012) has confirmed this, pointing to the problem of the increasing financialization and entry of financial actors and big corporations into the field of research and development of AI. Birhane et al. (2022) conducted a quantitative analysis of the affiliation and funding sources of the 100 most influential (and most-cited) papers presented at the ICML and NeurIPS conferences for the years 2008/9 and 2018/19. In the ten-year span, corporate-affiliated authors and funding increased from 43 to 79%, while Big Tech's presence increased from 11 to 58%. At the same time, around 82% of university-affiliated papers were written by authors that attend elite universities. This shows signs of extreme concentration of research and innovation in the hands of corporations and elite universities, which raises many different concerns. Birch et al. (2020) call this the innovation-finance nexus, which developed due to an increasing boom in academic entrepreneurship and a neoliberal marketplace for scientific knowledge. This leads to research and development mainly focusing on profit-making applications, "innovating in order to create (…) new mechanisms, devices of instruments of data ownership and control that are designed to extract value through the ownership and control of personal data" (ibid.) and not on the social consequences of what they produce.

Through their textual analysis of the 100 ML papers Birhane et al. (2022) concluded that the values most frequently exhibited in the papers are "performance (87% of papers), building on past work (79%), generalization (79%), efficiency (73%), quantitative evidence (72%), and novelty (63%)." While these values seem neutral, the authors warn that they are both socially and politically charged, especially in a context where they are defined and operationalized in ways that centralize power. Furthermore, of the 100 texts, only 29% make any mention of societal need, and only 3% make a rigorous attempt to present links connecting their research to societal need. 98 papers contained no references to potential negative impacts. While "values related to user rights and stated in ethical principles appeared very rarely if at all: none of the papers mentioned autonomy, justice, or respect for persons" (ibid.).

3 Socially Harmful Aspects of AI

The key concern lies in the fact that Big Tech companies own the intellectual property rights, operate with colossal research budgets, employ the most sought after data scientists, possess vast amounts of data as well as the centers to store it, own telecommunications networks, and, crucially, cultivate relevant relationships with those in power. They are the ones setting the agenda for AI development (Dyer-Witherford et al. 2019). The platforms might be technically free for users, but they are a two-way market—we are paying for the services with our data. This extractive system creates a profound asymmetry between who is collecting, storing, and analyzing data, and whose data is collected, stored, and analyzed (D'Ignazio and Klein 2020). Even though users produce the data, they are not in control of what happens to it, or in whose hands it ends up and for what purpose.

In the modern era, data has replaced land and the means of production as the most significant asset around which political struggles will revolve. As Harari (2018a) puts it: "Those who control the data control the future not just of humanity, but the future of life itself." The possibility of monitoring and controlling individuals gives companies that exercise control over the development of AI enormous political power. Dyer-Witherford et al. (2019, 3) make a salient point: "Machine intelligence is the product not just of a technological logic, but simultaneously of a social logic, the logic of producing surplus-value." The authors deem AI as a culmination of the process of workers' alienation of control over what they make, how they make it, and of their relationships with fellow human beings (ibid.).

Furthermore, as new technologies will cause many workers to become obsolete, the advancement of AI is also leading to the loss of individuals' economic value. It seems that for the next few decades, human intelligence will still exceed computer intelligence in various fields and that new jobs will appear as old ones start to disappear. However, these new jobs will demand a high level of technical expertise, leaving all those performing routine labor unemployed (Kelly 2020). As AI continues to improve even jobs that demand high (dynamic) cognitive capabilities will start to slowly disappear. According to West (2018), there is a

50% chance that AI will outperform all human tasks in 45 years and automate all jobs in the next 120 years. Study results vary and indicate that 14–54% of US workers have a high probability of seeing their jobs automated over the next 20 years (West 2018).

All of this is why many economists and technology insiders claim (Rotman 2014), that digital technology platforms are one of the main reasons for rising inequality all over the globe, concentrating power and profits while automating many middle-class jobs. Piketty in his work *Capital in the Twenty-First century* (2017) observes that wage inequality in the United States is "probably higher than in any other society at any time in the past, anywhere in the world," and much of the Western world is following suit. The Covid-19 epidemic has only made the situation worse while at the same time shed light on just how much the wealthy are extracting from the rest of the world—while many households lost income and employment, the owners of Big Tech gained 637 billion in wealth (Woods 2020). And since we have been relying on digital technologies to study, keep in touch, entertain ourselves, and do our jobs—it is ever more necessary to question how Big Tech is operating and what kind of influence this has on society at large.

Aside from economic power, Big Tech also wields more and more political and social power. Simončič (2021) points out that due to the progress of AI development it is easier than ever to undermine democracy, and companies have actively been doing so—or at least made it easier for others to do. From covert manipulation of voter preferences through micro-targeting consumers with customized ads based on personal data, which infringes on the autonomy and agency of each individual, through bots, echo chambers, and the resulting polarization of society, emergence, and proliferation of fake news, to "*big nudging,*" a practice in which governments or other actors use "Big Data and AI to exploit psychological weaknesses to steer decisions—creating problems such as damaging social cohesion, democratic principles, and even human rights" (Vinuesa et al. 2020). Another issue to consider is the use of AI and digital technology for surveillance and censorship of particular social groups (Zuboff 2019).

Many of these issues stem from our belief that technology is neutral and that the implementation of technological solutions or improvements

248 K. Simončič and T. Jerele

is inherently better for the functioning of a particular system. But it is not so. Research and development is influenced and encoded with the values and personal preferences of the researchers, interests from academic institutions, funding agencies, corporations, and so on. Recently reports have emerged of the "coded bias" in algorithms and datasets, ranging from racial and gender discrimination within facial recognition systems (Buolamwini and Gebru 2018), racial discrimination within algorithms that help predict repeat offenders (Angwin et al. 2016), and gender discrimination within Amazons hiring algorithm, that through previous hires learned to exclude women and anyone that has "women's" written in their resume (Dastin 2018). D'Ignazio and Klein (2020) point to the lack of diversity within AI firms and elite universities. Only 26% of those in computer and mathematical occupations are women, and out of those only 12% are women of color (while making up 22,5% of the US population); women comprise only 15% of AI research staff at Facebook and 10% at Google; women computer science graduates in the United States peaked in the mid-1980s at 37%, today they represent only 26% of graduates. These numbers indicate that "modern AI is being increasingly shaped by a small number of organizations that are less diverse than the broader population" (Ahmed and Wahed 2020).

Another example of this logic is the impact that Big Tech and Big Data have on the environment. Even though many AI enthusiasts and proponents hail the new technology as key to saving environmental issues, the reality is far more complex. AI and data centers require enormous amounts of energy to operate (Dyer-Witheford et al. 2019). To provide uninterrupted service leads cloud companies to develop several layers of backup, including diesel generators in case of electricity shortages to keep the servers working, which produces greenhouse gas emissions with consequential impacts for climate change, and chemical batteries that are known to pollute groundwater supplies (Mosco 2015; Lucivero 2020). Because of advances in cloud computing and the growth of the use of Internet services, some estimates indicate that data centers have the fastest-growing carbon footprint from across the whole ICT sector (Lucivero 2020). According to a Greenpeace report from 2017 the global IT sector, which is largely US-based, accounted for around 7% of the world's energy use (up 4% from 2014, when the estimate was around 3%). This is more than some of the largest countries in the world, including Russia, Brazil, and Japan. Considering that energy does not come from renewable sources, the cloud has a significant accelerating impact on global climate change (D'Ignazio and Klein, 2020). Two other issues to be considered are the disposal of computing hardware and the indirect effects of ICT relating to users' behaviors and practices, both of which add on to the environmental impact of ICT technologies (Lucivero 2020).

All of this leads to the conclusion that AI, as it's being developed today, is a potential source of social harm and points to the need to "democratize" AI (Fei-Fei 2018), i.e., allow everyone to create AI systems (Reidl 2020). Changing the conditions in which AI is being developed is a necessary first step to a democratized AI; i.e., AI that could, instead of producing social harm, be a source of social good, a term which broadly refers to an action that will result in a benefit available to the general public (Law Dictionary, n.d.) or something that benefits the largest number of people in the largest possible way, also known as common good (Kenton 2021).

4 Democratization of AI

4.1 Toward AI for Social Good

The concept of AI for social good has been gaining traction in the AI community (Hager et al. 2019; Floridi et al. 2020; Cowls et al. 2021). The idea of "social good" is inevitably linked to democracy, as actions beneficial to the general public can hardly be determined any other way than from the bottom up, by letting people decide what matters to them most. When tech companies talk about the democratization of AI they talk about the simplification, standardization of AI that would enable its use for non-experts as well as about possibly granting open access to cloud services to its users, scholars, and other companies (Suddman 2019). However, as observed by Schneider (2018), democratizing something is not only about ensuring access to it but also about»ownership, governance, and accountability.« Democratization not only means access to its use but, more importantly, the possibility of control (Lomonaco and Ziosi 2018). Suddman (2019) goes even further, claiming that the concept of democratization also encompasses the goal of serving good purposes and solving global problems that the majority of the population faces.

For now, there is only a limited understanding of what»AI for social good« in fact constitutes (Cowls et al. 2021). Floridi et al. (2020, 1774) define it as:»the design, development, and deployment of AI systems in ways that (i) prevent, mitigate or resolve problems adversely affecting human life and/or the wellbeing of the natural world, and/or (ii) enable socially preferable and/or environmentally sustainable developments.« Green (2019) points out that the lack of a unifying definition is problematic since by deciding what to work on, what data to use, and what solutions to propose, computer scientists in fact engage in political activity. When there is a lack of reflection with the social and political context, such»solutions« for social good might actually do more harm in the long term than good (Green 2019).

Specific areas of application, such as urban computing, health, environmental sustainability, public welfare (Hager et al. 2019), and various frameworks for the design and development of ethical AI have likewise emerged (Floridi et al. 2018). Floridi et al. (2018), for example, lists enabling human-self realization, enhancing human agency, increasing social capabilities, and cultivating societal cohesion as core opportunities and beneficence, non-malfeasance, autonomy, justice, and explicability as the core principles of an ethical framework for a»Good AI Society.«

There are already several initiatives that aim to use the advances in ML and AI to contribute to social good from a variety of sectors, such as the AI for Social Good (AI4SG) (Tomašev et al. 2020) and AIxSDG that aim to determine how AI can advance the United National Sustainable Development Goals (SDGs) or DataKind, an NGO, that brings together data scientists and social change organizations to collaborate with the goal of maximizing social impact (DataKind 2012). The University of Chicago (2013) has, for example, established a Data Science for Social Good (DSSG) program while private actors, such as Google (2019) and Microsoft (2019), have launched programs with similar goals.

Defining the values of future AI applications is necessary. Yet, while ethical frameworks serve as beacons and point us to where we should head, they are merely the foundation needed to achieve meaningful change. Furthermore, by emphasizing the socially beneficial effects AI can have, the socially harmful effects it has today are somewhat forgotten. A more exhaustive solution that could have tangible immediate results and change the structure of Big Tech that now has a de facto monopoly on developing AI, is needed. Rao (2020) notes that:»for AI to be truly democratized users need to have control over what they run, when they run, and how they use the results of the run« (Rao 2020).

4.2 Cooperatives as Guidelines for a Democratized Big Tech

One way to drastically democratize AI and steer it toward AI that contributes to social good is by applying the cooperative model of running a business to Big Tech, as the model encompasses all of the three elements necessary for the democratization of tech put forward by Schneider (2018, 21): ownership, governance, and accountability. Seeing that the cooperative's purpose is to provide benefits to its users (the University of California, n.d.) (which is in the case of Google, for example, 4 billion people) conceding ownership and decision-making to them might contribute to a shift toward solutions that benefit all or at least the majority of the global population.

Cooperation is not a new concept, seeing that tribal societies, for example, have always practiced some type of cooperation as they recognized the advantage of hunting and gathering in groups rather than individually. The oldest continuing cooperative business in the United States was a mutual fire insurance company in Philadelphia started by Benjamin Franklin in 1752 and the Fenwick Weavers Society in Scotland, which was founded in 1761, and sold discounted oatmeal to workers and assisted workers with savings, loans, emigration, and education (Carrell 2017). The application of cooperative principles to a business organization with an explicit mention of cooperation as an economic system started a few decades later with the Rochdale Society of Equitable Pioneers in 1844 in Great Britain (Holyoake 1893).

The Rochdale Pioneers cooperative was born from the work of activists and thinkers such as the Owenites, who were very active in Rochdale in the 1830s, as well as dr. William King who took Owen's ideas and made them more practical. To Owenites, who theorized and established a number of utopian communities according to communitarian and cooperative principles, the term»equitable« characterized a society in which the exchange of goods and labor would be fairly rewarded and capitalist exploitation eliminated (ibid.). Currently, there are, according to the International Cooperative Alliance, 3 million cooperatives in existence on the global level and at least 12% of global citizens are cooperators in at least one of them. 10% of the employed global population thus works in cooperatives (ICA n.d., b) and the 300 largest cooperatives on the planet generate around 2,146 trillion USD (Monitor n.d.). Most cooperatives are located in Asia, particularly in India and China (Eum 2017).

A cooperative is a people-centered enterprise, owned, controlled, and run by for their members to realize their common economic social, and cultural needs and aspirations (ICA n.d., a). Each member has a vote, regardless of their equity share, unlike investor-owned corporations (IOC), that are owned and controlled by outside shareholders according to their investment share who may or may not use the services of the business. Profits earned in the cooperative business are reinvested in the business and/or a share returned to members, while in IOC profits are returned to shareholders based on their ownership share (Farm Credit n.d.). Cooperatives are driven by values of self-help, self-responsibility, democracy, equality, equity, and solidarity as well as honesty, openness, and social responsibility. The goal is not only ensuring greater shareholder value, but first and foremost creating a sustainable business that generates jobs and prosperity in the long term (ICA n.d., a).

Changing the ownership structure of Big Tech could serve as a first step away from socially harmful AI toward AI for social good or common good, i.e., benefiting the largest number of people (Kenton 2021). This could be done following the seven principles, essential to the ethos of cooperatives, which are derived from the principles that the Rochdale pioneers set out for themselves in 1844. The principle of *voluntary and open membership (1)*, which stands for inclusiveness and the prohibition of discrimination could translate to greater diversity in the ranks of cooperative members, which would contribute to the development of AI that better represents all humanity (Kurimoto et al. 2015). Similarly, the second principle of *democratic member control (2)* stands for the fact that cooperatives are organizations controlled by their members who actively participate in setting policies and making decisions (ibid.). In line with the third principle, *member economic participation (3)*, members contribute to the capital of the cooperative, receive limited compensation, and allocate surpluses to the development of the cooperative as well as to other activities approved by the membership. *Autonomy and independence (4)* of the cooperative are of particular importance in the case of AI, meaning that members would be the ones steering the direction of AI development as opposed to a corporation focused on making a profit. The fifth principle, *education, training, and information (5)*, emphasizes the importance of decentralizing and dispersing knowledge, which a cooperative could provide for its members. The sixth principle, *cooperation among cooperatives (6)*, asserts the importance of cooperation and solidarity with others who have the same principles, as working together helps achieve the goal of creating a more sustainable and equitable economic future for all, Lastly, the *concern for the community (7)* serves as the seventh principle signaling that cooperatives work for the sustainable development of their communities, in particular the local communities in which they operate (ibid.).

There are three different work and employment forms in cooperatives: employees, worker-members, and self-employed producer members. Most cooperatives employ some individuals that work in the cooperative enterprise based on the employee-employer relationship without being members (employees), while worker-members on the other hand work in the cooperative and at the same time partly own it. Self-employed individual producer members, such as fishermen, farmers, artisans, etc., commercialize their products and services through cooperatives or, alternatively, provide cooperatives with production inputs (Eum 2017). Having space and flexibility for different kinds of involvement with the cooperative could be a big benefit to tech companies, as it could differentiate between workers and users, while still acknowledging both in the decision, production, and end processes.

Calzada (2020), looking at the emergence of platform and data cooperatives in Tallinn, Glasgow, and Barcelona finds that Covid-19 has invigorated the interest in cooperatives, but that they are still created randomly by entrepreneurial prerogative, without following a wider policy agenda from the public or private sector. In the past few years the number of cooperatives in tech, i.e., worker-owned cooperatives that operate in the IT industry, has been growing, confirming that the agile mentality that tech people apply when it comes to business, can likewise be applied to governance (Sheffield 2018). An example is CoTech, a growing network of tech cooperatives in the UK comprising 30 tech businesses that collectively employ 250 staff. Platform cooperatives, mutually owned by participants in the platform that connect producers with consumers in transport, accommodation, culture, catering, and in other sectors, have likewise been popping up. But, as Qualthrough (2021) observes, it's very difficult for them to compete with existing platforms' deep pockets.

Woodcock and Graham (2019) maintain that the states should play a much bigger role in facilitating platform cooperatives, by nationalizing existing ones or running them themselves. However, nationalization presents a whole other set of issues—the state running the cooperatives would mean trusting the elected officials to lead it in a way that embodies the basic cooperative principles and since most governments are tirelessly lobbied by the tech industry and abide under the neoliberal economic policy of the lean state, it is doubtful that they could be the solution. Besides, nationalization without implementing any other changes would merely transfer power and control from the ultra-wealthy to the elected and unelected officials, reminiscent of the situation in China, where social control, powered by AI, is thriving. When envisioning turning Big Tech companies into cooperatives, the idea is that the companies would be owned by its members, i.e., producers of data, implying that the power over what kind of future we want is put into all of our hands, not just the selected few.

10 Democratizing the Governance of AI: From Big Tech ... 255

Despite its commendable principles, running a business in the form of a cooperative does not automatically mean it will be run democratically. A study shows that in Slovenia, for example, in times of Yugoslav socialist self-management 50,6% of respondents replied that they never attended workers' council meetings (Whitehorn 1978), indicating that only half of the workforce was actively participating in the management of the company. One must keep in mind though, that Yugoslav self-management was a specific system, where any major decisions had to go through the blue-collar dominated workers' councils, when in reality only management was capable of making sound business decisions which only increased the sense of alienation inside of the work collectives (Ness and Azzellini 2011).

Another common criticism of cooperatives is that it's difficult for them to find investors or capital since lending institutions are not prone to making business loans to new business models due to the higher risk they pose to them and that, furthermore, most investors want to invest their money in a business that aims to maximize profit for the shareholders and not, primarily, compensate their workers-owners. Yet, service worker cooperatives, for example, whose main expense is the payroll, may not require large investments or capital. Some critics likewise believe that worker cooperatives are not scalable (Keng 2014), however this argument is clearly disproven with the existence of companies such as Mondragon that employ more than 80,000 workers.

It is likewise necessary to acknowledge that cooperatives established in the capitalist market must naturally compete with other, potentially exploitative firms, making it difficult for them to survive (Luxemburg 1900). As Faber (2002, 64 65) points out, this can lead to the situation where "the employees only have agency insofar as this agency acts in the interests of the company." Mondragon, for example, was unable to attract top managerial staff, so they had to raise the wage ratio from 1:5 to 1:12. Government subsidies that would assist cooperatives in their participation on the capitalist market would be a welcome solution to this problem. Naturally, the way institutions work in the real world is never a perfect reflection of their fundamental values, meaning constant improvements of implemented systems are inevitable. Yet, this doesn't mean that a system based on democratic, humanistic values that strives

5 Discussion

The idea of transforming Big Tech into cooperatives owned by its members can easily be dismissed as a fool's daydream. How could it possibly be done and why would Big Tech owners ever relinquish their boundless power? Is there any chance that social media users look up from the infinite»scroll« and start recognizing the value of their data and demanding something in return? Short of an imminent disaster shaking everyone to their core, it's hard to imagine. Another relevant question that presents itself is whether AI can ever be detached from capitalism and thus put social good before profit and the collateral social harm; Dyer-Witherford et al. (2019), for example, claim that it can't. According to Land (2014), AI is a technology that implements the logic of capital at its very core and this coupling of capital and AI leads not to human emancipation from capitalism, but, rather, to capital's emancipation from humans and consequently to human extinction.

Aside from changing the ownership structure of Big Tech and turning them into cooperatives, many other solutions for AI that are democratic, more inclusive, open, decentralized, and directed toward social good exist. Breaking up Big Tech is essential, but no substantial change will be achieved if in the end there are only more medium-sized companies that behave in the same way. One of the crucial goals to strive toward is to educate more people in ICT technologies and diversify research and development communities. Governments need to step up and ensure more privacy and rights for users of platforms worldwide. Currently, there are ongoing debates in the EU, USA, and elsewhere about privacy and data governance, which is an important first step to secure our data and start discussing the regulation of AI on a global scale. UNESCO has opened its first International Research Centre for AI in Slovenia, whose mission is "to generate relevant statistics on AI, AI-related applications and associated technological innovations and (…) work on legal, ethical and social implications of AI, through both awareness-raising and capacity-building efforts in the global North and South" (UNESCO 2019).

Following the example of the Defund the police movement in the United States, Barenregdt et al. (2021), for example, call for defunding of Big Tech, by which they mean abolishing the conditions that allow Big Tech to hold excessive control over ICT infrastructure and by redirecting its excessive revenues to support socially beneficial aims. The authors point out that, to defund, in the context of abolitionism, means to give voice to local communities to decide how to redirect the funds now invested in enforcement and imprisonment, which is what they propose for Big Tech as well, starting with radical democratization of ICT design and governance (Barenregdt et al. 2021).

Posner and Weyl (2019) on the other hand argue that the production of data that occurs as we, for example, use social media, should be considered as labor and remunerated accordingly. Recognizing data as labor could also serve as a desired earning opportunity for citizens affected by rising inequality. The authors propose the creation of data labor unions that would advocate for the rights of data workers against the tech companies (ibid.).

Since the commercialization of science and technology has led to a restriction of access to data and tools and has been limiting access to the benefits of the developments in AI, a vast number of academics and software engineers are advocating for solutions that enable to open innovation (Birch et al. 2020). Proponents emphasize that basic hardware and software components already exist and that these tools should therefore be available to all. An interesting initiative along these lines is the movement to create decentralized data markets on blockchain infrastructure and to connect data owners (governments, businesses, NGOs, etc.) with experts in software development and machine learning (Lauterbach 2019). Ocean Data Foundation, for example, is a non-governmental organization (NGO) that offers solutions for aggregating and navigating vast amounts of ocean data, drawing open institutional ocean data, the industry, independent scientists, by liberating and contextualizing that data (Ocean Data Foundation, n.d.).

At the Institute for Human-Centered AI (HAI), founded at Stanford, an initiative calling for a National Research Cloud (NRC) that would enable academic and nonprofit researchers with access to computing power and government datasets needed for education and research, has been launched. With the goal of democratizing AI research, education, and innovation HAI lobbied US congressmen and achieved the establishment of a National AI Research Resource Task Force that will study the possibilities of implementing NRC across the United States (Stanford University n.d.).

Privacy-sensitive alternative social networking sites, such as Diaspora, Friendica, Libertree, and identi.ca are popping up. Diaspora, for example, is a social networking site that consists of a potentially unlimited number of interoperating servers where user data is not stored and managed centrally (Sevignani 2012). The Diaspora software is produced according to "peer-production", i.e., a mode of production that relies on self-organizing communities of individuals who come together to produce an outcome (Sevignani 2012).

One of the proponents of distributed, decentralized, and democratized development of AI, Ben Goertzel, has co-created Singularity.net, the first and only existing decentralized platform that allows AI to cooperate and coordinate at scale and enables open access to of global network of AI algorithms (Montes and Goertzel 2019). Another notable effort toward liberation from Big Tech is DECIDIM, a free and open-source system for participatory governance approaches, now being used in Barcelona, Milan, and Mexico City that helps citizens, organizations, and public institutions to self-organize democratically (Decidim n.d.).

Furthermore, numerous initiatives addressing racial, gender, and sexual discrimination within AI research and development exist. *Algorithmic Justice League* fights against racial bias in facial recognition technology, *Queer in AI* has made it their "mission to raise awareness of queer issues in AI/ML, foster a community of queer researchers and celebrate the work of queer scientists" (Queer in AI, n.d) and *Black in AI* is a "place for sharing ideas, fostering collaborations and discussing initiatives to increase the presence of Black people in the field of Artificial Intelligence" (Black in AI, n.d.). Another project worth mentioning is *RadicalAI,* which aims to expose "how AI rearranges power and dreams up and builds human/AI systems that put power in the hands of the people" (RadicalAI, n.d.).

As these initiatives indicate, in order to mitigate the negative effects of AI and new digital technologies, there are many things that must be done, however the reorganization of Big Tech's ownership structure seems like a good place to start. While cooperatives might not be a panacea for the troubles new technologies are creating, we must nevertheless keep imagining what another world would look like. Imagining can be a constructive exercise in creating AI that could potentially be socially beneficial and the principles that apply to cooperatives, in the very least, serve as a useful example of a democratized form of ownership over technologies that will affect generations to come.

Whatever we do, we must start right away. There is an urgent need for a democratic debate about which technology do we, as individuals and as a global community, want to be implemented and which we do not, and all new technologies need to be tested for bias against marginalized communities and groups. But most importantly, for a just and good society, we must shift power from the few monopolistic corporations, their ultra-rich owners, and shareholders, and give it to the many.

Acknowledgements The research leading to this chapter has received funding from the Slovenian Research Agency, under the research project "Human Rights and Regulation of Trustworthy Artificial Intelligence" (No. V5-1930).

References

Abeba Birhane, Pratyusha Kalluri, Dallas Card, William Agnew, Ravit Dotan, and Michelle Bao. 2022. The Values Encoded in Machine Learning Research. In 2022 ACM Conference on Fairness, Accountability, and Transparency (FAccT 22). Association for Computing Machinery, New York, NY, USA, 173–184. https://doi.org/10.1145/3531146.3533083

Ahmed, Nuri Mahmoud and Muntasir Wahed. 2020. "The De-democratization of AI: Deep Learning and the Compute Divide in Artificial Intelligence Research." ArXiv abs/2010.15581: n. pag.

Amadeo, Kimberly. 2021. "What Is a Monopoly?" *The Balance.* Retrieved from: https://www.thebalance.com/monopoly-4-reasons-it-s-bad-and-its-history-3305945. Accessed on 20.9.2021.

Angwin, Julia, Larson, Jeff, Mattu, Surja, and Kirchner, Lauren. 23.05.2016. "Machine Bias." ProPublica. https://www.propublica.org/article/machine-bias-risk-assessments-in-criminal-sentencing. Accessed on 5.9.2021.

Barendregt, Wolmert, Becker, Christoph, Cheon, EunJeong, Clement, Andrew, Reynolds-Cuéllar, Pedro, Schuler, Douglas, and Suchman, Lucy. 2021. "Defund Big Tech, Refund Community." *Tech Otherwise.* https://doi.org/10.21428/93b2c832.e0100a3f.

Birch, Kean et al. 2020. The problem of innovation in technoscientific capitalism: Data rentiership and the policy implications of turning personal digital data into a private asset. *Policy Studies, 41,* 468–487.

Black in AI. https://blackinai.github.io/#/about. Accessed on 12.9.2021.

Bosshardt, William, and Lopus, Jane S. 2013. "Business in the Middle Ages: What Was the Role of Guilds?" *Social Education,* 77(2), 64–67.

boyd, danah, and Crawford, Kate. 2012. "Critical Questions for Big Data: Provocations for a Cultural, Technological, and Scholarly Phenomenon." *Information, Communication, & Society,* 15(5), 662–679.

Buolamwini, Joy, and Gebru, Timnit. 2018. "Gender Shades: Intersectional Accuracy Disparities in Commercial Gender Classification." *Proceedings of Machine Learning Research,* 81(1–15), 2018 Conference on Fairness, Accountability, and Transparency.

Burrows, Peter. 2018. "How the AI cloud Could Produce the Richest Companies Ever." *MIT Technology Review.* Retrieved from: https://www.technologyreview.com/2018/03/22/144507/how-the-ai-cloud-could-produce-the-richest-companies-ever/. Accessed on 20.07.2021.

Carrell, Severin. 2017. "Strike Rochdale from the Record Books. The Co-op Began in Scotland." *The Guardian.* Retrieved from: https://www.theguardian.com/business/2007/aug/07/retail.uknews. Accessed on 27.8.2021.

Calzada, Igor. 2020. "Platform and Data Co-operatives Amidst European Pandemic Citizenship." *Sustainibility,* 12, 8309. https://doi.org/10.3390/su12208309.

Cowls, Josh, Tsamados, Andreas, Taddeo, Marirosaria, and Floridi, Luciano. 2021. "A Definition, Benchmark and Database of AI for Social Good Initiatives." *Nature Machine Intelligence,* 3(2), 111–115.

D'Ignazio, Catherine, and Klein, Lauren. 2020. "The Power Chapter." In *Data Feminism.* Retrieved from: https://data-feminism.mitpress.mit.edu/pub/vi8obxh7. Accessed on 26.8.2021.

Dafoe, Allan, Bachrach, Yoram, Hadfield, Gillian, Horvitz, Eric, Larson, Kate, and Graepel, Thore. 2021. "Cooperative AI: Machines Must Learn to find Common Ground." *Nature*. Retrieved from: https://www.nature.com/art icles/d41586-021-01170-0. Accessed on 25.8.2021.

Dastin, Jeffrey. 11.10.2018. "Amazon Scraps Secret AI Recruiting Tool That Chowed Bias Against Women." *Reuters*. Retrieved from: https://www.reu ters.com/article/us-amazon-com-jobs-automation-insight/amazon-scraps-secret-ai-recruiting-tool-that-showed-bias-against-women-idUSKCN1M K08G. Accessed on 23.8.2021.

DataKind. 2012. https://www.datakind.org. Accessed on 13.8.2021.

Decidim—Free Open-Source Participatory Democracy for Cities and Organizations. https://decidim.org. Accessed on 13.8.2021.

Döpfner, Mathias. 2018. "Jeff Bezos Reveals What It's Like to Build an Empire—And Why He's Willing to Spend $1 Billion a Year to Fund the Most Important Mission of his Life." *Business Insider*. Retrieved from: https://www.businessinsider.com/jeff-bezos-interview-axel-springer-ceo-ama zon-trump-blue-origin-family-regulation-washington-post-2018-4. Accessed on 17.8.2021.

Dyer-Witheford, Nick, Kjøsen, Atle Mikkola, and Steinhoff, James. 2019. *Inhuman Power. Artificial Intelligence and the Future of Capitalism*. London: Pluto Press.

Eum, Hyung-sik. 2017. "Cooperatives and Employment: Second Global Report." *International Cooperative Alliance*. Retrieved from: https://www. ica.coop/sites/default/files/publication-files/cooperatives-and-employment-second-global-report-625518825.pdf. Accessed on 15.8.2021.

European Commission. 2017. "Attitudes Towards the Impact of Digitisation and Automation on Daily Life: Report." Publications Office. Retrieved from: https://data.europa.eu/doi/https://doi.org/10.2759/835661. Accessed on 15.8.2021.

Fairbairn, Brett. 1994. *The Meaning of Rochdale: The Rochdale Pioneers and the Co-operative Principles (Occasional paper series)*. Centre for the Study of Co-operatives, University of Saskatchewan. Retrieved from: http://www.col umbia.edu/~hauben/amalgamated/history/35/Meaning_of_Rochdale.pdf. Accessed on 25.8.2021.

Fei-Fei, Li. 2018. "How to Make A.I. That's Good for People." *The New York Times*. Retrieved from: https://www.nytimes.com/2018/03/07/opinion/artifi cial-intelligence-human.html. Accessed on 14.7.2021.

Feiner, Lauren. 2020. "House Democrats Say Facebook, Amazon, Alphabet, Apple Enjoy 'Monopoly Power' and Recommend Big Changes." *CNBC*.

Retrieved from: https://www.cnbc.com/2020/10/06/house-democrats-say-facebook-amazon-alphabet-apple-enjoy-monopoly-power.html. Accessed on 17.7.2021.

Federal Trade Commission. "Monopolization Defined." Retrieved from: https://www.ftc.gov/tips-advice/competition-guidance/guide-antitrust-laws/single-firm-conduct/monopolization-defined. Accessed on 25.06.2021.

Floridi, Luciano, Cowls, Josh, Beltrametti, Monica, Chatila, Raja, Chazerand, Patrice, Dignum, Virginia, Luetge, Christoph, Madelin, Robert, Pagallo, Ugo, Rossi, Francesca, Schafer, Burkhard, Valcke, Peggy, and Vayena, Effy. 2018. "AI4People—An Ethical Framework for a Good AI Society: Opportunities, Risks, Principles, and Recommendations." *Minds and Machines*, 28(4), 689–707.

Floridi, Luciano, Cowls, Josh, King, Thomas C., and Taddeo, Mariarosaria. 2020. "How to Design AI for Social Good: Seven Essential Factors." *Science and Engineering Ethics*, 26(3), 1771–1796.

Fuchs, Christian. 2019. *Rereading Marx In The Age Of Digital Capitalism.* London: Pluto Press.

Google. 2019. "Google AI for Social Good." https://ai.google/social-good/. Accessed on 24.8.2021.

Green, Ben. 2019. ""Good" Isn't Good Enough." In *Proceedings of the AI for Social Good workshop at NeurIPS*. Retrieved from: https://www.benzevgreen.com/wp-content/uploads/2019/11/19-ai4sg.pdf. Accessed on 27.8.2021.

Faber, Brenton. D. 2002. *Community Action and Organizational Change: Image, Narrative, Identity.* Carbondale, IL: Southern Illinois University Press.

Hager, Gregory D., Drobnis, Ann, Fang, Fei, Ghani, Rayid, Greenwald, Amy, Lyons, Terah, Parkes, David C., Schultz, Jason, Saria, Suchi, Smith, Stephen F., and Tambe, Milind. 2019. "Artificial Intelligence for Social Good." arXiv preprint arXiv:1901.05406.

Harari, Yuval Noah. in Dickson, Ben. 2018a. "AI, Big Data and the Future of Humanity." Retrieved from: https://bdtechtalks.com/2018a/01/31/yuval-harari-wef-ai-big-data-digital-dictatorship/. Accessed on 10.8.2021.

Harari, Yuval Noah. 2018b. "Why Technology Favors Tyranny." *The Atlantic*, 322(3), 64–73. Retrieved from: https://www.theatlantic.com/magazine/archive/2018b/10/yuval-noah-harari-technology-tyranny/568330/. Accessed on 13.7.2021.

Howell, Sean. 2019. "Big Data and Monopolization." *Antitrust: Antitrust Law & Policy eJournal.*

Holyoake, G. Jacob. 1893. *The History of the Rochdale Pioneers.* 10th ed. London: Sonnenschein.

International Cooperative Alliance (ICA a). "What Is a Cooperative?" Retrieved from: https://www.ica.coop/en/cooperatives/what-is-a-cooperative. Accessed on 15.8.2021.

International Cooperative Alliance (ICA b). "Facts and Figures." Retrieved from: https://www.ica.coop/en/cooperatives/facts-and-figures. Accessed on 15.8.2021.

Kelly, Jack. 2020. "U.S. Lost Over 60 Million Jobs—Now Robots, Tech And Artificial Intelligence Will Take Millions More." *Forbes*. Retrieved from: https://www.forbes.com/sites/jackkelly/2020/10/27/us-lost-over-60-million-jobs-now-robots-tech-and-artificial-intelligence-will-take-millions-more/. Accessed on 23.9.2021.

Keng, Cameron. 2014. "If Apple Were a Worker Cooperative, Each Employee Would Earn At Least \$403K". *Forbes*. Retrieved from: https://www.forbes.com/sites/cameronkeng/2014/12/18/if-apple-was-a-worker-cooperative-each-employee-would-earn-at-least-403k/. Accessed on 15.9.2021.

Kenton, Zachary, Tom Everitt, Laura Weidinger, Iason Gabriel, Vladimir Mikulik, and Geoffrey Irving. 2021. Alignment of language agents. arXiv preprint arXiv:2103.14659.

Kuhlman, Caitlin, Jackson, Latifa, and Chunara, Rumi. 2020. "No Computation Without Representation: Avoiding Data and Algorithm Biases Through Diversity." Retrieved from http://arxiv.org/abs/2002.11836. Accessed on 19.8.2021.

Kurimoto, Akira, Draperi, Jean–François, Bancel, Jean-Louis, Novkovic, Sonja, Shaw, Linda, Wilson, Mervyn, and Cracogna, Dante. 2015. *Guidance Notes to the Co-operative Principles*. International Co-operative Alliance: Consult. Em, 10, 2016.

Land, Nick. 8.3.2014. "The Teleological Identity of Capitalism and Artificial Intelligence: Remarks to the Participants of the Incredible Machines 2014 Conference." formerly available at http://incrediblemachines.info/nick-land-the-teleological-identity-of-capitalism-and-artificial-intelligence. Accessed on 15.8.2021

Lauterbach, Anastasia. 2019. "Artificial Intelligence and Policy: Quo Vadis?" *Digital Policy, Regulation and Governance*. ISSN: 2398–5038. Retrieved from: https://www.emerald.com/insight/content/doi/10.1108/DPRG-09-2018-0054/full/html?skipTracking=true.

Lucivero, Federica. 2020. "Big Data, Big Waste? A Reflection on the Environmental Sustainability of Big Data Initiatives." *Sci Eng Ethics*, 26, 1009–1030. https://doi.org/10.1007/s11948-019-00171-7.

Lomonaco, Vincenzo, and Ziosi, Marta. 2018: "On the Myth of AI Democratization." Retrieved from: https://medium.com/ai-for-people/on-the-myth-of-ai-democratizationa472115cb5f1. Accessed on 26.8.2021.

Luxemburg, Rosa. 1900 (1986). *Reform and Revolution*. London: Militant Publications. Retrieved from: https://www.marxists.org/archive/luxemburg/1900/reform-revolution/index.htm. Accessed 20.10.2021.

Menaldo, Victor. 2021. "Breaking up Big Tech: A Solution in Search of a Problem." *Venture Beat*. Retrieved from: https://venturebeat.com/2021/02/11/breaking-up-big-tech-a-solution-in-search-of-a-problem/. Accessed on 24.8.2021.

Microsoft. 2019. "Microsoft AI for Humanity." Retrieved from: https://www.microsoft.com/en-us/ai/ai-forhumanitarian-action. Accessed on 29.7.2021.

Monitor Coop. "Large Cooperatives at the Forefront of Recovery." Retrieved from: https://monitor.coop/en. Accessed on 28.8.2021.

Montes, Gabriel Axel, and Goertzel, Ben. 2019. "Distributed, Decentralized, and Democratized Artificial Intelligence." *Technological Forecasting & Social Change*, 141, 354–358.

Mosco, Vincent. 2015. "Marx in the Cloud." In *Marx in the Age of Digital Capitalism*, edited by Christian Fuchs and Vincent Mosco. Boston: Brill.

Ness, Immanuel, Azzellini, Dario. 2011. *Ours to Master and to Own: Workers' Control from the Commune to the Present*. Haymarket Books.

Ocean Data Foundation. "What Is the Ocean Data Foundation." Retrieved from: https://foundation.oceandata.earth/about. Accessed on 13.8.2021.

Piketty, Thomas. 2017. *Capital in the Twenty-First Century*. Cambridge, MA: The Belknap Press of Harvard University Press.

Posner, Eric A., and Weyl, E. Glen. 2019. *Radical Markets. Uprooting Capitalism and Democracy for a Just Society*. Princeton University Press.

Radical AI. Retrieved from: https://radicalai.net/. Accessed on 12.9.2021.

Rao, Anand. 2020. "Democratizing Artificial Intelligence Is a Double-Edged Sword." Retrieved from: https://www.strategy-business.com/article/Democratizing-artificial-intelligence-is-a-double-edged-sword. Accessed on 24.7.2021.

Riedl, Mark. 2020. "AI Democratization in the Era of GPT-3." *The Gradient*. Retrieved from: https://thegradient.pub/ai-democratization-in-the-era-of-gpt-3/. Accessed on 24.8.2021.

Richter, Felix. 2021. "Amazon Leads $150-Billion Cloud Market." *Statista*. Retrieved from: https://www.statista.com/chart/18819/worldwide-market-share-of-leading-cloud-infrastructure-service-providers/. Accessed on 22.7.2021.

Rotman, David. 2014. "Technology and Inequality." *MIT Technology Review.* Retrieved from: https://www.technologyreview.com/2014/10/21/170679/technology-and-inequality/. Accessed on 17.8.2021.

Qualthrough, Edward. 2021. "Why 'Platform Cooperatives' Have Yet to Challenge Big Tech." *Tech Monitor.* Retrieved from: https://techmonitor.ai/regulation-compliance/why-platform-cooperatives-have-yet-to-challenge-big-tech. Accessed on 7.9.2021.

Queer in AI. https://sites.google.com/view/queer-in-ai/home. Accessed on 12.9.2021.

Sevignani, Sebastian. 2012. "The Problem of Privacy in Capitalism and the Alternative Social Networking Site Diaspora." *tripleC: Communication, Capitalism & Critique. Open Access Journal for a Global Sustainable Information Society,* 10(2), 600–617.

Sheffield, Hazel. 2018. "Tech Co-operatives Are Leaving the Startup Race Behind." *Wired.* Retrieved from: https://www.wired.co.uk/article/cotech-tech-cooperatives-blake-house-outlandish. Accessed on 2.9.2021.

Shen, Lucinda. 2017. "Former U.S. CTO: The "Robot Apocalypse" Could Happen. Here's How YouStop It." *Fortune.* Retrieved from: https://fortune.com/2017/11/14/megan-smith-cto-robot-apocalypse-elon-musk/. Accessed on 27.8.2021.

Simončič, Katja. 2021. "Vpliv umetne inteligence na človekove pravice in na nastanek družbene škode v različnih družbenih domenah." In *Pravo in umetna inteligenca: Vprašanja etike, človekovih pravic in družbene škode,* edited by Aleš Završnik and Katja Simončič (fothcoming). Ljubljana: Inštitut za kriminologijo pri Pravni fakulteti v Ljubljani.

Schneider, Nathan. 2018. *Everything for Everyone: How the Co-Op Revival Is Powering the Next Economy.* Public Affairs.

SUBCOMMITTEE ON ANTITRUST, COMMERCIAL AND ADMINISTRATIVE LAW, UNITED STATES. 2020. Retrieved from: https://fm.cnbc.com/applications/cnbc.com/resources/editorialfiles/2020/10/06/investigation_of_competition_in_digital_markets_majority_staff_report_and_recommendations.pdf. Accessed on 12.7.2021.

Stanford University, Human-Centred Artificial Intelligence. "National Research Cloud." Retrieved from: https://hai.stanford.edu/policy/national-research-cloud. Accessed on 6.9.2021.

Suddman, Andreas. 2019. *The Democratization of Artificial Intelligence.* Verlag, Bielefeld.

Thiel, Peter. 2014. *Zero to One: Notes on Startups, or How to Build the Future.* New York: Crown Business.

Tomašev, Nenad, Cornebise, Julien, Hutter, Frank, Mohamed, Shakir, Picciariello, Angela, Connelly, Bec, Belgrave, Danielle C. M., Ezer, Daphne, van der Haert, Fanny Cachat, Mugisha, Frank, Abila, Gerald, Arai, Hiromi, Almiraat, Hisham, Proskurnia, Julia, Snyder, Kyle, Otake-Matsuura, Mihoko, Othman, Mustafa, Glasmachers, Tobias, de Wever, Wilfried, Teh, Yee Whye, Khan, Mohammad Emtiyaz, De Winne, Ruben, Schaul, Tom, and Clopath, Claudia. 2020. "AI for Social Good: Unlocking the Opportunity for Positive Impact." *Nature Communications*, 11(1), 1–6.

University of California. "What Is a Cooperative?" Retrieved from: http://sfp.ucdavis.edu/cooperatives/what_is/. Accessed on 12.8.2021.

University of Chicago. 2013. "Data Science for Social Good." Retrieved from: https://dssg.uchicago.edu/. Accessed on 12.8.2021.

UNESCO. 2019. "Slovenia to Host International Research Centre on Artificial Intelligence under the Auspices of UNESCO." Retrieved from: https://en.unesco.org/news/slovenia-host-international-research-centre-artificial-intell igence-under-auspices-unesco. Accessed on 17.9.2021.

U.S. Dep't of Justice. 2008. "Competition and Monopoly: Single-Firm Conduct Under Section 2 of the Sherman Act." Retrieved from: https://www.justice.gov/atr/competition-and-monopoly-single-firm-conduct-under-section-2-sherman-act-chapter-2. Accessed on 20.8.2021.

Vinuesa, Ricardo, Azizpour, Hossein, Leite, Iolanda, Balaam, Madeline, Dignum, Virginia, Dmoisch, Sami, Felländer, Anna, Langhans, Simona Daniela, Tegmark, Max, and Nerini, Franseco Fuso. 2020. "The Role of Artificial Intelligence in Achieving the Sustainable Development Goals." *Nat Commun*, 11, 233. https://doi.org/10.1038/s41467-019-14108-y.

Walch, Kathleen. 2020. "AI Laws Are Coming." *Forbes*. Retrieved from: https://www.forbes.com/sites/cognitiveworld/2020/02/20/ai-laws-are-coming/. Accessed on 22.9.2021.

Webb, Amy. 2019. *The Big Nine*. New York: PublicAffairs.

West, Darrell M. 2018. *The Future of Work: Robots, AI, and Automation*. Brookings Institution Press.

Whitehorn, Alan. 1978. "Yugoslav Workers' Self-Management: A Blueprint for Industrial Democracy?" *Canadian Slavonic Papers*, 20(3), 421–428.

Woodcock, Jamie, and Graham, Mark. 2019. *The Gig Economy: A Critical Introduction*. Oxford: Polity Books.

Woods, Hiatt. 2020. "How Billionaires Saw Their Net Worth Increase by Half a Trillion Dollars During the Pandemic." *Business Insider*. Retrieved from: https://www.businessinsider.com/billionaires-net-worth-inc reases-coronavirus-pandemic-2020-7?op=1. Accessed on 23.8.2021.

Zuboff, Shoshana, and Karin Schwandt. 2019. The Age of Surveillance Capitalism: The Fight for a Human Future at the New Frontier of Power. Profile Books.

Index

A

Academic entrepreneurship 244, 245
Accountability 37, 65, 70, 72, 112,
  114, 117, 118, 147, 185, 186,
  194, 197, 199, 200, 227, 249,
  251
Activists 252
Addictive design 109
Advertising 86, 87, 89–91, 94, 242,
  243
Agriculture 210, 211, 229
AI ethics 104, 184
AI for social good 240, 241, 249,
  250, 252
AI governance 101, 103, 104,
  111–113, 115, 117, 118,
  128–130, 184
AI guidelines 183, 230
AI monopolies 241
AI Regulation 142, 143, 208, 209,
  217–219, 226, 228–230
Algorithm 3, 5, 7, 9, 11, 13–18,
  23–26, 40–42, 48, 59, 60,
  65–67, 72, 77, 78, 80, 82,
  84–89, 91–94, 105, 106, 108,
  109, 111, 122, 125, 143, 147,
  153, 154, 156, 161, 163–171,
  173–176, 185, 195, 198, 199,
  241, 243, 248, 258
Algorithmic audits 93
Algorithmic impact assessment
  (AIA) 114
Alibaba 240, 243
Alienation 246, 255
Al-Khawaja-test 17
Amazon 86, 240, 242, 248
Amazon Web Services (AWS) 63,
  64, 66, 67, 69, 71–73, 243
Apple 122, 240, 242

© The Editor(s) (if applicable) and The Author(s), under exclusive
license to Springer Nature Switzerland AG 2023
A. Završnik and K. Simončič (eds.), *Artificial Intelligence, Social Harms
and Human Rights*, Critical Criminological Perspectives,
https://doi.org/10.1007/978-3-031-19149-7

270 Index

Artificial Intelligence (AI) 3, 12, 22, 57, 58, 78, 92, 94, 101, 122, 142, 143, 145, 146, 148, 150, 151, 156, 169, 176, 183, 207, 239
Asimov 166, 174
Attitude 107, 108, 198
Auditing 93, 194
Authentication 35, 40, 105
Authorication 38, 219, 220
Automated decision-making (ADM) 78, 104, 105, 185, 198
Automated weaponry 63
Automated weapons 58, 59, 65, 66
Automation 220
Automation bias 15, 16
Autonomous systems 26
Autonomous Weapons Systems (AWS) 58–60

Baidu 240
Beneficence 217, 218, 226, 230, 250
Bias 8, 15, 24, 25, 41, 82, 87, 88, 93, 102, 105, 106, 108, 109, 122, 144, 152, 154, 162, 164, 172, 176, 194, 198, 258, 259
Big data 9, 10, 25, 92, 112, 243, 244, 248
Big Nudging 247
BigScience Large Open-science Open-access Multilingual Language Model (BLOOM) 105, 106
Big tech 58, 101, 113, 114, 119, 240, 241, 243–248, 251, 252, 254, 256–259
Big tech monopolies 243

Biometric 35–49, 105, 151
Black box 9, 16, 85, 93, 120, 185
Blackstone-ratio 41
Border surveillance 107

C

Candidate selection 87
Candidate sourcing 86
Carbon footprint 248
Case-based reasoning 168
Climate change 143, 209, 214, 216, 226, 229, 248, 249
Cloud computing 243, 244, 248
Coded bias 248
Code of conduct 156
Collision avoiding mechanisms 213
Combatant 63, 64, 66, 72
Commodities 244
Common good 125, 249, 252
Community 36, 103, 107, 110, 122, 148, 150, 224, 249, 258, 259
Compliance 43, 66, 67, 70, 71, 103, 119, 126, 148–152, 156, 184, 220, 221, 225
Computability 170, 172
Computational complexity 163, 167, 170, 172, 173, 175
Computational ethics 161–168, 172–176
Computational power 35, 243
Computer science 107, 108, 165, 168, 172, 173, 184, 208, 248
Computer vision 103, 104, 107, 119, 121–123, 125, 126, 130
Confirmation bias 106
Conflict 58, 60–69, 72, 73, 104, 118, 147, 170

Index **271**

Consequentialism 166, 167, 169, 175
Cooperatives 241, 252–256, 259
Corporate responsibility 186, 189, 193, 199
Corporations 60, 127, 188, 245, 248, 253, 259
Covid-19 109, 247, 254
Criminal law 7, 9, 19, 46, 119
Critical criminology 102
Customers' preferences 88

D

DALL-E2 106
Damage 62, 85, 102, 121, 146, 147, 213, 219, 221, 222, 225, 228, 230
Damage prevention 146
Database 7, 21, 37, 39, 41–46, 82, 88, 122, 123, 125
Data collecting 216
Data collection 46, 81, 108, 152, 244
Data processing 11, 119, 121, 126, 130
Data protection 20, 21, 38, 44, 45, 49, 90–92, 103, 119–121, 123, 124, 126, 128, 130, 147, 185
Data scientists 246, 250
Data workers 257
Decentralized AI 256, 258
Deepfake 106, 124
Defence 69, 114
Degrading treatment 9, 10, 25
Democracy 106, 125, 144, 145, 247, 249, 252
Democratization of AI 249

Democratized AI 249
Deontological ethics 103, 107, 117, 129, 167, 169
Deontological rules 167, 168
Digital capitalism 244
Digital ethics 110, 111
Digital governance 111
Digital Humanities 121
Digital regulation 111
Discrimination 21, 23–25, 48, 77–89, 91, 93, 94, 103, 119–121, 144, 185, 192, 194, 226, 229, 253, 258
Diversity 109, 147, 196, 248, 253
Do-no-harm principle 166
Drones 58, 60–69, 72, 73, 211

E

Echo chamber 106, 247
Effective remedy 37, 185, 189, 193, 197, 200
Elite universities 244, 245, 248
Empathy 13, 108, 162
Employment 70, 77–86, 89, 90, 94, 104, 247, 253
Employment Equality Directive 80, 83, 87
Engineering 57, 103, 108, 114, 122
Environmental harm 209, 210, 212, 216
Environmental impact 111, 129, 131, 249
Equality 4, 7, 41, 45, 79, 88, 90, 125, 144, 145, 192, 193, 219, 252
Equality of arms 16–18
Equity 146, 252
Ethical awareness 107

Index

Ethical concerns 57, 64, 65, 106
Ethical fading 164
Ethical Guidelines 102, 142–146, 149, 150, 152, 227
Ethically permissible decision 175
Ethical reasoning 163, 165, 169
Ethical theory 167, 169, 174
Ethics assessment 101, 103
Ethics governance 102, 118
Ethics tuning 108
Ethification 111
European Convention of Human Rights (ECHR) 5, 9–13, 15, 16, 18–26, 79
European Data Protection Supervisor (EDPS) 126–128
European Research Area 126
EU values 145, 152
Explainability 48, 126, 147
Explainable AI 11, 17, 18, 26

F

Facebook 86, 89–91, 240, 242, 243, 248
Facial/face recognition 36, 39–43, 45–47, 57, 185, 248, 258
Fair trial 12, 16, 18, 21, 24, 37, 48, 185
Feedback loop 24, 194
Filter bubble 106
Financialization 245
Forensics 35–38, 41–43, 47–49
Function creep 46, 48

G

Gas emissions 248
Gender 24, 25, 46, 84, 90–92, 258

Gender discrimination 248
Gender Equality Directive 81, 83, 90, 92
General Data Protection Regulation (GDPR) 37, 38, 44, 48, 85, 91, 119–121, 124–128, 130
Goods and services (access to and the supply of goods and services) 78, 81–84, 89, 90, 92, 94, 145, 147
Goods and Services Directive 81, 83, 92
Google 91, 105, 114, 240, 242, 243, 248, 250, 251
Governance initiatives 112
GPT-3 105
Grievance mechanisms 190, 192

H

Harm 66, 88, 101, 103–105, 107, 110–112, 114, 185, 188, 196, 198, 199, 207–216, 218–227, 230, 231, 243, 250
Harm prevention 209, 212, 215, 218, 221, 222, 225–227, 229
High-risk AI systems 152, 156
Human agents 155
Human autonomy 146, 147
Human bias 15, 93, 164
Human control 59, 64, 67, 72, 73, 147, 219
Human intervention 36, 42, 48, 58, 59, 64, 65, 146, 147, 223
Human involvement 208
Human oversight 152, 227
Human rights 8, 9, 36, 58, 67, 77, 79, 81, 116–118, 125,

128–130, 142, 144–146, 183–200, 209, 217
Human rights due diligence (HRDD) 184, 188–197, 199, 200
Human rights impact assessment (HRIA) 193, 194, 196, 197

IBM 114, 196, 240
Identifiable individual 120
Identification 9, 35–42, 44–49, 105, 122, 147, 151
Identity 40, 45, 47, 84, 124
ImageNet 122
Impartiality 13, 15, 16
Inclusive AI 144, 156, 256
Independence 13, 14, 19, 109
Infallibility 47
Inferences 143, 152, 153
Infocentrism 162
Informational self-determination 22
Informed consent 126, 128
Inhuman treatment 10
Innovation 48, 114, 149, 150, 242, 243, 245, 257, 258
Innovation-finance nexus 245
Intellectual property rights (IPR) 119–121, 224, 227, 246
Intelligent 23, 57, 60, 63, 71, 161, 162, 208
International community 59, 62, 67, 68, 72
International humanitarian law (IHL) 66, 67, 70–72
International human rights law 67, 102, 103, 148, 183–187, 192, 193, 199

International law 64, 67, 69, 70, 73, 186–188, 199, 209, 219, 220, 226
International legal accountability 66
International legal framework 69, 73, 186, 188, 229
Internet of things 243
Investment asset 244
IP monopolies 244

Jus ad bellum 64
Jus in bello 64, 69

Kant's categorical imperative 169, 170
Kant's ethics 108, 117
Killer robots 63, 72

Label 42, 128, 170, 171
LaMDA 105
Large Language Model (LLMs) 105, 106
Law enforcement 21, 35–38, 43, 45, 46, 49, 106, 151
Legal certainty 184
Legitimate interest 48, 126, 127
Liability 5, 85, 93, 124, 208, 216, 218, 219, 221–223, 225, 228, 230
Lock's ethics 108, 117, 129

Machine learning algorithms 163

Machine learning (ML) 25, 87–89, 105, 121–124, 130, 153, 163–166, 175, 176, 185, 192–194, 197, 208, 211, 212, 243–245, 250, 257, 258
Mark Everingham Award 122
Microsoft 114, 198, 240, 243, 250
Militarisation 60
Military 60, 61, 63, 65–68, 71, 93, 142, 224
Modern warfare 57, 58, 60–62, 72
Monitoring *ex ante* 101
Monitoring *ex post* 101
Monopolies 242
Moral Machine 108

N

narrow AI 208, 212, 223
Natural disaster management 210, 215
Naturalistic fallacy 164, 171
Natural language processing tools 105
Neural network 109, 124, 163, 170, 171, 210
Non-combatant 66
Non-discrimination 37, 41, 84, 88, 89, 125, 144, 147, 193
Non-maleficence 112, 217, 218, 227
Non-mandatory basis 152
NP-complete class of problems 174
Nullum crimen, nulla poena sine lege 19

O

On-demand network access 243
One-way video interviews 87
Online marketplace 242

OpenAI 105
Owenites 252

P

Permissibility of action 169
Personal data 20, 22, 37, 38, 44, 45, 48, 85, 90, 91, 103–106, 109, 119–130, 147, 185, 241, 247
Personal digital data 243
Personalized pricing 91
Persuasive design 113
Philosophy 117, 155, 165
Police database 46
Political struggle 246
Positive discrimination 78, 92, 93
Predatory pricing 244
Price discrimination 82, 91, 92
Price-fixing 242
Privacy 20, 38, 44–46, 57, 58, 90, 93, 106, 109, 112, 124, 144, 185, 186, 195, 209, 217, 256
Private businesses 183, 184
Profiling 78, 81, 82, 106
Proportionality 4, 21, 45, 66
Proxy information 78
PSPACE-complete class of problems 173, 174
Public hearing 16, 17
Pufendorf's ethics 108, 117, 129

R

Race Equality Directive 80, 83, 90
Racial discrimination 24, 248
Reddit 243
Red line 118
Reinforcement learning 60, 171, 172

Reliability 37, 42, 43, 47, 48, 125, 126, 148, 211
Research Ethics 117
Responsibility 48, 65–68, 70–73, 112, 143, 147, 154, 155, 187–192, 194, 198, 199, 208, 217, 219, 220, 227, 252
Right of confrontation 16
Rising inequality 247, 257
Risk 8, 11, 17, 22, 24, 37, 38, 41, 46, 63, 66, 70, 77, 85, 103, 105, 106, 112, 115, 121, 128, 129, 144, 145, 147, 148, 152, 184, 185, 190, 194, 195, 199, 210, 211, 214, 216, 223, 227, 228, 255
Risk assessment 4, 7–9, 16, 17, 24, 70
Risk management 218, 227
Robot judge 12–17, 19, 26
Rule of law 4, 20, 125, 144, 145

S

Sandboxing 118
Satellites 211, 213–216, 224, 225
Science and Technology Studies (STS) 110
Scientific research 120, 125–128, 130, 131
Scientific research purpose 124, 126, 127
Self-management 255
Sentencing 4–12, 14–23, 25, 26
Sentencing guidelines 7, 8
Sentencing support system 8, 14, 17, 19, 26
Shareholders 240, 252, 255, 259
Social good 249–251, 256

Social harm 102, 209, 212, 213, 218, 220, 240, 249, 256
Social impact 103, 107, 109, 130, 147, 151, 250
Soft law 111, 112, 142
Software distribution 242
Solidarity 144, 217, 218, 229, 252, 253
Space activities 212, 213, 219–221, 223–225, 227
Space debris 213–215, 224, 225
Space law 208, 209, 225–230
Standardization 8, 42, 49, 105, 249
strong AI 59, 208, 212, 216, 222, 223, 227, 230
Supervision 147, 219–221, 223, 225, 227
Surplus-value 246
Surveillance 24, 36, 39, 43, 59–61, 72, 105, 119, 185, 247
Surveillance capitalism 113
Surveillance state 244
Sustainability 147, 150, 151, 188, 190, 210, 211, 216–218, 228, 229, 250
Symbolic logic 163, 165, 175
System 1 reasoning 166
System 2 thinking 166

T

Targeting 81, 82, 89
Targeting criteria 87
Tech cooperative 254
Technology 4, 8, 11, 27, 39, 41, 42, 45, 58, 60–63, 67, 73, 88, 105, 109, 110, 112, 114, 124–126, 142, 155, 156, 185, 195, 208, 210, 213, 216, 220,

276 Index

222, 224, 230, 243, 247, 248, 256–259
Tencent 240, 243
Text and data mining 120
The Labelled Faces in the Wild 122
TikTok 243
Traceability 146, 147, 155
Traffic management 211
Training data 15, 41, 122, 154, 164, 170–172, 176
Transparency 5, 8, 9, 23, 26, 37, 48, 91, 112, 125, 126, 129, 146, 147, 185, 194, 195, 197, 199, 217, 219, 225–227, 241
Tribunal 12, 13, 26
Trolley problem 108, 169, 175
Trustworthy AI 72, 125, 141, 147, 151, 156, 165
Two-way markets 246

U

Unemployment 127

United Nations Guiding Principles on Business and Human Rights 184, 188
United Nations (UN) 58, 69, 72, 116, 183–188, 224
Usage of drones 67, 72, 73
Utilitarianism 167–170, 174, 175
Utility of actions 174
Utility theory 169

V

Virtue ethics 107, 117, 129, 167, 168
Voter manipulation 247

W

Wage inequality 247
War 59, 61, 64, 66, 67, 69, 183, 230
Warfare 60, 63, 65, 67, 69, 70
Worker-owned cooperatives 254